PUSHED

PUSHED

STATE OF OKLAHOMA VS. AMBER HILBERLING: THE INSIDE STORY OF THE MURDER CASE THAT RIVETED THE BIBLE BELT

J.R. Elias

ARABELLE PUBLISHING

ARABELLE PUBLISHING
174 Watercolor Way
Santa Rosa Beach, 32459

First published in the United States of America, 2016
Copyright © 2016 by J.R. Elias

Arabelle Publishing, all rights reserved
ISBN: 153900015X
ISBN 9781539000150
Printed in the United States of America
Cover photo and author photo by Tommy Parker

This is a work of non-fiction. It also contains first-hand observations and opinions of the author.

dedicated to
Kimberly T.
forever kind, courageous, honest

Contents

" I will spend the rest of my life paying for this."
Amber Michelle Hilberling, June 7, 2011

Prologue

On the afternoon of June 7, 2011, Joshua Blaine Hilberling, 23, fell to his death from a 25th-floor apartment window in Tulsa, Oklahoma. Within two hours, Tulsa police charged his 19-year-old wife Amber, who was seven months pregnant at the time, with his murder.

The case dominated local media coverage for years and has continued to garner intense national and international attention. Josh's death led to other court cases, heated family conflicts, and untold rumors and speculation about what really happened between the young couple.

Very little of the actual story has ever been reported, until now.

I was one of Amber Hilberling's attorneys. Her family reached out to me the morning after she was arrested, and I agreed to help for one reason: I believed in her. I stood by Amber and her family, helping them try to navigate a treacherous storm of unwanted troubles. I never anticipated the challenges that would await.

Since the morning I met Amber, I've read and heard many false things about her, her marriage to Josh, her family, Josh's family, the murder trial, her legal defense, the other cases that arose from Josh's death, and, of course, what happened that tragic afternoon.

Amber and I agreed: it's time for the truth to come out.

This is the true and tragic story of Amber and Josh Hilberling. Of the turbulence that led up to the events of June 7, 2011. Of what exactly happened that fateful day. And of what happened after: the dramatic murder trial, the legal strategies and infighting, the prosecution's troubling tactics, family turmoil, lies, betrayals, romance and infidelity, greed, defamation, and the toll the grueling case took on the lives of those involved.

Every word of what follows is true.

Part One: Josh and Amber

JUNE 7, 2011

She pushed him.

He stumbled backward into the corner of their 25th-floor apartment living room, losing his balance and crashing into vertical window blinds. The glass behind the blinds gave way on impact.

His upper body began to fall through the hanging blinds, disappearing into the rays of sunlight that suddenly pierced the room. He reached out and tried to grab the sides of the window opening, looking at her in panic for one fleeting moment.

Then he was gone.

She lunged forward and tried to catch him, shards of collapsing glass dropping on both of them. She caught his right leg for a split second, her hands gripping his tennis shoe as the rest of his body continued to plummet.

Joshua Blaine Hilberling was six-foot-four, young, muscular, thick, athletic, 225 pounds. She had no chance. His shoe came off in her hands.

She bent forward through the broken window and let go of the shoe. It fell through the air, trailing above her husband. She clutched the metal frame, oblivious to the jagged pieces of glass piercing her skin, and watched her husband fall.

"JOSH!!!" she screamed.

He twisted and turned in the air, screaming loudly as he descended, his arms flailing, spending the last moments of his life trying to brace for impact.

He landed loudly on the concrete parking lot below.

He was 23 years old.

At the window high above, his wife stood and screamed in horror into the Tulsa sky.

Amber Michelle Hilberling was 19 years, eight months, and six days old the day she killed her husband.

She was seven months pregnant with their first child, a son they'd already named Levi.

2

Amber pulled away from the window and stumbled backward, bracing herself against the living room wall. Blood from her hands smeared the white paint.

She rushed out of the apartment and ran down the hallway to the nearby elevator bay, dripping blood onto the tiled floor. She pressed the buttons frantically, screaming, crying, trying to stay on her feet.

More drops of blood stained her white tank top, maroon jogging pants, and white tennis shoes. Her thick brown hair was unbrushed, pulled back in a careless ponytail.

A repairman named Armando Rosales hurried out of the Hilberlings' apartment after her, having heard her screams. He joined her at the elevator. In a surreal coincidence, Rosales was in the Hilberlings' bedroom at the same moment Josh went through the living-room window – repairing a small window Josh had just shattered in a fit of rage.

The two realities that had brought Rosales to Apartment 2509 — Josh's aggression, and the dangerously-thin windows of the University Club Tower building — would loom over the court battles that soon arose.

She cried to him, sobbing: "My husband fell out the window!"

The elevator doors opened and she lunged inside, pressing 1 and holding herself up against the wall. She was, Rosales described, "all hysterical."

"Is he dead?!" she cried. "Is he dead?! Is he dead?!"

As the elevator descended, the door kept opening on other floors to faces immediately stunned by the sight inside: a pregnant young woman bleeding, frantic, shouting desperately about her dead husband.

"My husband fell from the 25th floor!" she yelled to strangers. "Is he dead?!"

"Call 911!" Rosales shouted to some.

The door finally opened on the first floor. Amber rushed out through the lobby, then out the front door to find her husband. She turned right and ran, still bleeding from her hands and wrists, fresh fingernail scratches and imprints still on her upper back. She ran through the curved front driveway of the apartment building, toward nearby green grass and parked cars, screaming for her husband.

"Josh! Josh!"

Maybe he was alive, she thought. *Maybe the ambulance is on its way. Maybe they can fix him.*

He wasn't there.

She stopped, confused, then looked up at the west side of the building, the sun shining brightly above her. The cylindrical University Club Tower rose 377 feet in the air, an iconic – though visibly aging – building just southwest of downtown Tulsa.

Far above her, white blinds fluttered out through the shattered window of Apartment 2509.

She looked up and down the building, then put it together.

He must have landed on the parking garage. The garage protruded from the round building, wrapping around its first eight floors.

She looked at the top of the garage. There, lying against the black railing at the edge of its top level, was Josh.

She could see him.

"Josh!"

She ran back inside, back to the elevator, screaming again for her husband. A crowd had started to gather. Witnesses had heard her yells, seen the bloody, pregnant, woman running out of – and now back into – the building. Word was spreading about the fall.

The apartment manager, an overweight middle-aged man named Brad Blake, had come out of the office on the right side of the lobby. He angrily confronted her about her noise, then joined her in the elevator and continued. "Shut up and be quiet!" he yelled at her. "You're not helping the situation!"

Amber couldn't manage a response. She looked at him, confused, then crumbled to the floor of the elevator, sobbing, blood on her skin and clothes.

The door opened on the eighth floor. She rose to her feet and ran down the hallway, bursting through the door leading to the outside parking level.

She started running to her right, the wrong way.

"He's over here," Blake told her.

She turned and saw her husband.

Josh was sprawled across an empty parking space, his broken body lying next to a concrete parking curb alongside the perimeter railing.

Amber ran to him and fell to her knees, wailing.

"Josh! I didn't mean to do it!" Blake heard her cry out. "I didn't mean to push you! Wake up! Wake up!"

She rolled him onto his back, into her lap. She tried to hold his broken upper body and put things back into the shapes she had known. She held him in her arms, her body bent over his as she tried to talk to him, comfort him, revive him.

He was still handsome, somehow. He had always been hand-some. His hair still brown. His eyebrows still dark. His cheekbones still high. She whispered to him, stroked his hair, and kissed his cheeks.

She looked up into the sky and screamed.

"Fix him!" she yelled. "Someone fix him!"

She screamed so loudly that residents far above could hear. Some went to their windows and looked down. Others heard the screams from across the street, hundreds of yards away.

It was just after 4 p.m. The June sky was clear and blue, the air windy but uncomfortably hot, temperatures in the mid-90s. The morning news had reported a rash of water main breaks in Tulsa, citing the recent heat wave.

The door to the 8th-floor parking level opened again. Emergency responders rushed to the couple, Amber still hold-ing Josh in her lap, readjusting his clothing. One firefighter at the scene later said Amber was so upset the first responders worried she would jump off of the parking garage herself. They helped her to her feet and tried to pull her away.

"Let me go!" she cried out, struggling against them. "Let me see him! Fix him! Fix him!"

A paramedic put his arm around her. "You don't want to re-member him this way," he said. "Come on."

Amber draped her arm around his shoulder and obeyed. He guided her away from her dead husband, trying to console her.

She stopped after just a few steps and vomited on the parking lot concrete. Her sunglasses fell off her head near the vomit; she never picked them up. The first responders helped her to a decorative hay bale near the door. They sat her on it and continued to try to talk to her and calm her down while monitoring her vitals.

After a few minutes she tried to stand. She fainted.

The paramedics tended to her, giving her oxygen as she lay on her back, on the ground some 30 feet away from her husband.

Another paramedic knelt by Josh, who was now also on his back, his head turned to the left, his eyes lifeless. He wore an orange Oklahoma State t-shirt, blue gym shorts, and black socks. His left tennis shoe was still on. His right shoe, the one Amber had grabbed and pulled off, had landed some 35 feet away. His phone was on the ground nearby, having shot out of his pocket on impact.

The paramedic assessed him, found him unresponsive, pulseless, and having suffered obvious traumatic injury. Josh was pronounced dead at the scene.

Tulsa police officer Amber McCarty and Detective Christine Gardner arrived. They approached Amber, who was now sitting up in a daze, emergency responders surrounding her. At McCarty's request, the paramedics left her and the detective alone with Amber.

McCarty began asking Amber questions, but Amber could only manage one thought in response, which she repeated over and over: "When are they going to fix him? When is the ambulance going to take him and fix him? When are they going to fix my husband?"

3

The oxygen mask burned her nostrils, so Amber pulled it off. Two police officers were now standing above her. She looked around and saw more police officers now on the scene, looking at her and Josh, along with the paramedics and firefighters. Suddenly scared, she asked to borrow a paramedic's cell phone.

She called her grandmother, Gloria Bowers.

"Josh fell out the window," she sobbed. "I pushed him and he fell and he's dead! I didn't mean to push him! I'm going to jail, Grandma! I'm going to jail!"

Her grandmother said she was on her way. Amber hung up, and the paramedics led her to the eighth-floor elevator, then back down to the first floor. A crowd had already started to form in the lobby and just outside the front doors.

By now, eight firefighters, three paramedics and 13 police officers were on the scene, moving between Josh's body on the parking garage, Apartment 2509, and the crowded first floor. Two police officers were assigned to guard the apartment. Three were from the special investigations unit. Two were from homicide. One was assigned to transport witnesses. One to record the

HELLO
LOVELY READER

In the true spirit of gratitude (yes, we practice what we preach) we'd like to express a heartfelt thanks for buying this journal.

Here we are all helping one another. Beautiful. Can you feel that warm glow inside?

So this little bookmark should come in handy doing what little bookmarks do best.

We get it. You're thinking... *wow, can these guys be any cooler?* Well believe it or not, yes we can and here's how: every honorary Tortoise (that's you) can save a few hard-earned pennies on a shiny new journal or other cool W.O.T. stuff.

Perhaps you feel like spreading the love and treating a friend, family member or complete stranger? We actively encourage it but it's totally your call.

Simply go to *www.thewayofthetortoise.com* and add the discount code when prompted to get your lovely goodies.

Discount code: LOVEYOURTORTOISE

No rush, take your tortoise-time.

Happy journaling.

Peace out,
Klaus and Gal

scene. One to supervise. One helping where needed. One arrived to get the information necessary to go obtain a search warrant for the apartment.

Detective Justin Ritter assigned Officer Don Holloway to stay with Amber and bring her downtown. Holloway walked into the building around 4:40 p.m. He spotted Amber in the lobby by the elevator, blood on her white tank top. He told her he needed to take her downtown. Amber asked if she could wait for her grandmother, and Holloway consented.

Amber saw one of her uncles approaching the building. She rushed outside, sobbing, and he wrapped her in a hug. Holloway saw media vans and cameras converging and quickly took Amber and her uncle back inside, parking them in a conference room near the manager's office.

As Amber talked to her uncle, Officer Holloway stood nearby and listened.

Her uncle asked her what had happened.

"He fell," Amber answered, according to Holloway. "He fell back into the window. I reached out to try to grab him; I grabbed his foot but he fell and I watched him fall."

She started to cry again.

The police chaplain arrived, then made contact with the families of both Josh and Amber. Two men from the medical examiner's office came later to take legal control of Josh's body. Another man from a funeral home later arrived to transport the body to the medical examiner's.

By now, a swarm of local media vans was on the scene, filming from just outside the building's front doors.

Amber sat in the conference room waiting for her grandmother to arrive. Until then, she told the police, she wouldn't talk.

But she had already said enough.

Between 4 and 5 p.m., more than 10 people had already heard a distraught Amber admit to pushing Josh out the window.

The window repairman, Armando Rosales, had heard her say it. Witnesses at the elevator bays had heard her. Others had heard her outside the building as she ran in search of her husband. The apartment manager had heard her. Paramedics, firefighters, and police officers had heard her.

By mid-evening, police had collected statements from many of the people who had heard what Amber had said.

From Tulsa firefighter Dan Newbury: "As we stood with the wife she said 'I don't want to go to jail. I can't believe this happened. I pushed him, I pushed him and he hit the desk and went out the window. I can't believe this happened.' As we kept her seated she then said 'I tried to grab him but he was too heavy. I didn't mean to push him out the window.'"

From paramedic Jason Whitlow: "She was fixing his clothing and extremely upset. She was removed from the side of the body and sat on the ground. ... We moved her away from the scene to try and calm her down. Shortly after she stated 'I didn't mean to push him.'"

From Tulsa Fire Department Captain Robert Peters: "[Amber] was standing/sitting with EMSA personnel when she stated that she did not want to go to jail. 'I can't believe I did it' then she paused momentarily then stated 'I can't believe I pushed him out the window.'"

From Armando Rosales, the window repairman: "[She said] 'my husband fell out of the window! I pushed him! I pushed him through the window! Is he dead?'"

Gloria and another of Amber's uncles arrived at about 4:45 p.m. By that time, the police had already identified Amber as their one and only suspect in the death of Joshua Hilberling.

Gloria found Amber inside, hysterical, and immediately tried to calm her down. "She was crying and in shock," Gloria remembers. "My concern was to try to keep Amber calm. I was scared she would go into labor."

Holloway told Amber he had to take her downtown. Gloria said she was coming with them. Holloway walked them to his patrol car, guided them into the backseat, and drove them to the downtown detective division. Listening to them talk in the car, he heard Amber say: "I pushed Josh and he fell into the window."

They arrived at the station around 5:00. Holloway walked the two into a second-floor interview room and closed the door, leaving the two of them alone to talk.

At 4:49 p.m., Detective Dave Walker called Detective Jeff Felton and assigned him to the case. Felton arrived at the scene around 5:20 p.m., a few minutes after Amber and her grandmother were placed inside the interrogation room downtown. Felton talked briefly with University Club Tower employees, then went to the eighth level of the parking garage and observed the body. He then drove to the detective division to interview the two window repairmen, whom Officer Glenn Barnes had taken downtown for witness statements.

After interviewing the repairmen, Felton went to the interview room where Amber and Gloria waited.

Amber immediately invoked her Fifth Amendment right to remain silent.

"I think my mom is getting an attorney for me," she told the detective. "She doesn't want me to make a statement until I have an attorney with me."

A short time later, attorney Darrell Bolton called Felton and told him he would be representing Amber. Bolton said he would visit Amber the next day, then call Felton and allow Amber to provide a statement. But Bolton neither visited Amber nor took the case.

After getting off the phone with the attorney, Detective Felton returned to the interview room and informed Amber she was being arrested on charges of second-degree murder.

By now, Amber and Gloria had been in the room for more than an hour, talking the entire time. Amber had told her grandmother that she and Josh had been arguing, fighting in the living room, when she pushed him. She said he tripped over things behind him, then fell into the wall and through the blinds. As she had said repeatedly on the scene, she told her grandmother she had never meant to push him up and out the elevated living room window.

What Amber and Gloria didn't know was that the police had been in a nearby monitoring room the entire time, observing their conversation and recording it. The prosecution later gave Amber's defense team a copy of this videotaped conversation. All references to the couple's living-room fight were missing from this video. The prosecution would blame these omissions on technical issues.

4

In the hours leading up to the fateful push, Amber and Josh had been arguing.

Again.

And Josh's anger had become physical.

Again.

When Tulsa police photographed Amber after bringing her downtown, her right shoulder still bore physical evidence of their last fight. About two inches below the top of her shoulder, just above her shoulder blade, were two red scratch marks. Just above those scratch marks were three imprints in the shape of fingers.

That's where he grabbed me, she told me later, when I showed her the photos. *When we were fighting. Just before I pushed him off of me.*

Minutes before leaving the marks on his pregnant wife's body, Josh's anger had also left its mark on the couple's apartment. He had hurled a clothes basket across their bedroom, breaking a small sliding window. That broken window had brought repairman Armando Rosales to Apartment 2509.

Rosales was struck by Josh's anger the second he arrived at the apartment. Rosales described Josh as "angry" and "upset" and later testified that Josh "was not real nice to me."

As soon as Rosales had entered the apartment, he could tell Amber and Josh had been arguing. It was, he says, "obvious."

The subject of their argument was nothing new. It was the same thing they had been arguing about for months.

"Drugs and partying," Amber says. "All he cared about was drugs and partying. We were about to have a baby, and all he would do was go out every night with his friends and party. Doing drugs, selling drugs, drinking, while I'm sitting home alone. I just wanted him to grow up."

It was Josh's drug problems, in fact, that had just brought them to the University Club Tower a few weeks earlier.

For the previous six months, the two had been living at Eielson Air Force Base in Alaska, just southeast of Fairbanks, where Josh was stationed as a new airman. He had enlisted in the Air Force the previous summer, just before he and Amber married, and the newlyweds had moved to the Alaska base in mid-October of 2010.

There, they had a home in military housing, friends on the base, a routine, and were soon expecting their first baby. Josh had his job with the Air Force, with income and benefits. They had a start on life, a plan, a future.

Then, just like that, it all ended.

The Air Force kicked Josh out.

The military police had launched multiple criminal investigations into Josh during his short stint in Alaska. They had been at the couple's home on numerous occasions responding to reports of domestic violence. Multiple police reports identify Josh as the domestic violence "offender" and his pregnant wife as the "victim." He was arrested on at least one occasion. The police also issued a "no-contact" protective order against him at one point, ordering him to move into a nearby hotel and not go near his pregnant wife. The police and other witnesses had seen the bruises and injuries on her body.

The police had also been investigating Josh for his alleged manufacturing and use of illegal drugs. He was caught manufacturing synthetic marijuana, also known as "spice" or "K2." He had also been selling prescription drugs.

After just six months, the Air Force had seen enough of Josh Hilberling.

He was discharged for misconduct on May 6, 2011. With no place to go, he and Amber abruptly returned to Oklahoma. They were back home without a plan, without a job, without money, without a place to live.

And their baby was due in weeks.

In mid-May, Amber's mother, a nurse, and her stepfather, a plastic surgeon, let the couple move into their vacant second residence, a posh apartment at the University Club Tower near downtown Tulsa.

It wasn't the life Amber had planned, or wanted. And it got worse almost immediately.

On his first day back in Tulsa, Josh was back with his old friends, partying and taking Oxycontin, a drug known on the street as "Oxycotton." According to webmd.com, the drug, when taken in pill form as intended, is a slow-release pain narcotic. Its active ingredient is a morphine derivative, the same ingredient found in Percodan. When bought on the street, it's crushed and snorted to deliver a powerful and fast high that many users say is better than heroin.

Josh loved it.

Amber had discovered his drug habit when they were dating, but he assured her he'd have to quit before he joined the Air Force. In the days before he reported for duty in Alaska, he had tried to quit cold turkey. It wasn't easy.

Amber's grandmother remembers seeing him the day before he left. "He looked rough," Gloria says. "I asked Amber what was wrong with him. She said Josh thought he was coming down with a cold or flu. All he did was lie back in the chair, totally out of it."

During their first week in Alaska, Josh was viciously sick. Nausea, cramps, diarrhea, vomiting, anxiety, profuse sweating, and irritability. Amber tended to him, went to the store for all kinds of medicine, and worriedly called her grandmother every day for advice. His symptoms seemed to be getting worse. Amber was scared. She kept insisting he go see a doctor. He kept refusing. They'd argue about it.

Finally, he told her the truth. He didn't have the flu. He was coming down off of Oxycontin.

His withdrawal symptoms subsided after about a week, and Amber thought his addiction was behind them. She was wrong. In time, he found a source in Alaska.

She could tell when he was using just by looking at him. His eyes, the faces he made, his body language. His behavior changed too. Sober, Josh was happy, fun, playful. On Oxycontin, he was sullen, withdrawn, irritable, angry.

And violent.

Back in Tulsa, Josh spent most of May partying with his old friends, using drugs again, drinking, and coming home late to his pregnant wife, often well after midnight. They argued regularly about his lifestyle, Amber wanting him home with her, Josh apologizing and promising changes.

The two had planned to move into a rental house near midtown Tulsa in mid-June, but they had no income. Amber wanted

Josh to start working. They argued about that. "I deserve time off," he'd tell her. He told her he was going to start selling Oxycontin for income. They argued about that, too.

They argued about priorities. About planning for the baby. About being a family.

She begged for a crib throughout May. He told her they couldn't afford it. But he was planning a trip with buddies to the four-day Bonnaroo Music Festival in Tennessee beginning on June 9. Eminem was headlining. Ticket prices were in the hundreds. Neither had a job. They usually didn't have enough money for gas to get around town.

On Saturday, June 4, three days before his death, the two exchanged the following texts:

Amber: Who is paying for Tennessee again?

Josh: I am a

Amber: Lol! How are you gonna do that?

Josh: I will just be able to

Amber: Okay. Buy me a crib and then you can go.

Josh: Ok it will have to be after I get back

Amber: No. Before

Josh: Can't say

Amber: Then you can't go. Sorry

Josh: Im going

Amber: Okay

Josh: Why are you doing this shit to me wtf did I do to you. ???

Amber: I'm not gonna discuss this while you're high. Enjoy yourself.

He later told her he was going to sell Oxycontin at Bonnaroo, then use that money to buy a crib for Levi.

That plan, Amber said later, "made me sick."

She had had enough. In early June, she told him to move out, and that she wanted a divorce.

The text messages between the two clearly establish this: Amber told Josh she wanted a divorce, and that he needed to move out of her parents' apartment.

Yet the opposite was repeatedly told in the popular, and false, public narrative the media quickly adopted and pushed. Josh's father told the lead detective it was Josh who had just broke the news to Amber that he was leaving her that day. Then at the murder trial, the district attorney told the same story in her closing argument.

Text messages the two exchanged in the last few days of Josh's life paint a clear picture of their disintegrating marriage, and of Amber being the one to say she wanted a divorce.

The nights of June 4, 5, and 6, the last three nights of Josh's life, were repetitions of the same script. Josh was out with his friends, partying, doing drugs, texting his wife promises and apologies. Amber was home alone, frustrated, pulling away.

That Saturday afternoon, the two had planned to go to Target to fill out their baby registry for her upcoming baby shower. Instead, Josh took the car they were using, which belonged to Amber's mother, and was gone with his friends for hours. Amber was stuck at her grandmother's house. At 6:25 p.m., Amber finally texted him that she needed the car.

Amber: I need to go to the apt. You have the key.

Josh: Gotta take Brandon home.

Amber: Just bring me the car. And then I'll leave you alone.

Josh: In a little

Amber: I'm gonna call my mom. And she won't be easy to deal with.

Josh: Haha your going to call ur mom go ahead ill bring you the car and be gone.

Amber: Just bring me the car and do what you want.

Josh: Ha I can't believe you your going to call ur mom on me!

Amber: That's only if you refuse to bring me her car.

Josh: Haha oh mommy get me your car back

Amber: You don't have to be mean anymore

Josh: You stop acting like a brat and ill stop being mean

Amber: You'll never stop being mean.

Later that same night, at 1:10 a.m., the two had the following text message exchange:

Josh: I'm staring at the stars.

Amber: How do they look?

Josh: Not the same without you.

Amber: Well I hope it's special with whoever else you're with.

Josh: Nobody is with me and I wanna come home with you. But I can stay somewhere else.

Amber: Where are you and how did you get there?

(No response for 29 minutes)

Amber: You're alone yet still can't text me back.

Josh: Sorry Been trying to get ahold of Jordan my bags are in his truck and he Went to the bar.

Amber: Okay…Answer my question.

Josh: I'm at chris terry's house and chris got us earlier.

Amber: Party over there I'm guessing?

Josh: Not really

Amber: Hmmm. Okay

Josh: Well U can come get me and we can go home.

Amber: There's no gas in the car like at all. And you didn't give me money.

Josh: I got five bucks.

Amber: Idk if I could even make it there. What have you bought tonight?

Josh: There is a qt [a Tulsa gas station] right next to the house

Amber: I don't wanna see you if you've done any pills tonight

Josh: I have not just drank a few beers and smoked

Amber: For someone who felt so shitty you sure had some fun

Josh: I'm at 11th and Utica past Utica right on troost and white house on the right.

Amber: If I come get you it doesn't mean I'm not gonna feel the same.

Josh: What do you mean?

Amber: You're not being a huge douche bag anymore just bc you need to stay at the apt.
          It's whatever. I'll come get you and take you home and leave you alone.

Amber picked Josh up between 2:30 and 3:00 a.m. and drove him back to the apartment. She got in bed. He went into the living room and played video games.

At 3:16 a.m., she sent him a text message from bed: "Will you turn that down please."

The tension from the night before was still lingering when the two woke up later that Sunday, June 5. Amber told him she was going to go spend some time at her grandmother's to clear her head. She was close with her grandmother, Gloria, and had been turning to her more and more for comfort and support. Amber had told Josh many times that she was "scared of being alone" at night in the apartment while he was out partying. In texts, in person, over the phone.

But it wasn't enough to bring him home. So she'd often drive to her grandmother's, where she knew she wouldn't be alone.

At 1:46 p.m. that Sunday, she texted him this: "While I'm gone it would be help if you would do some really long, hard thinking about what you want from here on out. Not only with us and Levi but with everything in your life. I'll do the same today and we will talk when I get home Okay?"

Josh didn't respond.

That evening, Amber drove back to the apartment to pick him up and take him to a barbecue dinner. He was gone. Out with buddies again.

"I'm crying like a fucking idiot," she texted him. "I used the very last of the gas to come get you. I'm so so so stupid."

The two then had the following exchange, beginning at 6:46 p.m.:

Amber: I'm more upset now than ever before with you bc I'm trying to make someone love me and care for me the way I do for them and it's just a huge failure and making me stressed and sick and miserable. I can't take your lack of compassion and concern for me anymore. You're not trying the slightest bit!! Like at all!! You had weed on you too! How could you do that at a time like this??! What is wrong with you to make you think that's appropriate! You're horrible!

Amber: I want a divorce.

Josh: Well this sucks.

Amber: You made it this way. Only you. Selfish, selfish you.

Josh: Ya I know everything is always my fault.

Amber: No it's not. But this time, yes it definitely is. You want me and you want Levi with us yet you haven't done the slightest thing to work for it. I have. I'm always trying my best. You think you can do what you want and think how you want and still keep me bc you have always been given excuses. Well no more. I have to decide how I want to be treated and this is not it. So looks like my only option left is leaving you.

Josh stayed out with buddies again all that evening. At 8:41 p.m. he texted her that he'd "be home tonight" and join her at her doctor's appointment the next morning.

"If it's after ten then just stay somewhere else," she texted back.

Josh later texted her that he was "on my way." It was 12:39 a.m.

Amber: I don't want you coming here anymore.

Josh: Ten min is all I ask for ill be home!!

Amber: This is not your home. You're just staying here.

Josh: I wanna have a home with you im sorry I been such a shit im done of and always try to spend time with my friends when I should spent it with you

Amber: Don't text me that stuff

Josh: Why? I wanna be with you and only you I love always when your with me! I won't lose that

Amber: Are you drunk or something?

Josh: Nope that's how I feel! I have thought about a lot of the way I been and how you don't deserve that and I know I can be so much of a better man!

Amber: Sorry but I can't believe you.

Her skepticism proved prescient. The very next night, Monday, June 6th, Josh again went out with buddies, again leaving Amber home alone, again promising her he'd be home soon, and again breaking the promise. Amber called her grandmother crying. He came home after midnight again. He was high again. Amber refused to talk to him.

Earlier that day, Amber's grandmother had confronted Josh directly. Amber and Josh had been at Gloria's house visiting. Another one of Gloria's grandchildren, a two-year-old, was playing nearby. Gloria told Josh she wanted to talk to him. She told him she wasn't happy with how he had been treating Amber, that he needed to quit the drugs, quit the partying, and start growing up.

He responded in anger.

"He blew up so quick," Gloria recalls. "He started cussing me. F-this and F-that. I was not going to put up with that kind of attitude."

Neither was Amber. She told her grandmother that day, and then her uncle, the same news she had told Josh the day before. She was going to file for divorce. They were going to move out of the apartment. Amber would move back in with her mom without Josh, have the baby, get a job, and go back to school. Josh was on his own.

When Josh came back to the apartment late that night, after midnight, Amber didn't bother reacting. They both went to sleep and stayed in bed late that Tuesday. Around 1 p.m., Amber got up, poured herself a bowl of cereal, and texted some friends.

Josh would be dead in three hours.

Her grandmother called to see how she was doing, still concerned about the events of the day before. Amber told her she'd be coming back over soon, to be away from Josh while he packed his things. He was headed with friends to the Bonnaroo Festival in Tennessee, and had already loaded up the few items he had at the apartment into a green duffel bag. Amber told Gloria to keep her phone close in case she ran out of gas on the way over. She'd bring laundry, too, something she often did at her grandmother's.

By then Josh was up and about. He and Amber started to talk about things. She told him she needed the apartment key to give back to her mother, and that he needed to find a new place to stay when he got back from the music festival. He agreed with the plan.

Josh started texting some buddies, wanting to join them at a nearby pool. He couldn't use Amber's mother's car anymore, so he asked them to come pick him up. They didn't. They told him they'd get him later. Josh texted his dad, asking him if he could get a ride from him. His dad also said no. The exchanges do not show urgency or concern.

He and Amber continued to talk. The conversation again turned to Josh's partying and drug use. The music festival, Josh insisted, wasn't just a buddy trip. He was going to sell pills there and come back with money for them. Amber wanted him to get a real job.

They argued.

"I don't view you as a respectable man," she said.

It was that line, Amber said later, that set him off. He became angrier. He told her he wasn't going to join her at her father's upcoming wedding.

At 2:53 p.m., a friend of Amber's texted her: "So what's been going on in your life?"

Amber replied: "I can't really talk about it right now."

She got ready to leave. She had her sunglasses on top of her head, her purse and keys nearby. She went to pick up her clothes basket from their bedroom, but it still had some of Josh's clothes in it. She emptied it onto the floor, separated Josh's clothes, and put her own back in.

"What are you doing?" Josh asked.

"I'm not doing your laundry. You're leaving. I'm just doing my own."

"Fuck that!"

Josh picked up the basket, dumped her clothes out of it, and angrily threw it across their bedroom.

It shattered the small bedroom window overlooking the room's exterior balcony. Shards of glass fell on both the inside carpet and the balcony cement outside.

Josh glared at her then stormed out of the bedroom. Amber's thoughts turned to how mad her mom was going to be about the damage. She walked over to the window and started picking up the pieces of glass. She called the downstairs office and told them about the broken window. She vacuumed the carpet, then walked outside to the balcony and started to sweep up the broken glass.

She came back inside and the two started arguing again, this time about the window Josh had just broken. This time, they were louder.

Amber went into the bathroom and began to cry and vomit into the toilet. The downstairs neighbor later testified in detail about hearing these sounds. Josh came into the bathroom wanting to talk. He told her he wanted to make things work, but agreed they needed a break. They started to argue again about the window.

"You need to grow up!" Amber finally yelled, according to the downstairs neighbor.

Josh was in the bathroom with her for about two minutes. He left the room and texted his friends again, still looking for a ride.

They were still lounging at the pool and didn't want to leave. Later, they told him.

A few minutes later, the building's window repairman, Armando Rosales, knocked on the door. He had already been in the building repairing another window.

Josh, still angry, asked him how much the window repair would cost.

"I told him around $150.00," Rosales recalls. "He got very angry and asked his wife if her mother was going to have to pay for it. She said no, that they will have to pay for it."

For Rosales, it was just the latest of many broken windows at the University Club Tower, a problem he later attributed to the high-rise building's negligent use of dangerously-thin window glass throughout its 32 floors. He knew what to do and went right to work. He walked into the bedroom, then out its exterior door and onto the balcony. He was going to clear out the broken pieces, board the window, and order a new pane of glass.

Amber went back to cleaning up the glass mess inside the bedroom.

When she finished, she walked into the living room where Josh was apparently gathering some of his things from the television stand. They started to exchange words. Another neighbor heard them arguing.

Soon Rosales heard what he described as "scuffling" in the next room. The sounds of a fight. From what he heard, he thought Josh was in the living room beating Amber.

Then, a large crash. He felt the walls shake.

Rosales worried that Amber "must be knocked out." He decided he "better get inside and help her."

Her.

The only other person at the scene, the one person who sized up the situation, the dynamic between the two, had made a determination as to who was the threat and who needed help.

Josh's physical advantage over Amber was as clear to Rosales as it would have been to anybody. Amber stood nearly a foot shorter than her angry husband, her mobility limited by her basketball-sized pregnant belly. At her normal weight she had been about 100 pounds lighter than him.

Thinking Josh was in the other room beating up his wife, Rosales took a moment to mentally prepare himself to confront Josh. Rosales was considerably older and smaller than Josh. He tried to get himself ready for a fight.

Then his cell phone rang. It was his partner, Antonio De Paz, who had been outside on the ground below.

"Someone fell out the window!"

"Oh my god!" Rosales thought to himself. "He jumped!"

He.

Rosales's perception was that Josh had been upset enough to commit suicide.

He hurried in from the balcony, through the bedroom and into the small hallway, then turned left into the living room.

The room was empty.

Amber was out in the hallway, bawling, on her way to the elevator. Josh was 17 floors below.

Rosales saw the large window shattered, a chunk of blinds gone, the blue sky now shining into the living room of Apartment 2509.

5

As news spread of Josh's death, his family and friends launched an orchestrated public attack on Amber.

Led by Josh's stepmother Jeanne, who had never hidden her dislike of Amber and Amber's family, they began blitzing the media and the lead detective assigned to the case with stories painting Amber as a mentally ill woman who had been the physically abusive one in the relationship.

Jeanne publicly, and falsely, reported that in the moments after Josh's death Amber had actually been cockily "smiling" at bystanders and that she showed "no remorse" at the scene. But Jeanne had not been at the scene. There had been more than 20 eyewitness accounts, each of them unwaveringly consistent in their descriptions of Amber sobbing, wailing, crying hysterically, even vomiting and passing out.

Jeanne's story was a lie.

But the truth didn't matter. Her false account was soon reported as gospel in local, national, and even international media reports.

Jeanne and the small campaign group quickly created a public narrative that baited the willing media and captured the public's fascination. The pregnant, teenage girl, standing five-foot-five, was cast as the mentally-ill monster who had purposefully pushed her large husband up and out an elevated 25th-floor window. And the six-foot-four, 225-pound husband, a former college football player who had recently gone through basic training, a man who had just been thrown out of the Air Force after chronic domestic abuse incidents and drug investigations, was cast as the gentle, law-abiding, military hero who had been beaten around and killed by the maniac.

It made for a hell of a story. The media and public ran wild with it.

So did the prosecution.

Lead Detective Jeff Felton, for instance, had originally recommended a second-degree murder charge after having gone to the scene, interviewed witnesses, and learned of Amber's actions and statements.

But then he called Josh's family. Josh's father, Patrick, told the detective that Amber had assaulted Josh numerous times while the two lived in Alaska. He didn't tell the detective, though it's not clear whether he even knew the truth, about Josh's history of domestic violence against his pregnant wife. He also told the detective it had been Josh who had just informed Amber he wanted a divorce in the moments before his death. The couple's text messages prove otherwise.

Felton apparently believed what he heard. After that call, the detective amended the second-degree murder charge to first-degree. The main distinction between the two charges is the mindset of the defendant. To make a first-degree murder case, the state has to prove that the defendant deliberately intended to kill.

The next morning, four of Josh's friends called the same detective and pitched the same exact narrative. They each accused Amber of having been physically abusive while she and Josh had lived in Alaska. None of the four had been to Alaska or witnessed anything they reported to the detective. When boiled down to the specifics they offered, they told the detective the following: they had heard that Amber once had pushed Josh, had once thrown a shoe at him, and had once knocked a floor lamp onto him as he lay on a couch.

They spread the same narrative across the Internet and with multiple media outlets.

The Tulsa media instantly had its storyline, and it was sensational.

Local TV newscasts quickly brought in experts to insist that, yes, such a history of domestic violence by a woman is possible. What Amber was accused of was plausible, they educated their viewers.

When these newscasts used photos of Amber, they would regularly use the mugshot from when she was arrested for Josh's murder. For images of Josh, the media used photos of him smiling in his Air Force uniform, the American flag draped behind him. They inaccurately referred to him as an "airman," a term used exclusively for active members of the U.S. Air Force, ignoring the fact that he had been quickly discharged for misconduct. Josh's stepmother aggressively pushed this falsehood, telling the media that she and her husband were "proud military parents" until Josh's death.

CNN's Nancy Grace called Josh "a gentle giant" and reported on national television that he had "filed multiple temporary protective orders" against Amber, another falsehood.

As to what had happened when Josh and Amber were alone in the living room, Jeanne Hilberling reported that Amber had "charged him with all her insanity strength and pushed him out the window." She told another reporter: "When you're trying to leave, that's the most dangerous time." The media reported her fiction as news. One of London's largest newspapers, the *Daily Mail*, reported that Amber had "viciously pounced" on Josh after he had told her "he was leaving her."

Soon after the death, the local Fox affiliate, Fox 23, aired a story on its nightly newscast painting Amber as mentally ill. The anchor, Chera Kimiko, began the piece by reporting that unnamed "friends and family" of Josh "question the mental state of" Amber and "have said they noticed issues."

Kimiko then cut to reporter Sharon Phillips, who stood outside the University Club Tower and began her report as follows:

"Yeah that's exactly right, Cheri. Friends and family members of Josh say they noticed Amber having frequent mood changes, and we talked with a man this afternoon who says he's experienced that most of his life and he didn't realize what was wrong until later in life. According to the Mental Health Association, one out of four people are living with a mental illness."

Phillips stood outside Amber and Josh's apartment building as she reported this as breaking news: *anonymous sources say they think a pregnant teenager may have had some mood swings.*

She then introduced her interview subject, a man who didn't know Amber, or Josh, or anyone involved, a man who had nothing to do with the case at all. Instead, the man went into detail about his own diagnosed bipolar disorder, spoke of once believing he was Jesus Christ, of being institutionalized for mental illness, of once believing he had to get to the White House to meet Jimmy Carter, and of now having had years of medical treatment for his problems.

Scrolling at the bottom of the screen the entire time: "Victim's Family Questions Mental Health" of Amber.

At the very end of the long piece, Phillips added a toss-in disclaimer: "Amber Hilberling has not been diagnosed with a mental health disorder to our knowledge."

To our knowledge.

On June 8th, the day after the death, another local news report accused Amber of "a pattern of domestic violence." Local and national media had quickly picked up on the theme, and it spread like wildfire.

Predictably, the public tide against the 19-year-old was instant, strong, and merciless.

She was vilified.

Hate websites were created with names such as "Put Amber Hilberling Away For Life" and "Amber Hilberling Is Guilty." Internet commentators, often hiding behind anonymity and fake names, made scores of false accusations against Amber. They accused her of being a drug addict, of being on drugs at the time of the incident, of being an adulterer, a prostitute, a serial husband beater, and of intentionally murdering her husband. They insulted her parents and her siblings. Josh's stepmother and stepsister actively participated. Some put Amber's family's address on the Internet and encouraged others to show up. They called Amber a "whore," a "bitch," a "cunt," a "murderer." They called for her to be "tortured."

One commenter wrote: "Throw a rope around her neck and let her hang 10 feet off the ground."

Another wrote: "She needs to die already. Execute her ugly ass."

6

Amber and Josh started dating in April, 2010, having met at a party in downtown Tulsa.

Josh was 21, Amber 18.

"We clicked instantly," Amber recalls. "We fell in love quickly. We spent every second together. It was great."

For Amber, their budding relationship also meant something else. A way out. Her teenage years, she says, weren't easy.

Her life changed when she was 12, she says, around the time her mother Rhonda filed for divorce from her father, Mike Fields. The couple engaged in a heated divorce fight that lasted 31 months and embroiled the couple's three children. During that battle, Rhonda obtained an emergency protective order against Mike that remained in place for nearly 14 months. Their acrimony created tension between Amber and her mother. After one argument during the divorce, when Amber was 13, her mother placed her in a youth facility overnight. Four years later, at 17, Amber moved out of the family's home, staying with a friend in Texas for a couple months. She came back to Tulsa and moved back in with her mother, who had remarried.

It was a few months later when Amber met Josh.

Photographs from their first months together show two attractive young adults, often in each other's arms, beaming as they looked at each other. Josh had a wide, toothy smile, dark hair, thick eyebrows, long eyelashes, and the tall, muscular body of an athlete. Amber was a head turner with long brown hair, alluring eyes, a confident smile, a knack for makeup, and a shapely figure. They were young, beautiful, and in love.

In short time they were spending their days and nights together. Talking about their lives, their dreams, the troubled homes they each hoped to leave behind, their futures. They didn't want to be apart.

But they were going to have to be. Josh was headed to the Air Force soon. First he'd be off to basic training, then he'd be stationed far away. They had a decision to make: stay together, which meant getting married and living together in military housing, or break up.

They chose to stay together.

On May 10, Josh left Tulsa for boot camp in San Antonio, Texas, at Lackland Air Force Base. For the next eight weeks, Amber wrote Josh a letter every single day. When he graduated, Amber made the trek from Tulsa to San Antonio for Josh's graduation ceremony.

Josh then went to the Air Force's civil engineering school in Wichita Falls, Texas, for a month. On his weekends off, he would race back to Tulsa to be with Amber.

After completing the courses, he'd have an eight-week leave before heading to the Air Force base in Alaska. He made sure Amber was coming too. As soon as his leave began, Josh married Amber in a brief ceremony in Wichita Falls. They then had a reception back in Tulsa.

Their plan was to spend their leave in Tulsa, staying with Amber's parents and spending time with family and friends before starting their new lives together far away.

For the first time, they were going to live together as husband and wife. The life they had lay in bed at night talking about, dreaming about, laughing about.

That fantasy had been fun for them to imagine.

Reality was something completely different.

7

Josh's phone would buzz at all hours with both texts and calls. It bothered Amber. They'd be snuggling and talking, and he'd interrupt things to get up and respond to a text. They'd be watching TV, and he'd have to stop for the phone.

She knew it wasn't other girls. He would show her his texts.

The calls and texts were from his customers. He was selling them "Roxies."

"Roxies" are the street name for Roxicodone pills, an opioid narcotic with the same active ingredient as Oxycontin – oxycodone – but sold in tiny blue pills with immediate-release effect. In other words, Roxies worked faster than Oxycotton. Some say it's a quicker, more powerful high than heroin. They'd typically sell on the street for at least $30 a pill.

Josh told her it was just temporary, the only way he could make some quick money before Alaska. But Amber would complain, and they'd argue. Finally, they reached a compromise. He'd turn off his phone while they spent time together. He told her he'd cut down on the selling, and that he'd stop selling for good when his military service began.

He'd also have to quit using at the same time, he promised. She didn't like the way the drugs made him act, brooding and angry and irritable. But he liked the way it made him feel. He told her he'd started on it when he was 19.

Amber wasn't about to judge, having already become accustomed to alcohol and drug abuse in her own home. Court records reflect that her mother Rhonda and stepfather, a Tulsa physician named Bryan Whitlock, have publicly accused each other of a history of alcohol and drug abuse. Her younger brother has been in and out of prison for drug-related crimes. Amber says the behavior runs in both sides of her family.

Josh's drug use gave her no reason to turn and run away.

Amber freely admits she had already tried pot herself before she met Josh. Then they smoked some together. She tried his pills, gamely trying to share the experience with him when they were dating. She didn't like them, she says. But mostly, she hated what they did to her boyfriend.

Still, she says, she thought the drugs were just a phase. He told her about his plans, his dreams for his future, their future. She believed him. She wanted those dreams to come true because they matched her own. After everything she had been around for years, the one thing she wanted most, as she would remind Josh in their last argument, was to be with a "respectable man." In a respectable home. A respectable marriage. A respectable life.

Josh understood, Amber says, having come from a home with troubles of its own. They both wanted something different than what they knew. During his eight-week Air Force leave, Josh and Amber moved in with her parents. Briefly. After just two weeks, they moved into the house of Josh's stepbrother, Scott Askew.

That's when their own troubles got worse.

"He was taking pills every day at Scott's," Amber remembers, "and we started fighting about it a lot. I didn't even know where he would get them."

He'd lie to her, denying he was taking them. But he'd go into the bathroom, lock the door, and she could hear him in there snorting. She didn't have to bother asking what he was doing.

"I could taste it in his mouth. And his personality would totally change. His pupils would get tiny. He'd turn into a complete jerk. He couldn't ejaculate. Usually he was sweet and fun loving. Not when he was on Oxy."

Josh's brother had no idea, Amber says, or he'd have kicked them out.

It was during this same stretch when Josh started getting physical with Amber for the first time. She told herself it was just the drugs, that it would stop when they went to Alaska, when he'd have to be clean.

"He threw me around the bedroom at Scott's a few times," Amber remembers. "I remember crying to Scott once, telling him he had thrown me."

She remembers Scott's wife, Monica, seeing him yell in her face, grabbing her arms and pushing her backwards.

Amber's grandmother once saw Josh angrily throw Amber off of a chair.

And there was the night he pushed Amber down on the concrete driveway. It hurt, she remembers.

And the time "he picked me up off the bed and threw me into the closet doors." That hurt, too.

There were other incidents, more than she can remember. They were getting to be almost routine. Josh was becoming, in Amber's words, "pushy and shovey."

But like Josh's drug use, his physical abuse was another fact of life to which Amber was already accustomed. Amber and her mother Rhonda have both spoken openly of the domestic violence cycle in their family. Rhonda once obtained a protective order against her husband Bryan, accusing him of physically abusing her. He was then arrested for violating the order, according to court records. Rhonda has shown me bruises on her body she alleged were from her husband, and friends of the family have told me about other incidents of his domestic abuse. The two have separated and reconciled on numerous occasions.

Still, Amber was gradually becoming more concerned about Josh's anger. She began opening up to her confidant, her grandmother Gloria, telling her about Josh's abuse. Amber was scared it wouldn't stop.

Once they got to Alaska, she told herself, it would get better.

Everything would get better.

She was wrong.

8

Things turned cold and violent in Alaska.

From the moment they arrived at the military base in mid-October, nothing went as planned. Nothing went right.

Their house wasn't finished when they got there, so the Air Force put them up in temporary housing for 30 days: a tiny hotel room with a bed, a TV, and a small bathroom.

Josh would leave in the morning and work all day on the base, leaving Amber alone in the hotel room with no phone, no car, and no money. She'd sit around all day, bored, staring at the ceiling, the walls, the television screen, waiting for her husband to come home, never sure when he'd walk through the door.

And then when he'd come back to the hotel in the evening, "he'd just smoke pot and play video games," Amber remembers. She'd ask him to do things with her, give her attention, but he'd tell her he was "too tired."

It wasn't long before they had picked up right where they had left off in Tulsa, frequently arguing again. Only now, Josh was getting more physical, and more often.

During one argument, Josh angrily picked up the hotel room's TV set and threw it, breaking it. He called the hotel manager and said it "fell." The hotel moved the couple to another room.

"He was throwing things a lot," Amber says. "He was getting rough."

The two started counseling. They saw a marriage counselor together, and each started seeing a counselor individually. For a while, Amber says, it helped.

Things improved when they first moved into the house on base. "We were getting along great," Amber remembers, "for the most part."

They'd argue some about money. Josh would get paychecks from the Air Force but keep them to himself. If Amber said she needed money for something, he'd tell her to ask her parents. He wouldn't agree to open a joint bank account or let her add her name to his, so she couldn't go buy groceries or other basics. Some days she'd sit at home hungry, waiting for him to get home to share money for a meal.

She wanted to buy warmer clothes for the cold Alaska climate. But she couldn't.

Amber wanted to work herself, but Josh insisted she stay home.

She told him she couldn't figure out where the paychecks were going. The two barely had bills, living on base. But Josh would tell her it wasn't her business how, the paychecks were spent. It didn't take long before she figured out where the money was going. He had found a source and was using again.

One day Amber saw a package for Josh in the mail, sent from Tulsa. It was 75 Oxycontin pills. Josh admitted he had a friend send them to him.

He took them all within about one week.

"We started fighting about that again, all the time," Amber says. "He was getting high all the time with two other guys, [name redacted] and [name redacted], and I wanted it to stop."

Then, in early December, Josh learned some news that excited him. He told Amber that Alaska had outlawed "spice," the nickname for synthetic marijuana, so he could start making it at home and selling it for income. He told her he'd just ordered the ingredients and tools off of eBay.

"It was just $200!" he told her.

About the time his materials arrived, the couple received some news.

At a doctor's appointment on December 14, Amber learned she was pregnant. The two were elated. Amber hoped it would be the spark Josh needed to get clean. They went home from the appointment and excitedly started making plans for the baby.

That same day, Josh received an angry text message from his stepmother, Jeanne.

"It was not a good feeling to read on Facebook that Amber is pregnant," Jeanne texted him. "Our worse [sic] fear has come to reality. We figured when Cortney got knocked up - Amber would try to do the same. I am disappointed in you for being such an easy mark. You could've at least told us yourself. However, I guess all is well in crazyville. Rhonda is happy - and after all she is the one who decided you would have to be married ,very quickly'. Anyway - good luck - your [sic] gonna need it - hope you get as good as Amber in manipulating money from Rhonda."

Josh responded that "i was going to call you guys after I got off work" and told her they had "just found out this morning."

Jeanne: "Bullshit - Amber got pregnant on purpose. She was supposed to have an IUD placed last summer. Rhonda wants Amber to be just like her. Rhonda got pregnant when she was 18 and she wants the same for Amber. Your life is fucked - you are at the mercy of Rhonda and Amber. I don't feel sorry for you - cause you were warned. I wouldn't want to be you!!"

Josh: "I don't mind I got work and I'm going to school I got Amber and I got a kid on the way I'm blessed I'm not going to be sad about this its my life and I'm going to make it the best shit happens mom and life is not fair you taught me that cause if stuff went my way than life would be fair but its not so thats life. I just want you to be happy for me and I don't want you to feel sorry for me I don't need a pity party just be happy my life is going good I have nothing to complain about."

Jeanne would soon tell people the baby wasn't even Josh's.

The more Amber learned of Josh's home life, the more she understood his need to escape. To Alaska. To Texas. To friends. To drugs. And the more she heard and saw from Josh's stepmother, she told me, the more she understood Josh's dysfunctions and anger problems.

Understanding was one thing. Accepting was another. She wanted her husband to get clean. She insisted. When his eBay package arrived, Josh went into the kitchen, mixed the ingredients, poured them into a baking pan, and stored it in their turned-off oven. Amber was angry. She told him she didn't want it around her or their unborn baby.

"This is smelling up my kitchen!" she yelled at him. "Get this out of my house!"

She took the pan out of the oven and dumped the ingredients on the floor. They fought.

She had hoped the pregnancy would be the spark to help get him clean.

It wasn't.

On New Year's Eve, a neighbor saw Josh smoking spice upstairs at his house and reported him to the Air Force police. When Amber heard about it she went upstairs, angry. She yelled at Josh and, she admits, pushed him. Police soon arrived to investigate the neighbor's drug allegations. They found spice residue in the couple's vacuum, still lingering from the cleanup after Amber had dumped his pan out a couple weeks before. They searched Josh's computer and found his eBay receipts. Amber was terrified the Air Force was going to kick him out. She tried to blame it all on herself, but Josh stopped her. He confessed, sort of, telling the police he had "tried" to make spice once but it "didn't work."

The Air Force would soon learn better. Josh's drug habits were hardly a secret around the base. People talked. Oxycotton, spice, roxies, weed, alcohol. He had already developed a reputation.

"I witnessed it firsthand," the same neighbor later told me. "When I was over there, everyone was smoking spice around Amber and another neighbor who was also pregnant."

What about Amber, I asked, remembering the rumors. "I never saw Amber smoke it," she says. Not once.

The very next time the neighbor went over to their house, "people were drinking and Josh was smoking spice again." She watched as Josh, high, put on a helmet and told everyone to take turns punching and kicking him in head. He had one of his buddies videotape it, then watched after, laughing.

Amber blamed the drugs. This wasn't how he acted when sober, she says. This wasn't the real Josh doing this. *This wasn't my fun, sweet Josh.*

Spice, in particular, made him agitated, paranoid, and detached from her.

And more violent.

In one argument in their Alaska living room, he put his hands around her neck and choked her.

By now he'd started to occasionally punch her, usually in her arms or legs, seemingly trying to avoid the baby.

He'd grab her shoulders, pushing or shaking her, sometimes leaving scratches on her skin.

He'd throw remote controls, plates, glasses, cans of soda against walls.

He broke her iPhone in anger, throwing it down onto the floor and stomping on it. She got another one. He soon broke that one, too, throwing it against a wall.

He threw a glass candle at her while she was pregnant, just missing her head. It shattered against the wall behind her.

He threw a plate full of food at her. The plate shattered and food hit the ceiling, leaving stains that remained until the day they left the house.

He once threw a suitcase, which she had packed full of clothes to leave, down the stairs at her.

He threw his wedding ring at her several times.

And he threw her.

"He was always pushing me into furniture and walls," Amber remembers. "He would push me into closets. He'd always hold me down and throw me around. He'd pick me up and throw me off the bed."

He'd do this knowing she was pregnant.

One time he pushed her off the bed of a pickup truck onto concrete pavement below.

One neighbor once heard Amber screaming, "I can't breathe!" as she tried to get an angry Josh off of her.

Sometimes she would flee to her neighbors, running pregnant outside in the cold Alaska winter night. Sometimes Josh would chase after her. Other times he'd just lock her out.

Josh didn't deny the abuse. He went to counseling to seek help with his anger. He apologized often: to Amber, even to her grandmother. "He admitted he'd done a lot of stuff to Amber," Gloria said.

But nothing changed.

The counseling sessions could only do so much, Amber had complained, with the two of them not able to tell the therapists the whole truth. Josh had insisted they couldn't bring up what she believed was their most serious problem – his drug habits, which she felt led to his violence — because such an admission would risk getting him kicked out of the Air Force. Amber had urged him to see a therapist off base, someone whom he could trust completely, to help him get clean. He refused.

When things got bad, Amber would sometimes call home from Alaska in fear. "Bring me home!" she'd cry to her mom. "Bring me home!"

Amber didn't often talk to her father, Mike Fields, who still lived in Missouri. But she did tell him about some of the abuse. During one conversation, Amber mentioned to him that Josh had "pushed her down on the bed and got on top of her, bouncing on top of her, while she was pregnant," he told me. "I was surprised. I asked if he was just kidding around. She said, 'no, he was being mean, he was mad at me.'"

One of Amber's Alaska neighbors, Nicole Pasco, says she talked to Amber every day during the first few months of her pregnancy. Pasco quickly became her new confidant, filling the role Amber's grandmother had served in Tulsa.

"He kept Amber secluded," Pasco says. "No one heard her side of the story except for me."

One of Amber's closest friends back in Tulsa saw the same dynamic. "She would have to sneak to talk to me on the phone," Sylvia Treat says. "He didn't allow her to talk to anyone. She was always very, very, very fearful of him being mad."

Treat says Amber talked to her about "escaping," about buying a plane ticket back to Tulsa, sneaking to the airport while Josh was at work, and moving in with her. "Josh was very, very abusive to her up there. She would call me all the time crying. She was miserable there."

"It wasn't the Amber that I knew."

While Treat heard about the abuse from afar, Pasco saw it with her own eyes.

"I saw him hit her," Pasco says. "I saw bruises all over her. Some on her breasts, her arms, her legs. They'd just randomly appear, and I'd ask her about them. She'd cry and tell me about their fights. She said they would fight over petty stuff, like her wanting to get a job to raise money for the baby and him not wanting her to, him playing video games."

Her fiancé, Will, saw the bruises on Amber too.

Pasco says she reported Josh's domestic abuse to the military police, and she'd occasionally photograph Amber's injuries.

On January 2, 2011, another neighbor called the police to report that Josh had been physically abusive of his pregnant wife. The police arrived at the house, saw the injuries on Amber, and called for medical responders to treat her. The police report says Amber "was in obvious pain."

The police arrested Josh. They transported him to the 354th Security Forces Squadron, where they read him his rights under Article 31 of the Uniformed Code of Military Justice. Josh requested an attorney. The police report clearly identifies Josh as the "offender" and Amber as the "victim."

According to the report, the fight had started because Josh wanted Amber to cook dinner, and Amber wanted to order take-out. Josh became angry and started calling her names. Amber gave in, went into the kitchen and began making Josh dinner. But the two kept arguing. Josh confronted her in the kitchen, screaming in her face, knocking her dinner plate and drink out of her hands.

He pushed her and grabbed her chest, squeezing and twist-ing her breast so violently that it broke blood vessels and caused significant bruising. She slapped him and ran away. She first ran upstairs, trying to flee, but he chased her. She tried to leave the house but he physically blocked her. She finally managed to es-cape through the back door. She ran outside and climbed over the back fence, pregnant in the cold January night, and ran to the neighbors. They immediately called the police.

The Air Force Security Forces issued a "no-contact" protective order against Josh, prohibiting him from having any contact with Amber. They transported him to a hotel on the military base and ordered him to stay there, while Amber was allowed to remain in the home.

Josh and Amber soon ignored the protective order and start-ed to communicate each other. He was back home within days.

But the violence continued. Later that same month, the po-lice were at their house again. According to a police report dated January 31ˢᵗ, 2011, Josh threw a glass candle at Amber's head. It just missed her and shattered against the kitchen wall. Then he pushed her hard into the wall. Amber responded by slapping him and fleeing. Josh claimed that her slap caused him to hit his own head against a cabinet behind him. But Josh admitted to the police that it was he, not Amber, who had first been physical.

Finally, Amber had had enough. She called her mother.

I'm scared and unhappy and need to come home. Now.

Rhonda, who had been urging her to leave him, bought her daughter a plane ticket home. Amber came back to Oklahoma late that winter.

But she and Josh missed each other. They talked and texted. He made promises and apologies.

After about two weeks, Amber flew back to Alaska.

Within days the police were back again. On March 14, 2011, Josh became angry at Amber because, according to Pasco's written police statement, Amber had hidden his spice and pipe from him, hoping to prevent him from doing the drugs. Josh punched Amber, who was now in her second trimester and visibly pregnant, leaving a large bruise on her thigh.

Amber sent Pasco a text telling her to come pick her up quickly. Pasco rushed over.

"Amber was waiting outside, crying," Pasco remembers. "Josh was outside yelling at her. He went back inside and I took her to my house. There was this big, humungous welt on her leg."

Amber told her what had happened and showed Pasco her injuries. She said Josh had been high. "Josh kept calling her," Pasco says, "telling her to come home, and eventually she did." As soon as Amber left, Pasco called her first sergeant and the police.

The police soon arrived and obtained statements from both Amber and Josh. In his written statement, Josh wrote that he had "smacked" Amber. Amber again tried to protect Josh. She wrote in her statement that "he smacked my leg gently" and showed the police the leg with no welt, concealing the injured leg.

Amber told police she did not want to press charges.

"After that," Pasco says, "she wouldn't really talk to me much."

The police were back just nine days later, on March 23, 2011. According to Amber, Josh had been holding her down, yelling at her. He wrested her cell phone out of her hand and threw it, destroying it. She called the police and told them she wanted to go home to Oklahoma, to get away from Josh.

"I personally think it is in both of our best interests (including the unborn child) for us to separate and work on things from a distance until Josh's separation," she wrote in her police statement. The "separation" she references was Josh's pending discharge, an outcome the Air Force had already told Josh was inevitable given what had been discovered in the ongoing criminal investigations.

Witnesses say they called police on Josh other times, incidents in which no official reports were apparently filed.

In April, the two were in their car headed to Amber's five-month appointment with her obstetrician-gynecologist. She was excited to see the ultrasound. But in the car, the two started arguing again about Josh's drug use and the baby's future.

Josh pulled the car over and kicked her out. He told her to walk the rest of the way to the appointment. She had no money for a cab. She started walking.

Josh drove ahead and waited for her there.

When Amber finally arrived, crying and cold, the technician waiting with Josh saw how upset she was. She told Amber and Josh they needed to work out their problems before she'd conduct the ultrasound. Josh and Amber talked alone for a while, then told the technician they were ready.

She came back into the room and showed them their baby boy.

9

Amber kept giving Josh more chances.

The Air Force didn't. Six months of his behavior was enough.

The domestic violence incidents were piling up. There were numerous reports of him using, manufacturing, and selling illegal drugs, with at least one criminal investigation launched.

On top of those problems, his female co-workers had been complaining about his behavior on the job. "He had a reputation for beating his wife, and we didn't like that," Pasco says. "I was higher ranking than him, so I'd be hard on him. He was very lazy, and he'd just sit there and badmouth women all the time. He talked about how he wouldn't transfer his GI Bill to his wife because he didn't think she was smart enough to get a college education."

Pasco quoted some of his recurring lines: "'Women weren't as smart as men. Women shouldn't be in the military.'"

"He was misogynistic beyond all reason," says Treat, who had known both Josh and Amber for years.

Pasco says she and other female co-workers complained to their superiors about Josh's workplace behavior. The problems

0

got so bad, Pasco recalls, the Air Force transferred Josh to a new job that March to separate him from the female complainants.

Those complaints, though, weren't why the Air Force finally kicked him out.

"Everyone knew he was kicked out because of the drugs," Pasco says.

Another fellow airman, Matt Anacker, recalls Josh telling him "he was getting kicked out because of his bad rapport with the first sergeant and because of problems with him and Amber."

However many reasons there were, his superiors began planning his exit by spring. His official discharge record, DD Form 214, identifies only one official reason for his expulsion: "MISCONDUCT (DRUG ABUSE)."

Amber told her family in March that they'd be coming back home. But the return date kept changing. Josh told her he was waiting on "the paperwork" and his airline tickets. The continued uncertainty made Amber and her family nervous. She was nearing the third trimester of her pregnancy, and they didn't want her flying back from Alaska that late in her term. Finally they booked her a flight back to Tulsa at the end of April.

As bad as Alaska had been, the idea of Josh returning to Tulsa scared Amber even more. "All of his drug friends are there," she told her grandmother. "And I'm not going back to that. I'm not going to raise a baby in that lifestyle."

On her last night in base housing, Amber walked out the front door of their home, alone. She stood in the yard and took one last look at the starry Alaska night sky she had grown to love. She looked at the houses of her neighbors and friends, the ones she'd be forced to leave in the morning. She stood in the driveway and looked back at her own home. She thought of the flowers she had wanted to plant along the front of the house, the nursery she had been dreaming about, its colors and décor, the crib, the baby shower she wouldn't have with the other young Air Force moms... the life that wouldn't be.

Instead, she knew, they were on their way back to Oklahoma, hands out again, broke and jobless, begging to stay with relatives.

Josh saw it all differently, according to Pasco. "He was excited about getting kicked out of the Air Force," she says. "He was going to go to Tulsa and be with her."

Amber stayed on the front patio and cried, then collected herself and walked back inside. Josh was laying on the couch watching TV.

"You're sleeping on the couch tonight," she said, then marched straight up the stairs to finish packing for the next morning's flight. Josh laughed at her. She reached out over the stairway railing and angrily shoved the tall floor lamp.

About 10 minutes later she hauled one of her packed suitcases down to the front door. She saw Josh sitting up, bleeding from a spot next to his right ear. The lamp had hit him, he told her.

It had fallen sideways, into the arm of the couch, then over and onto the couch where he lay. His head had been turned to his left watching TV, and an edge of the lamp had hit him near his ear, leaving a two-inch cut. He went to the hospital to get it stitched. Amber went with him, the two making up on the way.

She said goodbye in the morning and headed back to Tulsa. His discharge was official a week later, on May 6. He was back in Tulsa the next day.

Soon after the plane landed, Josh contacted his old drug dealer in Tulsa and bought more pills.

One month later, he was dead.

10

About one hour after the death of Josh Hilberling, Officer Don Holloway walked Amber Hilberling and her grandmother down a hallway in the Tulsa Police Department's detective division. He opened the door to a small gray room and directed the two inside.

Still wearing her bloodstained clothes, Amber took a seat in the chair on the far side of the room's small, rectangular brown table, her back to the rear wall, unknowingly facing a hidden camera above the door. A bottled water sat on the table in front of her. Gloria sat in one of the two chairs on the other side of the table, this one backed up into the front left corner of the room.

For the next hour-plus, the emotionally ravaged 19-year-old tried to make sense of what had happened. She sobbed, cried, buried her head in her hands, dropped her head to the table, caressed her pregnant stomach and talked to her baby.

Police watched and recorded the conversation from a nearby monitoring room.

Notes taken by Officer Holloway reflect Amber telling Gloria details of the couple's final altercation in the living room. According to Holloway, the two had been arguing about Josh's plans to start selling pills again at the upcoming music festival when things turned physical.

This portion of the dialogue is missing from the video the prosecution later produced.

The video the prosecution later produced begins in mid-dialogue, with Amber crying and holding her head in her hands, talking mostly to herself, her description of the altercation having already occurred.

"I shouldn't be here..." she cried. "Josh is dead, and I'm here. I didn't just lose my husband. Jeanne and Patrick lost their son. Zach lost his brother. His grandma, his poor grandma's going to have a heart attack when she finds out that her little Josh is gone.

"All I keep seeing, I just held his broken body. I just kept looking at him."

With Amber crying and whispering "I can't believe this" to herself, Gloria talked on her cell phone to relatives trying to line up an attorney. She got off the phone and warned Amber that she's going to have to fight for herself and for her baby.

"But who fights for Josh?" Amber replied.

"He's in a better place," Gloria answered. "He's in God's hands right now."

"He's not supposed to be there."

"No," Gloria agreed, "he's not supposed to be."

"This isn't fair."

Throughout the recording, Amber continued to blame herself and express grief for Josh and Josh's family. Sometimes she spoke to her grandmother. Sometimes to herself. Sometimes to God.

Sometimes to Josh.

Her agony is palpable, her remorse self-evident.

"I just want to be with Josh. I just want to die."

"No, you don't," Gloria said.

"Yes, I do," Amber insisted, crying.

"You've got that baby there."

"This is Josh's baby."

"That's the only thing that Josh has got is that baby."

"He's supposed to be here," Amber whispered. "I'm such a bad person."

"Amber."

"No. I don't deserve to live. I don't deserve to be a mom. Josh deserves to be a dad. Josh isn't even a person anymore."

"You can't talk like that."

Amber put her hands on her stomach and looked down at her baby, crying. "I'm so sorry," she whispers to him.

"And you can't talk like that in front of them," Gloria said. "You've got to hold it together, baby."

"I can't stop seeing Josh fall," Amber said, wiping her eyes. "I just want to be back in bed, laying with him. That's never going to happen again. Why did he have to die?"

Gloria asked if Josh had been "doing pills today?"

"No," Amber replied. "He went out with his friends last night and smoked weed -- the person I couldn't even imagine being separated from is dead." She cuts her answer short and starts crying again.

"Josh!" she sobbed. "Josh!"

This was how she spoke throughout the video: not finishing a thought, not responding to a question, starting in one direction then veering into another. When her grandmother would ask her questions, Amber would respond by looking at her confused, as if she didn't understand, sometimes with only a blank stare and the question: "What do you mean?"

"I just want to see him smile again," she said. "This isn't fair. I just want to go back in time. I lost the person I love. The person I couldn't even imagine being separated from is dead."

She put her hands on her face and sobbed, then dropped her head to the table.

"Oh, Josh!" she sobbed. "Josh!!"

"How did this happen?!" she cried. "Why did he have to fall out a window? Fall out a window?! WHY?! Why did Mom put us in that apartment? Why were we there? Why didn't I just leave?"

"Were you both struggling?" Gloria asked. Her use of the word "struggling," and Amber's uncertain response, would become a focal point of the prosecution's case.

"What do you mean?" Amber responded.

"When you was-" Gloria started to refer to something specific but was interrupted.

"I can't get the image out of my head, of him falling out the window," Amber said. "I keep trying to tell myself this isn't real, it's all going to be over soon."

She whispered to herself. "I can't... this isn't happening... Josh is dead."

"His bones were sticking out all over his body," she cried. "His whole body was broken. And I just held him and kissed his cheeks and screamed at him to wake up.... This is going to turn into a nightmare."

"You'll just have to pray," Gloria told her. "We'll get through it."

"I don't deserve to pray. Josh hates me. I'm not going to be able to meet him in Heaven because he hates me. I killed him."

"Amber stop talking like that."

"What kind of person am I?"

"You're a loving person who has been abused by Josh just as well."

"No," Amber said. "I'm a horrible person. Who could do that? Who could do that? Push my husband and make him fall out the window? I wish I could just go back and know that if I pushed him that was going to happen!"

Gloria started to ask her the question the public would debate at length:

"Did you intentionally-"

"No, of course not!" Amber answered immediately, looking at Gloria incredulously.

Amber paused for a few moments, as if replaying things in her mind.

"I don't understand this whole pattern of events of the last year. Us getting married and going to Alaska, everything in Alaska, me being pregnant, coming back here, getting kicked out of Mom's house, going to the apartment, and then all for it just for Josh to fall out of a high rise building?"

"I wish y'all never would have went to the apartment."

"I mean, what are the chances?" Amber continued. "How many times has that happened? All Josh's friends, his family, they're going to know he died because he fell out of a high-rise apartment.

"And I just keep watching him fall over and over and over again in my head. Watching him flail and think that he, you know, my last thought was, 'please catch yourself.'"

She started to sob again.

"And I just want to know what was going through his head. If he knew he was going to die. If he said a prayer, or cursed my name, or just thought he could catch himself too. And then I just watching him hit the ground."

"For the rest of my life everyone is going to think I'm a murderer. My family, my whole family."

"Amber, we don't think that baby."

"All of Tulsa is going to know. I want to be the one that's dead. I want to be dead and I want Josh to be here."

"This can't be real. I still have my whole life ahead of me, and I was supposed to spend it with Josh. And now I'm going to go to prison, and Josh is dead and my baby is going to get taken away from me."

"I can't believe this. I can't believe Josh fell. I wish I could just get it out of my head."

"I know, baby," Gloria said.

"I just want to go to sleep. This is --" she paused and cried, then resumed, "What am I going to tell Levi?"

"That he had a handsome dad, and that he, he loved him, and you will show his picture to him, and you will show him and tell him the good things about his dad," Gloria tells her.

"But I know what really happened," Amber said, correcting her grandmother. It isn't the only time Amber's words seem to implicate Josh.

"What really happened?" Gloria asked. "You don't know what really happened. You all were in there, you were struggling."

"I can't believe he fell out the window," Amber responded. "Why did that happen?"

"Because it's an apartment up there with a view-" Gloria started to say.

"Why didn't I just leave? Why were we there? Why did he fall? Josh is dead?"

Amber grabbed the table with both hands and wept, then buried her head into her folded arms.

"I just want to know where he's at right now," she said, looking up. "He's probably talking to his grandpa."

"He's probably talking to his grandpa," Gloria agreed.

"But I wonder where he went," Amber said, implying she wasn't sure whether her husband had gone to Heaven or Hell.

She followed that with another telling remark: "I'm waiting for Josh to walk into the room and tell me that he's sorry and that he loves me so much."

Tell me that he's sorry. It was a line that would come up in closing arguments.

"I just keep seeing him fall. I wish I could just get it out of my head. It's never going to go away. Every time I close my eyes I'm going to see it for the rest of my life."

"I just want to go home," she whispered. "To my husband."

"Josh fell," she whispered again, to herself, her head shaking back and forth in her hands.

"I feel so guilty. For breathing, for not crying."

"You're in shock," Gloria said.

"But I feel guilty for just being here. I just want him to be in the hospital. I just kept screaming his name, screaming, saying 'Wake up! Please!' And I just waited for him to wake up. I just held him, his body broken to nothing. Every bone in his body was sticking out. And I just, his eyes were open, and I just looked at him and I just kissed him."

She began to sob again. "And I said 'I'm so sorry, please, I love you, wake up.'"

She buried her head in her hands again.

"This isn't happening. Little Levi... he's going to have to grow up without a dad, all because of me."

"Why did I do this? How? How could I do this? I want to die."

"Amber," her grandmother reacted.

"I miss him. I want to be with Josh, and Josh probably doesn't want to be with me. I just, I, I just can't imagine what it would feel like to lose Adam or Ariel, and Josh's family lost him... Why did this happen? This is only stuff that happens in movies"

"I killed him," she whispered.

"You didn't kill him, Amber."

"I know. But it was an accident that went wrong because of me."

Gloria told Amber to "be open and honest with your attorney" but that "your emotions right now, you're in shock."

"What if I'm not? What if I'm just a horrible person that can't cry?" Amber spent most of the video crying, sobbing, sniffling, and wiping her nose with her hands or shirt, yet often indicated her apparent belief that she hadn't cried.

"You're not," Gloria said. "You're human. You've seen your husband that you love die. That's shock. You're seven and a half months pregnant, you're carrying a child."

"I don't feel like I'm in shock. I just don't feel anything." She stopped and sobbed again. "I just keep hoping this all, that Josh is going to walk in here. But he's not."

Now she wept hard.

"God I can't take this," she cried, shaking her head. "I can't take this. I can't do this. I can't. I can't."

"Josh is dead," she whispered again. "Not only is he dead, but the way he died. I just wish it would leave my head, every time I close my eyes I see it. It's like torture, just, my subconscious just keeps playing it over and over and over again, as if one time seeing it isn't bad enough, I have to see it over and over and over."

She stopped and wept again, then resumed. "I just want to save him. I want to save him. I just want to, at least if I could go back and take back the push, at least I could save him."

"The push?" Gloria asked.

"I pushed him against the wall and he fe – Oh my god!" Again, Amber stopped herself in mid-thought and cried, burying her face in her hands. "At least I could catch him. I tried but it was all so fast. And I just want to know what his last thoughts were. What could you think? What could go through your head when you're falling to your death?

"Was he fixing to - where was the candle things?"

"There's like these big, there's like these stand-up candle things like this high, they're just like these little wire things. But he was fixing the TV, he was like messing with the TV right here, and the window's right here, and I pushed him and he fell out the window [unintelligible words while crying], fell, God, I'm never going to get over this, I'm never going to understand it. I mean I thought divorce was going to hurt. He's not even here, I can't even talk to him. Every time I pick up the phone I'm just going to want to text him."

Amber cried again, then picked up the bottled water and drank.

"Why is this happening?" she asked.

She later tried again to make sense of the last few moments of her husband's life.

"God... I just watched him fall, not doing anything, standing safely in my apartment watching him... I just kept saying to myself 'please catch yourself, please catch yourself'... I'm wondering why I was ever thinking he could catch himself, hoping he would just break his leg..."

Gloria: "You was hoping he would fall?"

Amber: "No."

Gloria: "Was you fixing to come over to my house?"

"I was waiting for him to leave. I didn't even yell at him or anything, I don't know what happened. He was the one walking around yelling at me, being mean, and I was just cleaning up the glass, I didn't say anything mean to him, didn't yell at him, just sat in the bathroom crying so hard I was throwing up. He came in there and said 'I've got all these options, what do you want to do?' I said 'please make your own decisions.' He said 'OK I will.' He said 'I want to work things out with you but we need to be separated for a while.' He had already talked to his dad, had just got off the phone with him. His dad was at work, he was going to pick him up after work, that's why he was going with his friend, he was on the phone with his friend, he had just hung up, I don't even know if he was on the phone, I don't know. I just came, he had dumped all my laundry out, and I was putting it all back in there, I just don't understand why. I wish I could go back and just have left."

Officer Holloway briefly returned to the room, took some biographical information, then left.

"I can't," Amber muttered after he left. "I can't do this. Josh is gone, for forever. I'm only 19. I have the next 60 years to think about this, to let it torture me. I'm never going to find someone that I love more than Josh. I'm never going to find someone as perfect for me as he was, and I ruined all of it."

She wept and slammed the palms of her hands down onto the table.

"God, why did I do this? God, I just want to go back."

"That wasn't the first time you all got in a fight," Gloria said.

Amber looked down at the cuts on her hands and wrists.

"He's dead," she said. "I touched his bones, all broken and sticking out of his body. Everything was bent backwards. I rolled him over and just held him, I didn't care... I want this to be over."

"I love you," Gloria offered.

"I can't believe this," Amber whispered. "Why? I'm going to have his baby and it's going to be just like Josh. And I'm scared because it's going to remind me of him every day. Look like him. And I was supposed to enjoy it with Josh. And I stole that from Josh, I didn't, I stole his whole life away from him. He's 23, he's supposed to- he's never going to watch - he's not going to be there when Levi's born, he's not going to watch him grow up, watch him get married, see him have grandkids... Oh my god!"

She sobbed again.

"It's OK, baby," Gloria attempted.

"No! Josh is gone!"

Gloria moved around to Amber's side of the table. She put her arm around her granddaughter, and Amber buried her head into her grandmother's left shoulder and wept.

"I'm so sorry," Amber cried.

Gloria kissed her forehead.

"What kind of person am I? I don't deserve to be here. How could I push Josh out the window? Why? Why?"

"Baby there was not-"

"I just want to be with him. I can't accept the fact that he's not here anymore. I refuse to do that. I'm not looking forward to all the nights I'm going to spend crying, waking up screaming, dreaming about him –"

"That's why we have therapists," Gloria said. "It will help."

"—dreaming about what happened, every time. I just see it, I can't get it out of my head now. I just can't imagine how his parents feel, or how his brother's going to feel, he's all the way in

Afghanistan. Him and his brother have grown up protecting each other.

"I'm such a bad person," she whispered. "Josh was so special. He is so special."

Detective Felton came into the room and introduced himself, then asked Gloria to step out.

"How old are you Amber?"

"Nineteen."

"How long have you guys been married?"

"I can't, I don't want to make a statement. I don't want this to turn out bad."

"OK, well um…"

"My mom I think is calling an attorney."

"Is that what you want to do?"

"And I'm not supposed to say anything until he gets here."

"OK. Who is your attorney?"

"I don't know."

"OK. What's your mom's name?"

"Rhonda Whitlock. Okay. And um, you know her phone number?"

[Omitted.]

"OK, let me just get all your information then, and we won't talk about the case at all. Amber?"

"I just can't."

"And we'll let your grandma come back in here."

"I just can't deal with this," she whispered.

"Can you tell me your name and stuff?"

"Amber Hilberling." Just saying their last name, Josh's last name, seemed to set her off. She started crying again. Felton soon called it quits.

"You want you grandma to come sit back in?"

"Yes please."

"OK," Felton said, standing up and walking out.

For a few moments, Amber was alone in the room for the first time.

She looked up and started talking to her husband.

"Josh, baby, I will never, ever forgive myself. I can't even begin to accept this. I want you to be here. Just come back, please. Please. I love you. I love you so much. I hope, I hope you are happy.

"I will spend the rest of my life paying for this."

Part Two: Pre-Trial

11

In the course of her trial preparation, Tulsa County Assistant District Attorney Michelle Keely telephoned Nicole Pasco, Amber's confidant in Alaska, to interview her as a potential trial witness.

Pasco says she told Keely about Josh physically abusing Amber. She says she told her about the bruises and welts on Amber's pregnant body, about Josh getting arrested for domestic violence, and about the protective order entered against Josh in Alaska. She says she told Keely about Josh's drug abuse and manufacturing, and the police's criminal investigation into Josh's drug offenses.

Keely told her specifically to not put any of that on the record, Pasco says.

Instead, Pasco says, the prosecutor told her she only wanted one specific part of her recollections put on the record: "Josh telling me about Amber hitting him," Pasco recounted to me later. "But I never saw that."

Pasco's detailed accounts of Josh's pattern of domestic abuse were evidence that would have been helpful to Amber, as they corroborated her assertion of self-defense. The district attorney's office did not share any of this evidence with Amber's defense team. I only learned about this when I tracked down Pasco myself.

Pasco told me in detail about her dialogue with the district attorney. I asked Pasco what testimony she told Keely she could have given.

"I would be comfortable testifying about him beating her," she says she told Keely. "But she didn't want that."

Instead, Pasco told me, the prosecutor told her to send her a written statement omitting any accounts of Josh's misconduct. What Keely told her to send, Pasco says, was an e-mail "about why *Amber* was mad at *Josh*" … and nothing else.

Pasco refused.

The state elected not to have her testify at trial.

Later in the case, the district attorney's office listed Pasco as a potential witness and produced its required summary of her testimony. The summary only contained a description of testimony that reflected poorly on Amber. It made no mention of what Pasco had told the prosecution about Josh's physical abuse of Amber or his criminal history.

Withholding helpful evidence from a defendant is against the law. It's known as a "*Brady* violation." Under the 1963 United States Supreme Court case of *Brady v. Maryland*, 373 U.S. 83, the district attorney's office is required to turn over to the defense all evidence and information that could be favorable to the defendant. I had also filed the necessary motion in the case requiring the prosecutor give us all such evidence.

The prosecutor's failure to disclose Pasco's statements wasn't an isolated incident.

What Pasco told me was just a hint of the bombshell *Brady* violation I would discover long after the case was over.

12

My cell phone rang early in the morning. It was Shawn Peters, a successful local realtor and a longtime close friend of mine.

She was frantic.

"Did you see the news?!?" she asked.

I hadn't.

"That's Rhonda's daughter!"

"Hold on," I said, walking from my bedroom into my home office. "Give me a second."

I pulled up the Internet and immediately saw the news coverage. It was everywhere.

A Tulsa man had fallen to his death from a high-rise apartment window the day before. His name was Joshua Hilberling. Tulsa police were holding his wife, Amber Hilberling, on suspicion of murder.

I didn't know Amber. But I knew her mother, Rhonda Whitlock, a close friend of Shawn's. I had met her a few months before, when Shawn had invited me to meet the two of them for happy hour.

"Rhonda's going to call you," Shawn said. "She needs help!"

Rhonda would call soon after.

I often wish I'd never answered.

13

JUNE 8, 2011

I was still reading a news article about Josh's death on my computer screen when my phone rang again.

It was Rhonda. She was fired up, crying and upset.

She was even, it struck me, angry. Angry at the police. Angry at the media. Angry at Josh. She insisted Amber had been wrongfully charged and was "innocent."

She asked me to help.

I said no.

I was doing my best to get rid of cases, not take new ones. I had closed down my law office months before, burned out after spending six years earning a living by engaging in unpleasant fights about money. Or as others call it, litigation. By the time Rhonda called, I was well on my way out of active practice, having whittled down my caseload from more than 100 to fewer than 10, finishing up the last few lawsuits out of my home office.

I could see the finish line. A new murder case didn't exactly fit my exit strategy.

But even if it had, I wasn't the guy for the job. My practice had been focused on civil litigation, not criminal defense work. The two are different worlds entirely. About the only time I ventured into the criminal courtrooms was to refer a case to another attorney.

"Call Allen Smallwood," I told Rhonda, referring her to one of Tulsa's most respected criminal defense lawyers.

Rhonda wasn't listening.

"She's my baby! She's my baby! She couldn't have done this!"

It sure looks like she did it, I thought, based on what I had been reading as we talked. She had pushed him and admitted it, the articles and Internet buzz were already saying.

"They're making it look like something it wasn't!" she said. "The media is trashing her! This wasn't murder! This guy was a druggie, he was abusive! This was self-defense! She needs somebody now!"

"Call Smallwood, Rhonda," I said. "Call him now."

I looked up his number and gave it to her.

"OK, OK. I will."

It wasn't long, though, before my phone was ringing again.

It was Rhonda.

Smallwood wanted more than they could afford, she said. I told her to try Clark Brewster, a friend who had built a successful practice by cherry-picking high-profile criminal cases and high-value civil cases. He'd love the headlines on this one, I thought, and might decide to work the case for free.

They called him. Then Rhonda called me back. Brewster's fee was also too steep, she said.

"I thought your husband was a plastic surgeon."

"We can't afford it," she said. She told me they'd been struggling through financial problems. "We don't have the cash. Please! My baby!"

I told her I'd make some calls, find her somebody, and call her back. I made a few calls at my desk, while I kept clicking through stories on my computer screen.

Rhonda's words replayed in my head.

Abuse. Self-defense. Nineteen years old. The media is trashing her.

I kept going back to the pictures of Amber in the breaking news stories. A pregnant teenager. Sitting down there in jail, probably no idea what to do, probably talking too much.

And I knew all about the media's ability to trash somebody. I was a journalist myself, having spent years in news rooms before scratching an itch to learn more about the law, and understood well how quickly the media could adopt a narrative and run wild with it, accuracy be damned.

I looked at the photo of Amber on my computer screen. I saw a scared kid.

I called Rhonda back. "Has anyone told her not to talk?" I asked. "Not to say anything to anybody? Not even to you?"

"I don't know. She hasn't talked to an attorney yet."

"The police need to know she has counsel," I said. "She can't talk to them."

"Can you just talk to her? Just tell them you're her attorney so they don't talk to her? Until we find somebody? Please! She needs help."

Rhonda was right. Amber did need help.

I ended the call, threw on a suit, got in my car and headed to jail.

14

JUNE 8, 2011

The room was small and white, with concrete walls, a small table, and two white chairs. A loud buzz, then the metal door opened. A female guard escorted Amber into the room, where I stood waiting. She wore the standard jail uniform, orange shirt and orange pants, her brown hair down.

I had never met her, but she seemed immediately relieved that I was there. The guard left, and I introduced myself. She shook my hand and smiled nervously. We sat down on opposite sides of the table, and the first words out of my mouth were this:

"You're not in here because you pushed your husband out a window," I said. "You're in here because you talked."

That message was the reason for my visit. To tell her not to talk to anybody about what happened. Not any police officers, detectives, guards, media, friends, or other inmates. No one. She said the only people she had talked to since being booked were her mother and grandmother, both over the phone.

They can listen to those calls, I told her.

They can?

No attorney has talked to you?

No.

Has anyone explained your right to remain silent?

No, not that I can remember.

I assumed they had read her rights to her, but she probably had been in a daze. I walked her through her constitutional rights, her right to remain silent, her right to counsel. I told her that her parents were finding her a criminal defense attorney.

She was soft spoken and polite. She struck me as shy but strong, though clearly still traumatized. I tried some small talk to help her relax, asked how she was being treated. We talked about her emotional mother, which finally made her chuckle a bit.

Before long, she started talking about what had happened the afternoon before.

She told me they had been arguing.

"He's been doing drugs and I didn't agree with it. Smoking weed and he was going to be selling Oxycotton tomorrow. He was supposed to be getting them today. He's sold before, that's how he made his living before he enlisted last year. He had a stash. He was pretty hard core about it."

The arguing got heated, she said. She told me about the laundry basket through the bedroom window. Her in the bathroom.

Them arguing, her vomiting. The knock on the front door, the window repairman in the other room. Then the two of them, back in the living room, arguing again.

Josh was by the TV stand against the living room's left wall. "Messing with stuff," Amber said, probably packing up his video game accessories. They started exchanging words again, Amber not remembering exactly what.

She remembered calling him a "coward," which made him angrier. And asking him, in a taunting manner: "Are you going to go get high?"

"He grabbed on, like we were pushing each other back and forth, but he grabbed on to me. He grabbed my shoulder and was digging his nails into me."

I could see her replaying the scene in her head. She looked down and closed her eyes.

"It all happened so fast," she said. "He stumbled backwards. Just... I don't even remember exactly how he fell out."

"He went backwards?" I asked.

"Yes."

"I pushed him into the TV, then he stumbled on everything. The TV, his own feet... It was... probably not the best spot to be fighting."

He made eye contact with her as he first went through the glass, she said, her eyes now watering.

"I saw him going into the window and I tried to catch him," she whispered.

She lunged into the window after him, grabbing the frame with her hands, and watched as he twisted in the air as if bracing himself for the landing. She saw him land and hoped somehow he'd survived.

I sat there trying to picture it all happening. I couldn't. A six-foot-four man fitting through a living room window? Going right through window glass, just like that, in a high-rise apartment living room? It didn't add up.

"It's hard to believe you can go through the glass like that," I said.

Amber nodded in agreement.

"How did he fit through?"

"I don't know. I've thought about that too. It doesn't make any sense to me."

She sat there replaying the scene in her head, trying to figure out how it all happened. How it was possible. She didn't get it.

Her answers, the way she worded them, the language she used... she struck me as genuine. Sincere. Years of litigating had made me a cynic, years of cross-examinations had helped me spot lies.

I believed her.

Across the table from me, I saw a vulnerable, scared, confused girl.

I didn't see a murderer.

She wiped her eyes with her hand, which was still bandaged. From the cuts at the window frame, she explained.

I asked her where exactly Josh had grabbed her.

"My shoulders," she said.

"I want to look at them."

She stood up and turned to her side, then pulled the top of her shirt down past her left shoulder. I didn't see any marks. Then she turned the other way.

There, on her right shoulder blade, were two scratches. Two thin horizontal red lines, narrowing toward each other at the left like a sideways V. She didn't know they were there. To my un-trained eyes, the lines were consistent with fingernail scratches. Consistent with what she had told me about Josh digging his nails into her before she pushed him off.

And above the scratches were marks in the shape of fingertips.

I snapped photos of the injuries with my iPhone, which I had snuck into the room despite the jail's prohibition against phones. I had seen the rule posted on the wall, but I had a gut feeling I might want photographs. Or more accurately, that Amber might need them.

I asked her if Josh had ever touched her in anger before Tuesday.

Yes, she said. Many times.

She started to tell me about Josh attacking her in January, him getting arrested, the protective order barring him from being near her.

There were other incidents, sure, she said. Other injuries. Bruises, welts, marks.

"But it doesn't matter," she said, her tone resigned. "I didn't take pictures. My friend had but I made her delete them. I normally didn't call the police because I didn't want him getting kicked out [of the Air Force]. So I have no proof of any of that. No one is going to believe me."

And, it was clear, none of that really mattered to her anyway.

She had just lost her husband.

It doesn't matter, she said.

"Amber, listen to me. They all matter."

She didn't see it. The importance of every incident. Every single time an angry man laid a finger on a woman, especially a pregnant one, mattered. Every one. The history of this behavior, the pattern. Things she would ultimately need at trial if she asserted self-defense. Whoever took the case, I wanted them to know. I wanted Amber to make sure they knew. I wanted her to understand.

But she had no interest in strategizing, in thinking about preparing a defense or winning a trial; she was only thinking about her husband.

Which made me root for her even more.

I needed to make her understand.

"The news is all over this," I told her. "Dateline NBC called. The media spotlight is not really great for you, obviously, because it's going to follow you for the rest of your life. But it also puts pressure on the prosecutors because they know everyone is watching them. They're macho, they don't want to lose a public, high-profile case, so they're going to be more determined to get a conviction here, OK? And you understand, first-degree murder carries with it the possibility of a death sentence, or life in prison. Your best hope right now is to be able to build a self-defense case. So I don't ever want you to tell me, or anybody else – whoever is helping you — 'oh well there wasn't any pictures, or that one didn't count, or it was just a little thing.' There are no little things here in a self-defense case. Every minor, little thing, I don't care if you didn't have a mark, don't care if it didn't hurt, every time he touched you or scared you or threatened you is your life-line, it's your ticket out of here."

She looked at me and nodded slowly.

"OK," she said.

Then she started to tell me about more incidents. More times Josh had left marks on her body. More times he had physically hurt her.

A lot more.

15

I wanted to get her out. Home with her family.

That was my first instinct as I told Amber goodbye and walked down the long corridors of the county jail that Wednesday morning.

I looked up her bond information. Her bond was set at $250,000. The District Attorney had charged her with second-degree murder, the police's original recommendation.

I called a criminal defense attorney for advice. Mark Collier, a longtime district attorney who had gone into private practice, was straight out of central casting. He was in his mid-40s but looked about 10 years older. He drank too much, smoked, and cussed like a sailor, often grumbling about the ugly divorce he was battling. He sometimes looked like he had just woken up on his office couch, his hair and clothes a mess. But his mind was sharp as a tack. He had forgotten more about criminal law than I'd ever known, and he was universally respected in the criminal courtrooms.

"Two-fifty?" he said. "That's pretty goddamn low for a murder bond. They'll try to raise that."

"How? When?"

"I bet the state files a motion to increase bond by tomorrow," he said, matter of factly. "If she's gonna post bond, she better do it now. Right fucking now."

And if Amber was already out, bond posted, Mark explained, it'd be less likely the judge would grant the state's motion to increase the bond and put her back in jail.

I called Amber's mom.

"We need to post bond right now, right away," I told her. I explained to her what little I knew about the bond process. If she used a bail bondsman, she'd need to come up with 10 percent of the bond amount. So, $25,000.

"There's no way," Rhonda said. "We can't. We can come up with some, but not that much."

I called Mark back. He had connections I didn't. He referred me to a friend of his, Rusty Roberts, a bail bondsman who Mark said might work with us if I dropped his name. I went straight to Rusty's office and pitched him face to face. I told him about Amber's situation, vouched for her, and used Mark's name as directed. I assured him that Amber's family would do whatever was needed. I did everything short of beg.

He said he'd post the bond if we could come up with $10,000.

I called Amber's mother back and told her to find the money, now. A few minutes later, an employee from her husband's medical office called me. "Rhonda told me where to find some cash. I can get $10,000 and meet you with it."

I drove across town and met the employee. She gave me an envelope full of $100 bills, and I drove it straight to the bondsman's office. I told him about the time crunch – Mark's prediction that the state would be moving to increase the bond, maybe as soon as today. He agreed to start the process on the spot.

"How long will it take?"

"It takes hours to process somebody out of jail," he said.

"The media is gonna swarm the jail when this gets out," I said. "It'll be a circus. Any way to get her out quicker?"

Roberts leaned back in his chair as if sizing me up.

"Let me make a call," he said.

Within minutes, we had struck a deal with the jail. They agreed to expedite the process and send Amber to meet me outside the back door. I drove back to the jail and pulled my SUV around to the fenced-in parking lot behind the complex. A jail officer came out and told me Amber didn't have a change of clothes. The blood-soaked clothes she had been wearing had been retained as evidence. I looked in my backseat and saw my gym bag. I opened it and showed the clothes to the officer.

"That'll work," he said.

A few minutes later, Amber walked out the back door of the jail wearing a red Nebraska Cornhuskers t-shirt, a pair of black men's gym shorts, and men's tennis shoes several sizes too big.

I opened the door to my car and hustled her in.

"Thank you!" she said, her eyes red. "Oh my god, thank you so much."

I sped away from the jail, almost in disbelief that we had gotten her out so quickly.

And Mark Collier had been right. Within hours, the state filed a motion to strengthen the bond, just as he predicted, eventually asking the court to increase her bond to $500,000.

"You're lucky to be out this fast," I told her. "A lot of things had to happen the right way to get you out."

I told her to not take her freedom for granted. To be smart. That people were going to want her back in jail. We'd have several conversations in the ensuing months about the lifestyle I wanted to see her living. How I wanted the jury to see a responsible young woman who was working, going to college, staying out of trouble, and raising her son.

I wouldn't get my wish.

16

JUNE 8, 2011

I drove Amber from the jail to Shawn Peters' house, where she would wait for her mom to get back in town from a trip.

Amber didn't want me to leave her. So I waited with her.

My adrenaline was running high. It was just the middle of the day, and I felt like I had already done about a week's worth of work. This felt nothing like the usual fights about money that had occupied my days, weeks, and years. But there was something else I wanted to do, and right away.

My thoughts kept going back to Apartment 2509, and what I could learn by getting inside and seeing it with my own eyes – and seeing it now. It had been less than 24 hours since Josh's death. I was sure the scene hadn't yet been put back in order. I wanted to see things before it was. There must be something there, somewhere, that could teach me something about what had just happened.

After Amber's family arrived at Shawn's, I borrowed one of their apartment keys and headed to the University Club Tower. I worried I'd be stopped, or that the apartment would be sealed shut. Neither was the case. And when I opened the door to 2509,

I saw immediately that my hunch had been right. The broken window was still open, warm gusts of air blowing into the living room. Eight of the 16 blinds were gone. The remaining eight, some broken, swayed in the breeze.

I took a quick look around the apartment. Other than the discomforting scene at the large living room window, and the small broken window in the bedroom, the apartment was clean and well decorated.

I walked over to the window. It was frightening. There was no balcony, no ledge, no safety bars, nothing. Just a TV stand, a chair, then a large hole in the wall that led straight down, a long way down, to a cement landing.

I looked at the four edges of the window frame. Pieces of glass still jutted out from its sides. There were still some on the carpeted floor. I pulled a piece of glass out of the window frame and held it in my fingers. It felt barely thicker than a piece of construction paper.

I would later learn exactly how flimsy the glass was: a mere nine one-hundredths of an inch thick. Less than one-tenth of one inch.

The glass felt barely thicker than a napkin. This was all that had stood between life and death. Nervously, I held my phone out through the opening and snapped a photo:

The window wasn't made of safety glass, which is normally used in high rises. The building's own window repairman, Armando Rosales, later testified in court that high-rise buildings normally use safety glass that is "usually one inch thick," or more than 10 times thicker than the thin sheets of glass put in the University Club Tower windows.

A national window glass expert, who had overseen the installation of more than a million square feet of high-rise windows in his 30-plus years in the field, would later testify he had never seen high-rise glass this thin.

Not once in his entire career.

I looked at the piece of glass in my hand and saw a defense for Amber.

To make any kind of murder case, first degree or second, the state was going to have to prove beyond a reasonable doubt that Amber knew Josh could go through that window glass. I thought back to her words in our first conversation.

It's hard to believe you can go through the glass like that.

There was no way Amber could have known, I thought. No way she could have guessed how bizarrely thin was the glass in this large living room window.

No one could have guessed. So would a jury, I wondered, ever believe that this teenage girl could have known?

I looked at this cheap, dangerous window glass and saw something else. A wrongful death lawsuit. A civil case against the University Club Tower.

Not only could this irresponsible choice of glass explain things and help Amber's defense, I started to envision, it could set her and her baby up with enough money to get on their feet, get a fresh start somewhere with a house and a college fund.

I had got there just in time. The window was boarded up later that day, the glass replaced. The incriminating shards of glass would be gone. But we now had real evidence, right here in my hand.

But I needed someone else's hands on it too. I didn't want to be the one sitting on a witness stand testifying about how we got the actual pieces of glass. An opposing attorney would try to impeach me as biased in favor of Amber, not properly trained in evidence collection techniques, not knowledgeable about broken glass. I needed to get someone else inside the apartment, someone independent, someone who could testify cleanly. Ideally someone with experience examining buildings.

A building inspector, I decided.

I started working the phones, Googling, calling the city, the fire marshal, inspection companies, looking for the right guy. Finally I got in touch with a longtime City of Tulsa building inspector named Carl Crager.

Carl immediately said something that stunned me.

"I was thinking about calling you," he said. My visit to the jail had apparently already put my name on the case. "This thing smells to high heaven. That window should be safety glass.

There's no way that kid should have been able to go through it like that."

My thoughts exactly, I said. Carl agreed to meet me at the apartment. He was a gentle, white-haired, sweet-spoken softie, the kind of guy you'd want your kids to have for a grandpa. He said he and his wife had already been praying for Amber, her family, and Josh's family. More important, for my purposes that day, he said he had been a building inspector for decades. He knew his stuff.

I met him outside the building and brought him up to Apartment 2509.

Carl picked up a piece of the broken glass and held it in his fingers. He looked shocked.

"That is unbelievable," he said. "I've never seen such flimsy windows in a high rise in all my life. These are just old household windows. In a high-rise apartment. No safety glass. In all my years…"

I pulled out more pieces, some between three and five inches long, and handed them to Carl. He put them in a large envelope I had asked him to bring. I asked him to seal the envelope when we were done, date it, initial it, and maintain possession of the envelope until we needed it for trial.

Carl pulled out a tape measure. The window was roughly 45 inches wide and 51 inches tall, about 16 square feet. Give or take a few inches, it was about four feet by four feet.

I looked at the window and replayed the scene. The window was four feet, three inches tall, which meant Josh had to have gone through at some kind of angle. He couldn't have fit through otherwise.

The bottom of the window was about 26 inches above the floor, which meant Josh's upper body would have been the first part of his body to go through the glass, unless he had performed some aggressive leap into the air.

The windowsill was only 1.5 inches deep, which meant the glass pane had been very, very close to the hanging white blinds it hid behind. I could tell by the positioning of the clips above that the blinds had been fully closed when it happened. Neither Amber nor Josh likely saw any window glass until his fall.

Taking in the whole scene, the only thing that made sense was that it had been an accident. Amber had only been staying in the apartment for a couple weeks. There had been an unusually thin sheet of glass hiding behind closed blinds. There had been a complete stranger just in the next room. Amber was on her way out the door, headed to her grandmother's with laundry.

There was simply no way she could have understood what was going to happen when she pushed Josh.

It was the same thing she had said at the jail.

It doesn't make any sense to me.

She was right. It didn't make sense.

17

JUNE 8, 2011

That Amber was out of jail so quickly – the day after being arrested — only added to the public's resentment of her. The backlash was swift. Josh's family complained about it. Local media quickly reported that she was "already" out of jail. The Internet trolls pounced, publishing inflammatory and threatening comments that frightened Amber and her family.

The court had quickly set the state's motion to strengthen her bond for a hearing that Friday. I knew the prosecutor, and the judge, would be feeling public pressure to put Amber back in jail.

Amber would need an attorney. A real criminal defense attorney – in other words, not me. I already had the sense I was going to stick around and help, but there was no way I'd be leading a murder case. That was no way to get my feet wet in the practice of criminal law.

Wednesday evening, hours after driving Amber from the jail, I met with her, her mother Rhonda, and her stepfather Bryan at Shawn Peters' house. We sat outside on the backyard patio and strategized. Rhonda and Bryan thanked me repeatedly for hustling to get Amber out of jail so quickly.

I took more photos of Amber in the backyard, close-ups of her injuries. I talked to them all about what I had seen at the apartment that afternoon, about the window glass and what it could mean. I showed them photos I had taken of it all.

We talked about the attorneys they could hire. Who they might afford, who they couldn't.

"Why can't you do it?" Rhonda asked again. "We trust you. Look what you've done already."

In a follow-up email, Rhonda wrote about all of the attorneys the family had spoken with and considered hiring. But, she wrote, "we CHOSE you."

They told me how they had been impressed by my hustle and success that day. But I suspect it was more than that. I think they could tell I believed in Amber, that I had genuine concern for her. They wanted that – someone who cared – helping their girl. It probably also helped that unlike the high-priced attorneys they had initially called, I hadn't even mentioned payment.

And though Bryan had no idea, his wife had already been leaning on me for months.

When Shawn had invited me to that happy hour a couple months before, it was partly because Rhonda had wanted my legal advice. She said she was planning to file for divorce and had some initial questions. I wasn't much help. I tried to steer as clear as possible from the emotional and often ugly dramas that unfolded daily in the divorce courtrooms. I referred her to an attorney who specialized in complex, high-dollar divorce cases.

But she had continued to call and text me regularly after the happy hour, picking my brain and seeking comfort. Sitting on Shawn's patio that Wednesday evening, she pleaded with me to stay by her side.

Amber wanted the same thing.

Finally, I offered a solution.

Hire a criminal defense attorney, I said, and I'll work the case with them. But they're in charge, and you pay them first. Things were going to get expensive, I knew.

They agreed. I called Mark Collier back and asked him to take the case, a call Mark said he figured was coming. I had told the family I suspected Mark might be more flexible on fees than Smallwood or Brewster, that maybe he'd take payments. Mark and I met with the family at a downtown restaurant the next night, in a private room near the back.

Mark agreed to lead the case. I was relieved.

He and I talked on the phone later that night. We'd work the case together. He'd be the captain; I'd do whatever was necessary. The next day, Rhonda called me into her husband's clinic, where she was working as the office manager. She gave me another envelope of cash, this one for legal fees. She told me to divide it up however I felt would be fair. I gave it all to Mark. I wanted him fully committed to the cause. I'd take a cut from a later payment, I told him. For now, I wanted him to get to work.

Of immediate concern was the bond issue. Just as Mark had predicted, the state wanted to double it. Amber's parents made it clear they wouldn't be able to come up that much cash. If the court ruled in the state's favor on its request for a bond increase, Amber would be back behind bars, back in the dirty jail I had just pulled her out of. Then probably delivering her baby in custody.

I couldn't allow that. I was scared for her and scared for her unborn child.

Mark didn't share my fear. "We'll win," he said, matter of factly shrugging off the upcoming battle. "Quit fucking worrying."

His detachment struck me. I understood it was the result of his years in criminal law: If a client gets hauled behind bars, so be it; it happens. But this was new territory for me. The idea of someone's very freedom resting upon the quality of my work was a pressure I had never felt. I had worked hundreds of civil cases, won jury trials in multiple courthouses, been through countless hearings, depositions, arbitrations, mediations, and intense legal fights in several states. I'd won my share of six- and seven-figure paydays.

But when we went to court to argue about Amber's bond, I found myself more nervous than I could ever remember being in my legal career. I knew my nerves were ridiculous, irrational. I thought about the criminal defense attorneys I knew and asked myself how the hell they did it.

As the prosecution began the hearing with its argument, I found myself acting like the kind of co-counsel I had always found annoying – writing Mark notes, reminding him of details I thought would boost our case, whispering to him. He shook his head.

I got this, his facial expression told me. *Relax.*

And he did. When the state finished, Mark stood and calmly countered their arguments point by point. He used criminal-law terms that were nearly foreign to me, and cited legal standards I hadn't heard about since law school. I could feel the nerves of Amber's family behind us, terrified that Amber would be leaving the hearing in handcuffs.

Come on, Mark, I rooted. *Come through. I vouched for you. Let's start off by kicking some ass.*

Mark nailed it. We won, and Amber was free to go back home with her family. They celebrated, relieved, hugging and wiping their eyes.

I was thrilled. But I hid my emotions and played it cool. "Nice work, Mark," I said.

He shrugged his shoulders like it was no big deal.

I was sure I had chosen the right guy to lead the fight.

Amber's family soon disagreed.

18

The public narrative about Amber and Josh was set.

The early campaigning from Josh's family, and the statements by the police and prosecution, had succeeded in crafting a specific storyline. Media reports and the Internet rumor mill, often interchangeable, were overwhelmingly pro-Josh.

Amber was mentally ill, the talk went. Deranged, physically abusive, an intentional murderer, even a drug addict. One friend of Josh's even told the lead detective that it was actually Amber, not Josh, who had been taking the Oxycotton and smoking the marijuana during their final weeks together in the University Club Tower. While she was pregnant.

If the state was going to try to sell any of these stories to a jury, I wanted us to be prepared.

So we set out to find the truth.

We quickly looked into the drug rumors. Just days after her arrest, we asked Amber to submit to a private, thorough drug screen. We insisted on a hair follicle screen, not a urine test, because a hair screen shows drug usage from the previous 90 days, whereas a urinalysis goes back just a few days.

The 90-day window would prove whether Josh's friend had told the detective the truth.

She willingly took the test. She passed completely.

She had been clean.

We researched the rumors that Amber had been physical with Josh. Amber hadn't claimed innocence in this area. She had admitted there were times she tried to physically fight back or push her husband off of her so she could flee to their neighbors. There were times she lost her own temper during their heated fights. Her accounts, though, were a far cry from the public story being painted.

I pressed her for more details. I interviewed witnesses. The stories never changed.

Once she threw a shoe at him, which hit him in his finger. She kicked him during a fight in Alaska. The night their neighbor caught Josh smoking spice, after Amber had told him she was scared the fumes could hurt the baby, she admits she lost her temper and pushed him. Josh called his family after that, high and upset, complaining that Amber was being mean and had pushed him. But usually she was no match for his physical strength. He could hold her arms or pin her down while laughing at her futile attempts to resist.

She told me about her single worst moment, on April 29, her last night in Alaska. The night she shoved the lamp that fell over and hit Josh's head. "That was my fault," she admitted. "I shouldn't have done it."

I wanted to find out if there was more.

I worked the phones, trying to reach people who had known Josh and Amber during their times together in Alaska or Tulsa. I talked to people who worked with Josh, their neighbors at Air Force housing, counselors, Air Force military police, friends and relatives. The witness accounts all matched up with what Amber had told me: Josh was abusive. They had seen the bruises, cuts, and welts on Amber.

I sent the Air Force requests for copies of all military police records pertaining to Josh and Amber. They resisted. I sent subpoenas and Freedom of Information Act requests, pestering officials until I got the records. The stack was disturbingly large. I scoured every page. The records were consistent with the accounts Amber and the witnesses had told me, down to the last details.

Within months, I had compiled a convincing arsenal of evidence demonstrating that Josh had assaulted Amber on numerous occasions, putting his hands on his pregnant wife in anger, striking her, leaving bruises and welts across her body. The evidence was ugly.

But the storyline I kept hearing was completely different.

The narrative dominating the news coverage and public dialogue was still about Amber's anger. It was anecdotal, light on specifics, but heavy with venom.

It was already a battle between truth and fiction.

I knew whom I believed.

Mark wanted to believe too, but early in the case he may have had his doubts. One day in June, he pulled me aside and said he wanted to find out if Amber was telling the truth.

He wanted her to take a lie detector test.

19

"I didn't think lie detectors were admissible," I said. I hadn't researched it, but I was aware courts generally did not allow polygraph tests as evidence.

"They're not," Mark said. "I just want it done."

Mark had tried more than his share of murder cases. I deferred to him, much as I would have expected him to do were we working a civil case together. I told Amber we wanted her to take a polygraph.

"Of course," she said, without hesitating. "Anytime. I'm telling the truth."

On June 20th, 13 days after Josh's death, Mark brought a professional polygraph examiner, Bill D. Brown, into his conference room to interrogate Amber. Mark and I left the two of them alone. They went over the details of what happened that afternoon in Apartment 2509, with Brown testing her for deception.

He delivered us his polygraph report the following day. Among Amber's statements were the following:

"Amber stated Josh pushed her, and she pushed him back... Amber stated Josh then grabbed her by the shoulders, and she pushed him away from her. She stated he tripped over a television stand, could not regain his balance, and fell through the window. She tried to grab him, but succeeded only in getting his shoe, which she then dropped outside the window."

Q: "Did you deliberately push Josh out that window:

A: "No."

Q: "Did you push Josh out that window on purpose?"

A: "No."

The report pronounced a clear conclusion: Amber had scored perfectly. "She was not practicing deception in her responses," it declared.

The lie detector test further confirmed what I had felt from day one.

Amber Hilberling was telling the truth.

20

The *Tulsa World* newspaper published an article headlined: "Autopsy Gives Clean Toxicology Report." It reported that the results of the medical examiner's autopsy of Josh Hilberling revealed that "neither drugs nor alcohol was found in his body."

The article failed to mention that the medical examiner's toxicology was limited, or that the report specifically identified the only eight drugs its toxicology screen could identify.

Notably, the toxicology screen did not test for the two illegal drugs Josh had, by all accounts, regularly used.

THC, the active ingredient in marijuana, was not one of the eight drugs for which the screen tested. And the report specifically made a point to state that its screen also does not test for Oxycodone, which the evidence demonstrates had been Josh's primary addiction.

But almost instantly, local, national, and even international media outlets parroted the *Tulsa World*'s misleading, incomplete report, proclaiming that Josh Hilberling had no illegal drugs in his system.

Once again the media had, either through incompetence or an intent to advocate a preferred narrative, not told the whole story.

21

It wasn't a secret that Josh's family never liked Amber or her parents.

Josh's stepmother Jeanne routinely badmouthed Amber and her family. Amber says Jeanne warned Josh that Amber was only marrying him to "spend his inheritance," an idea Amber found ludicrous. Josh had grown up in a modest, middle-class home. Amber's family was relatively affluent. If Amber was after money, it was fairly obvious that she wouldn't have married Joshua Hilberling.

When Josh tried to stand up for his wife, it made the situation worse. His parents wouldn't allow Amber in their home. According to other relatives, Josh's parents had the same prohibition against their other daughter-in-law, and similar strife with Josh's siblings.

For someone who talked daily with her own family, Amber was struck early on by how distant Josh was from his own. But she grew to understand why. She watched first-hand as Josh felt pushed further away from his own family.

Josh and Amber were both upset by how his parents handled the news of the baby. Jeanne freely told others she suspected the baby wasn't Josh's. Josh's father later asked me to provide him a DNA test confirming Josh's paternity.

Their accusation confused Amber, who had been essentially living in isolation in Alaska, without a car and stuck inside a house on the base. She was sure their living room television set hadn't impregnated her.

Still, Josh's father and stepmother said they wanted nothing to do with the baby. They would make good on their words later, refusing to even meet their grandson despite multiple attempts by and on behalf of Amber.

"This hurt Amber so bad," Gloria remembers. Gloria told Josh to stand up to his parents, to stand up for his wife and baby. Josh told her he couldn't. "You have to know my parents," he told her.

In the days leading up to their last fight, the subject of Josh's family problems had come up again in text messages between the two.

"You could have all the places in the world to go to, and all the people in the world to lean on but you choose to knock everyone down when you're mad," Amber texted. "Granted your family has done a really really shitty job of teaching you to be better than that but I can't give you that excuse anymore. It's not getting us anywhere by me allowing you to hurt me and our family as long as you're eventually sorry."

When Josh got kicked out of the Air Force, Amber says, his family found a way to blame even that on her. They didn't know the truth about Josh's behavior in Alaska, Amber said. They didn't know about his drug problems, his selling roxies, his using and manufacturing spice, the investigations.

And they didn't know about his physical abuse, his violence, his arrest, even the "no-contact" protective order issued against him, Amber says. When his parents did hear about their fights, she remembers, Josh would blame her. During some of his arguments with Amber, Josh would taunt her about derogatory comments he'd say his parents had made. "My parents want me to divorce you," he'd tell her. "They say you're after my inheritance." Amber remembers Josh telling her his stepmother "says you're just like your mother." "They say you trapped me by getting pregnant." And this line, which would haunt Amber later: "They say you're going to kill me."

When he returned to Tulsa just after being discharged, the cut by his ear still fresh, his parents were upset. They drove him to a domestic violence center that helped victims obtain temporary emergency protective orders for their own safety. They obtained one against Amber on the basis of the cut. The court set the matter for an evidentiary hearing to determine whether there was actual evidence to support maintaining it. No one showed up, and the court dismissed it.

It was immediately evident who had wanted the order that day. Josh reached out to Amber within minutes of arriving home from the proceeding. Then, as soon as his parents left for work, Josh drove across town and picked up his wife. He brought her back to his parents' empty house, where the two made love and talked. They then went to eat at Taco Bueno and spent the entire afternoon together. They were just as inseparable in the days that followed.

Josh apologized to Amber about the filing, then apologized to Amber's grandmother as well. He said his parents had "tricked" him into it and had threatened to "cancel" his modest inheritance if he didn't go along.

"You have to know my parents," he said. "I don't want to make them mad."

A few days later, Josh's stepmother called him. Unbeknownst to her, Josh put the call on speakerphone. Amber was sitting next to Josh, listening the entire time. On the call, Jeanne angrily told Josh she didn't believe the baby was his. The accusation upset Josh. They argued. He told Jeanne he wasn't going to stay at their house any longer with her "talking like that." The fight pushed Josh out the door. After the call, he packed up his things and drove across town to Amber's parents' house to resume living with his bride.

By the weekend, Josh and Amber would be living in Apartment 2509 at the University Club Tower.

22

Sixty days after the death of his father, Levi Hilberling was born.

Two days later, Levi went home with his 19-year-old mom to live at his grandparents' house in south Tulsa. He has lived there ever since.

Amber's brother posted a video of the hospital scene onto YouTube. It showed Amber and Levi, surrounded by smiling relatives taking their turns holding the newborn baby.

Below the video are public comments posted by viewers. The comments include the following: "What if the husband wasn't even the father," "Grandmother looks like Caitlyn Jenner and these are his role models," "Someone adopt him!" and "Too bad his father will never get the chance to hold him, thanks to the incubator that carried him for nine months!"

The video is set to the song "Never Give Up On Me" by Christian singer Josh Bates. Near the end of the video, he sings:

"You always erase all my mistakes,
You lift me up when I'm down.
Through the ages, Your love never changes,
You welcome me just as I am.

Pushed

You never give up on me,
No you never give up on me.
Though I'm weak and you're strong
You tell me I still belong
No you never, never give up on me."

As Rhonda holds Levi, swaddled in a blanket, Amber reaches out and tucks the blanket in tighter around his shoulders, trying to keep him warm, gazing fondly at her baby boy.

She's still wearing her wedding ring.

23

Over our first few months working together, Mark Collier and I saw eye to eye on almost everything. Every issue, every strategy, every decision.

Except for one thing: our media strategy.

The prosecution and Josh's circle had worked the media well. Their strategy was smart. The media was obsessed with the case, and their one-sided narrative had dominated the tone of the coverage.

The more I discovered the truth, the more frustrated I became. At the media, the prosecution, everyone pushing the falsehoods.

I wanted to fight back.

I wanted to take the evidence I had put together in the first couple months – the witness interviews, the police reports, Josh's criminal records, his arrest, the protective order against him, his drug problems – and strategically take it public.

Mark disagreed strongly.

He had sound reasons, which he argued in his colorful style.

"Listen, goddammit. It'll piss the judge off," he told me. "He'll have our asses, and it will backfire against Amber. No. We're not trying the case in the media."

Plus, he pointed out, *why show the prosecution all our cards? Let's save the good stuff for when it counts: trial.*

He also didn't think playing the media would work. It was too late. The one-sided narrative had become so dominant so quickly, he didn't think we could change it.

I knew Mark to be an excellent attorney. He had several murder trials under his belt, and had acquitted more than his share of defendants who probably had no business being acquitted. He called the shots, and for good reason.

But I was restless. Biting my lip was getting harder. Reporters from newspaper, television, and radio outlets were calling, texting, or emailing almost daily. National news programs. Dateline NBC. Anderson Cooper. British media. The talking heads discussed the case on Fox News, CNN, seemingly everywhere.

I kept wanting us to sit down with one of them. Just one. Start setting the story straight. Changing the narrative, if only a little bit. Correcting the falsehoods.

Mark and I went round and round.

"Don't fucking do it," he warned me. "Be patient. The truth will all come out."

It never did.

24

Amber and I grew close.

I'd meet with her regularly, update her on the case, answer her questions, and talk strategy. We'd go over evidence, things that could work in our favor, things that could hurt.

We'd talk about life. The baby. Her family. Dealing with the media attention, the public spotlight.

We'd talk about her future. She said she had wanted to be a Christian counselor, but was now thinking about going to law school. "I want to help others who've been wrongfully accused," she said. "I think this might all be God's plan for me."

We'd talk about Josh. About their time together. About her pain. Her regrets.

Most of her life, though, was about her baby boy. She rarely let him out of her sight, or out of her arms. If she went to her grandmother's or church, Levi came with. She worked part-time, at a department store a couple miles from her house, just a few minutes away if Levi needed his mommy. She was on the road to being the trial witness I had wanted: a devoted mother, a college student, and a young adult with a job contributing to society.

She would rave to me about Levi, telling me how smart he was, how much he reminded her of his daddy.

Sometimes she'd look down at him and cry. She didn't have to tell me why.

Her own mother was the picture of a doting grandmother. She was always there in those first few months, offering Amber breaks, cutting her own work hours to stand in as Levi's second parent. The tragedy had seemed to bring Amber and her mother closer, their bond stronger. Rhonda's protective instinct — for both Amber and Levi — had kicked in.

Levi would usually go off with Rhonda, his "Mi Mi," while Amber and I met in their den, reviewing the case and planning for trial. She needed to be ready to testify.

A defendant in a criminal case doesn't have to testify, and most don't. But self-defense cases are a different story.

From day one, our trial strategy was based on Amber asserting that she acted in self-defense. There was no one else in the living room. We couldn't make the self-defense case without Amber telling the jury what had happened on the afternoon of June 7.

But I wanted her to do more than that. I wanted her to tell the jury all about what had been happening long before June 7. I knew the details of the Alaska police records inside and out. I had heard details of Josh's abuse from multiple witnesses. Now it was time to put that history together for a jury.

I started with some rough sketches, some general ideas. Strategies Mark and I had kicked around and ultimately agreed on. How we're going to go into this, then that. What we'll be allowed to talk about here, what we probably can't there. We knew the judge wasn't likely to allow her to talk about Josh's drug problems, fair or unfair.

I went over the game plan with Amber. We started to work through the outline, piece by piece, meeting by meeting. We talked about how we thought the district attorney would try to attack her on cross-examination, what she'd ask, how she'd try to trick her.

I talked to Amber about her demeanor on the stand. The importance of listening to the question. Not arguing with the prosecutor. Being honest. Things the jury would be watching.

In time we started doing some dry runs. We started with some partial direct examinations, me questioning her, having her tell her story to the jury. She quickly became comfortable with the process, appearing relaxed, warm, and likable as she practiced.

We eventually moved into cross-examinations. Mark had talked about this particular prosecutor's style at trial: cold and ruthless, he warned, much as others had. We set out to prepare Amber for the worst. I'd ask her tough questions, trying to rattle or confuse her. She caught on quickly. She'd keep her poise, sometimes asking questions, never once flinching or complaining.

She listened, learned, and understood. It struck me how she never seemed worried. She fully believed she was going to win the case, and one day she told me why.

God has my back on this one, she said. *He told me.*

The more time I spent with her, the more I came to admire Amber. I admired her strength. Her courage. Her faith in God. Her ability to forgive, both Josh and his family. Her honesty, her willingness to admit her mistakes. She didn't try to pretend to be perfect. She regretted things she had done in her past, in her marriage, and took responsibility.

She'd go out of her way to defend Josh, to remind me that she loved him and forgave him, and that she was no angel herself.

She quoted the Bible. She spoke with humility.

Public Enemy Number One, I started to feel, was a better person than most people I knew.

For the first six months of working together, I saw a young woman who was strong, poised, and confident, looking forward to clearing her name, ready to put the tragedy behind her and raise her son.

And then she fell apart.

25

As the media frenzy escalated in the days after Josh's death, one University Club Tower resident decided to actively seek out a role in the story.

Nathan McGowan lived in Apartment 2508 at the University Club Tower, one residence down the hall from the Hilberlings. Homicide detectives had met with him inside his apartment during the evening of June 7, within hours of Josh's death. According to police records, McGowan offered no relevant information during that visit.

But that was before the case became a national sensation.

Nine days after Josh's death, with the case now dominating media coverage, McGowan suddenly offered the police a new and dramatic account of what he now claimed were incriminating details he claimed to have heard during the fateful confrontation inside Apartment 2509.

In this new account, McGowan informed police that in the precise moments before Josh had gone through the glass, McGowan had heard Amber's footsteps moving in a "left to right" direction toward the living room window. He also now reported that Amber had been "screaming" the words "No! No! No! No! No!" in the moments leading up to the sound of the crash. And even more, according to the police report, he now pointed out that he had "never heard a male's voice" during the altercation.

He would later volunteer to share this same dramatic story on a national television show.

McGowan's account of Amber yelling "No! No! No! No!" and moving "left to right" toward the specific window happened to perfectly match the story Jeanne Hilberling had told the media – a version of events now all over the Internet.

It was also the only witness account of its kind.

In the days after Josh's death, I interviewed and read the statements of numerous witnesses, including the man who had been in the couple's bedroom at the moment of Josh's death, and the neighbor directly below who had heard such intimate details as words the couple exchanged and the sounds of Amber vomiting.

No one, even those who had been much closer to the scene than McGowan, claimed to have heard anything like his account.

I wanted to meet him. I wanted to hear this new account in person.

I knocked on his apartment door on June 28. Of all the witnesses I interviewed, McGowan's demeanor stood out. He was nervous, twitchy, almost trembling as he told me what he claimed to have heard. His eyes darted around his living room, around the floor, as he gave me his account.

He told me he had been sitting at home alone on June 7, on his computer surfing the Internet, when he heard the noises. He walked me through what he alleged to have heard.

No! No No! No! No!
Footsteps traveling left to right.
Oh my God! Oh my God! Oh my God!

And then he started volunteering specific bits of information.

"I heard them argue two or three times before," he said, his eyes wide. "I even heard her yelling."

Her. His choice of words struck me.

It was the same claim he had apparently made to the police. "Mr. McGowan stated he never heard a male's voice," the report read.

I decided to follow up on this claim.

"Nathan," I asked, "Did you ever hear him yell too?"

He ran his hand through his hair. I noticed it was shaking. I made a point to look him in the eyes. He wouldn't look in mine.

"Well, um, yeah," he admitted. "I heard him yell too."

"How many different times?"

"A couple times."

Wait, I thought. He had eagerly volunteered – first to the police, and then to me – that he had heard the voice of an upset Amber Hilberling down the hall. But only after I pressed him did he finally admit he had heard Josh yell just as often.

What was he trying to accomplish?

It got weirder.

"I think she smoked pot, even though she was pregnant," McGowan suddenly offered, out of nowhere. I knew Josh's camp had pushed allegations that Amber had been the one with the drug problems; the rumors were all over the Internet. Had McGowan read these rumors while surfing the Internet and decided to parrot them? Or did he have some real evidence of his own?

"What makes you say that, Nathan?"

"I smelled pot from over there a few times. Strong weed."

"Any reason it would have been one person in particular smoking it instead of another?"

His eyes darted around the room again.

"Well... I guess I can't be sure," he said.

Twice he brought up that the police had been "right here inside my apartment" looking out his window after the death.

"*Homicide*," he said, emphasizing the word, seemingly in awe.

He struck me as a guy who had probably read every story, every rumor, out there about Amber and Josh Hilberling.

He troubled me.

I wrapped up our conversation and left his apartment.

I turned right, toward Apartment 2509 and the nearby elevator bay, then noticed something I had overlooked before.

I stopped in my tracks, stunned.

There, between Apartments 2508 and 2509, his apartment and theirs, was another door.

I opened it.

It was a concrete stairwell.

On both sides were thick cement walls made of rectangular blocks. The stairwell between the walls was about 15 feet deep and 10 feet wide. The half-turn staircase traveled the height of the 32-story building, with eight concrete steps in each direction and landing areas in between each flight. I took a photograph of the stairwell:

The stairwell added even more distance between McGowan and the incriminating "left to right" footsteps. I measured the stairwell, then went back into the Hilberlings' living room to evaluate McGowan's claim. The confrontation had occurred on the far left wall of the living room, the side farthest away from the neighboring cement stairwell and, eventually, the apartment of Nathan McGowan beyond.

It didn't add up.

McGowan claimed that while he had sat in his living room and surfed the Internet that fateful afternoon, he could also pinpoint that some 40 to 50 feet away, through two concrete walls and a cement stairwell and over in another apartment unit, Amber

Hilberling's footsteps — on soft carpet, no less — had specifically moved "left to right" toward one particular now-infamous window.

McGowan struck me as a guy caught up in the hoopla, excited to have been near something that was now making national and international headlines.

There was no way the prosecution would dare putting a story like this on the stand, I thought.

I was wrong.

26

Rhonda and Bryan were upset.

They called me one evening and asked me to come to their house to talk. Bryan picked up a stack of paper from the top of their bar and handed it to me. The papers were printouts of Internet pages, many of them marked with highlights and circles.

They were upset about statements people had been making on the Internet, mostly in comment sections below news articles and on "hate pages" devoted to Amber's case.

My initial reaction was what it had long been: ignore it all.

We already knew there had been countless ugly and false things said on the Internet about Amber, the case, her parents, her siblings, even me and Mark.

Having been a newspaper reporter myself, I had a rule to never even look at that garbage. I understood how easily false things could be said publicly, especially with just a few clicks of a keyboard in the Internet age. The comment section in particular struck me as the moral cesspool of society, a place reserved for uninformed cowards spewing hatred in the security blanket of anonymity.

I gave Rhonda and Bryan the same advice I had given others: never read the comments. In a case like this, I told them, the carnival barkers will have their day and it's best to just ignore it all.

They hadn't.

Bryan's face was red as he pointed me to some of the comments. Rhonda was trembling at times. I was skeptical at first, but I soon started to see their point.

Some of the comments were disturbing.

Particularly troubling were some lies and direct threats regularly posted on a Facebook page called "Put Amber Hilberling Away For Life."

Josh's stepmother, Jeanne Hilberling, had posted some vicious comments about Amber in the page's infancy, then appeared to have bowed out of the dialogue. Josh's stepsister, Carrie Askew, was among the page's regular commenters, aggressively fanning the flames with vitriolic and personal attacks against Amber and members of her family.

But one frequent commenter stood out. She went by different aliases on the page, but I ultimately pinned down one real name: Kristi Cassidy. Neither Bryan nor Rhonda had heard of her.

The day after Josh's death, Cassidy had even sent Amber a direct message on Facebook. She told Amber she hoped she would "rot in hell."

Since that message Cassidy had embarked on a steady Internet rampage about Amber and her family. She claimed she had inside information about the case, including a direct line of communication with the lead detective. She alleged she knew things not yet available to the public. Scores of others appeared to believe her, and her comments and allegations were available to anyone with Internet access.

Her inside sources, she claimed, had even informed her that Tulsa police had discovered "evidence" that Amber deliberately intended to murder her husband.

She falsely alleged that Josh and Amber had actually not had any argument the afternoon of June 7. His death, Cassidy claimed, was something Amber had plotted. "She wasn't going to let him leave HER so she killed him!"

She gave fake details about the scene at the University Club Towers. She falsely reported that after Josh fell, Amber had shown no remorse, no emotion, except for an evil smile she flashed at the bystanders.

"She knew what she was doing," Cassidy wrote. "She's a liar and a murderer."

She reported that Josh had never been abusive of Amber. "She's never had a mark on her," she lied in one post.

She repeatedly brought up business litigation involving Bryan's medical practice. She accused Amber's parents of having mental issues. She accused Bryan of having mangled Amber's face with a botched plastic surgery. She mocked Amber's family for what she alleged to be their financial and personal problems.

She alleged that Amber's unborn child wasn't Josh's.

But it wasn't just her lies that were bothering Rhonda and Bryan.

Cassidy had posted the address, and a photograph, of the Whitlocks' home, where minor children still lived, and called it a "murderers holding cell." This was in the same public conversation with people who were openly calling for Amber's murder. Within days of Cassidy's post, Amber's family reported seeing strangers in both their front and back yards.

Rhonda and Bryan told me they were scared. I understood.

They asked me to help, so I did.

I tracked down Kristi Cassidy, working my way through her fake online identities, and sued her. Not for money, but to shut her up.

It worked.

The very day we served her, her comments abruptly stopped.

I then started formal discovery, first demanding that she answer written questions under oath. Ironically, one of her responses revealed that she was guilty herself of the behaviors for which she had publicly accused and mocked Amber's family. I had demanded that she list all lawsuits and criminal cases to which she had been a party, and she responded with a list of 29 separate cases. She had been arrested herself for drug offenses. Her own legal history was a long track record of protective orders, civil lawsuits, a paternity case, debt collections, even a criminal truancy charge alleging her children were failing to attend school.

She was exactly what I had always assumed an Internet troll to be.

I then took her deposition in person, and we walked through some of her most offensive Internet statements. Under oath, she admitted she actually knew nothing about the many lies she had been publishing on the Internet, had no first-hand knowledge, and knew nothing about any actual evidence from the case.

We went statement by statement, line by line, accusation after accusation. She knew nothing, nothing, and nothing. Yet she had been publishing lie after lie on the Internet. And people, the public, had been reading it.

She agreed in writing to never again post online about the case, Amber, or Amber's relatives, which was all we wanted. My work quickly done, I then dismissed the lawsuit.

But where, I had wanted to know before I finished the deposition that day, had she come up with all of the strikingly specific lies? She lived in the city of Edmond, Oklahoma, some 100 miles from Tulsa. She didn't know the police investigators, didn't know Josh, and had no apparent connection to the case.

I pressed her on this question.

Had she just made up all of the lies and ugly, hateful attacks herself? Or had someone been feeding her these things to say? Was she just someone else's mouthpiece?

Finally, we got our answer.

Cassidy admitted under oath that she had, in fact, been communicating with one person involved in the case.

Jeanne Hilberling.

27

onths into the case, the prosecution gave us a copy of what
they claimed was the video recording of the conversation
between Amber and her grandmother in the police station an
hour after Josh's death.

We soon realized the 62-minute video was incomplete. Amber
and Gloria were already seated when the video began, and clearly
had already conversed. Their later dialogue appears to reference
earlier parts of their conversation not shown in the video. And
Officer Holloway's own notes identify portions of their conversation that did not appear on the version the prosecution produced.

The prosecution also produced a three-minute audio recording of Amber speaking with her grandmother that was taken on
Officer Holloway's iPhone. However, this audio recording was also
clearly not complete.

The prosecution blamed these omissions on "technical issues." I found the explanation troubling.

In fact, I found the recordings troubling in their entirety.

Amber had asserted her right to an attorney almost immediately. Her grandmother had repeatedly reminded the police of
this, telling them that Amber would not be making any statement.

The law – the Fifth Amendment, along with the United States Supreme Court case of *Miranda v. Arizona* and its progeny – prevented the police from attempting to obtain a statement from her after she asserted her rights.

Knowing they weren't allowed to get a statement from her, the police had done the next best thing: placed Gloria in a small room with Amber, fully aware by now that the two were close, then sat back and watched Amber talk for more than an hour. The lead detective, Jeff Felton, later admitted the tactic was simply another way to obtain a statement from a suspect: "A lot of times if that family member is going to be a calming influence, or they're gonna be, you know, help them - help prompt the individual to tell the truth about the situation, then it may be beneficial to have them in there."

This struck me as a violation of the *Miranda* rule, if not technically then in spirit. They weren't allowed to try to get her to talk, so they staged a scenario for the explicit purpose of getting her to talk?

It was an interrogation without interrogation, I felt, a circumvention of Amber's constitutional rights.

I researched the law and found some cases I thought supported my argument. I filed a motion to have the video excluded from evidence. The state countered, with ample legal authority on its own side, that no one has a reasonable expectation of privacy when talking inside a police station.

Mark told me I'd lose.

I argued it at a hearing and, as usual, Mark was right. The court overruled my motion and allowed the video into evidence.

The partial video, that is.

The strange omission from the video would gradually take on a life of its own. It wasn't until much later, when the prosecutor delivered her second and final closing argument of the trial, that it became clear just how much she had always intended to capitalize on the troubling omission of Amber's description of the living-room fight.

The video recording the state produced contained no clear description of what had actually happened in the living room, and no explicit reference to there having been an altercation between Josh and Amber. Officer Holloway's notes, however, established that Amber had clearly described this living-room fight to her grandmother during that same conversation.

That dialogue just happened to be missing from the video.

28

Since the moment I plucked pieces of glass from the window frame the morning after Josh's death, I knew I'd sue University Club Tower. I could feel the negligence in my fingers. The glass wasn't safe enough, period.

I started building the civil case immediately. As his widow, innocent until proven guilty in the murder case, Amber still had the right to represent Josh's estate as the plaintiff in a wrongful death civil suit.

If convicted in the criminal case, however, she'd lose that right. In that event, whomever the probate court appointed to serve as personal representative of Josh's estate would succeed her as plaintiff. *If* there was still a civil case, that is. A conviction would hurt the value of a wrongful death civil case against the building, as there would already be an adjudication that Amber was legally responsible for his death. At most, then, a civil lawsuit could find that another party shared partial liability with Amber.

When time allowed, I started researching. Learning about building codes, window codes, local rules, national standards. I started reading journals, book excerpts, trade literature. I studied the law. Who could be liable, what the defenses were, what I'd need to prove.

The more I worked on it, the stronger the case looked.

My plan was to get Amber acquitted in the criminal case, then shift my focus to what I thought was turning into a strong negligence case to be litigated in a civil court. If we went two-for-two, Amber and Levi could end up with a decent settlement or jury award to help them both get a fresh start.

Amber didn't show much interest in the civil case. But she did sometimes open up about her dreams of a fresh start. She and Levi, together, somewhere the hell out of Oklahoma, away from the drama, maybe a small town in the middle of nowhere. A little house, just the two of them. Amber back in school, maybe even law school someday. Somewhere away from all the cameras, away from the courtrooms, away from the prosecutors, away from the angry families.

A new beginning. Now all we had to do was win.

But as I worked to build that second case, I had no idea that someone close would soon be plotting to try to take it away.

29

"This is Rhonda Whitlock," my friend Shawn had said, beaming as she motioned across the hightop bar table. "Isn't she beautiful?"

It was a Friday afternoon, not long after Shawn had texted me an invitation to join her at happy hour. Shawn and I had remained close friends since dating years before. A caring, genuine, smart, and successful woman, Shawn was the rare person whose telephone calls or social invitations I would never decline, and this day was no exception.

Drinks in front of them, she and Rhonda sat inside a restaurant in Brookside, a dining and shopping district that aims to be a trendy spot in a staid city. I kissed Shawn on her cheek, shook Rhonda's hand, and took a seat at their table.

Almost immediately, Rhonda began telling me all about her marriage struggles and picking my brain for legal advice. I didn't do much divorce work, I told her, so I listened and offered generalities. She twice used the word "prominent" to describe herself and her plastic surgeon husband, though I had never heard of either. She mentioned her kids, including a daughter named Amber who had married an Airman and lived at an Air Force base in Alaska. Another daughter, a son, stepkids. The ex. The current. Abuse. Dramas.

As one round of cocktails turned into another, our conversation shifted into friendlier territory. Rhonda, who said she was separated from her husband, became more flirtatious with each sip, complimenting my looks more than once. At one point I excused myself to use the men's room near the back of the restaurant. When I came out, Rhonda was waiting in the hallway. She grabbed me and kissed me aggressively, pushing my back up against the wall. I was surprised, both by the kiss and the fact that I enjoyed it.

"Damn," she said after she pulled back. "That was good. You're going to be trouble."

She was right about the kiss, but wrong about the trouble. I had no plan to pursue her, that night or any night. I wrote the kiss off as a one-time moment. She wasn't the first lonely soul I had seen fueled by liquid courage, and I called it a night before the evening turned into a series of bad decisions.

Rhonda continued to text and call in the days and weeks that followed, sometimes with legal questions, sometimes with romantic hints or overtures. But I wasn't the right guy for either job. I was in the middle of my own divorce, holding out hope for a reconciliation with my wife, and nowhere near ready to chart a new course with Rhonda or any woman. So I viewed her as a friend.

She held on to other ideas. A few weeks after the happy hour, Shawn invited me to a party at a house in midtown Tulsa. She hadn't told me Rhonda would be there. Rhonda and her husband, that is. Apparently, I inferred, they weren't as separated as she had claimed. Rhonda shot me smiles and flirty looks throughout the evening, along with a couple suggestive texts. At one point she walked upstairs without her husband and found me talking to another group.

"Quick legal question," she said, pulling me away into a nearby empty room. She started to kiss me.

"We shouldn't do this," I said, uninterested in either a fling with her or a bullet from an angry husband. She said she understood, and I returned to the party.

———

I didn't tell Amber the whole story about how I had met her mother.

I didn't think it mattered. Once I was on the job helping Amber, all that mattered to me was her, her son, and her freedom.

But to my surprise, it wasn't Amber who would end up demanding most of my time and attention throughout the case. It was her mother.

With a full caseload, Mark Collier often didn't have time to promptly respond to Rhonda's calls and texts. He was in court daily, regularly juggling multiple criminal dockets in the same morning. So he relied on me to handle Amber's family. I was much more available, having already closed down my law office, stopped advertising for new cases, and begun my transition out of full-time practice.

When Rhonda or Bryan called, I answered. When they texted, I responded. When they asked to see me, I got in my car and headed their way, either to their home or Bryan's medical office.

Throughout Amber's case, Rhonda and Bryan continually turned to me for help, advice, support, and friendship. When they had other legal questions, they called me. They came to me for help in their defamation case and I quickly delivered, again at no charge given everything they were going through. Rhonda had a car accident during the case and immediately reached out to me for help. When their marriage hit its predictable valleys, she'd come to me wanting to talk. Bryan would reach out with questions and strategy ideas, and I'd listen. He had a sharp mind.

As Rhonda's reliance on me grew, as both an attorney and a friend, so, it seemed, did her feelings. A few months into Amber's case, Rhonda again started trying to test the romantic waters.

Her text messages would veer from legal questions to flirtatious comments to complaints about the media to outright propositions. Some texts left little to the imagination.

One afternoon she called and said I needed to come to her house to talk about Amber and the case. Soon after I arrived, she quickly pulled me into the powder bathroom near the front door and kissed me. Another day that same summer she arrived at my front door, unannounced, and soon made an even more aggressive advance inside my home.

I take responsibility for her flirtatious behavior. While she was aggressive, even forceful, I should have been more firm. I should have been more clear about boundaries, about my lack of a recip-rocal interest, instead of just trying to shrug it off or quietly hope the behavior would stop. For reasons that long predated Rhonda, saying "no" to a woman has always been a struggle for me. I have always been too protective, too worried about hurting a woman's feelings with rejection. My wife had admonished me more than once that I needed to "learn how to say no" to women. And with everything Rhonda was going through, that she would redirect feel-ings to me, a man trying to help her and her family, is something I should have anticipated and handled better. That's on me, not her.

But as her behavior became more aggressive, working on Amber's case became more difficult.

I took steps to try to change the dynamic.

Instead of meeting with Amber at their home, I started to ar-range for her to meet me elsewhere, away from her mother and stepfather. That seemed to upset Rhonda. It was only after the case was over that I fully understood why: Amber later told me that when we would meet privately, her mother would confront her suspiciously afterward and ask *Amber* if *she* was trying to sleep with me. The irony was rich.

Instead of replying directly to Rhonda's text messages, I start-ed to add her husband Bryan to my responses, turning the ex-changes into group texts. But that led to another problem: Bryan began asking me questions about Rhonda's previous direct text messages. He had apparently started to study their cell phone statements, and he'd pepper me with questions – usually late at night – demanding to know exactly what she had said in a text at a particular date and time. I wouldn't answer those questions, which angered him.

I found myself caught in the crossfire of their marital problems, suspicions, and insecurities. Their behavior was a distraction. I finally asked them both to stop texting me altogether.

But they wouldn't stop.

———

Working with Amber became the easiest part of the job. Amber rarely called me or Mark, content to wait patiently for our scheduled meetings and trust that the justice system would work. As she often said, she believed God had a plan and she trusted it to play out.

But the conversations with Rhonda were frequent and demanding. She'd cry, cuss, accuse, yell, interrupt, and argue. I understood her pain and sympathized, tried to listen, and, despite everything, often found myself admiring her strong-willed nature. She had been through a lot.

But Mark and I both felt that what Rhonda wanted more than anything else was attention. And that desire for attention was becoming more and more of a problem.

One day she called and texted us with an urgent plea.

"Please let me go on Dr. Phil!" Rhonda begged over the phone. "I want to go on Dr. Phil! He said he'd help! Please!"

Mark and I strongly agreed on our answer.

No way.

I only had a vague idea who "Dr. Phil" was, other than a TV personality. I had never seen his show and I doubted Mark had either. But neither of us was comfortable with the notion of Rhonda speaking her mind unchecked on a national television show. She was still too raw, still too angry and upset about a lot of things, as she let us know often.

She was mad at the media. She was mad at the police. She was mad at the prosecutors. She was mad at the judge. She was mad at Josh. She was mad at Josh's family. She was sometimes mad at Amber. She was mad at her son. She was mad at her own husband. She was mad at her ex, Amber's father. She'd later become mad at Mark, then eventually add me to the list.

We worried that if given a microphone, she would anger the judge and turn the jury pool more strongly against Amber than I feared they already were.

She continued to ask if she could do media interviews. She badly wanted to go on the "Dr. Phil" television show, and continued to ask for permission. We kept saying no.

After the case, we'd always tell her. *After the case.*

She didn't forget.

About six months into the case, I reconciled with my wife. Rhonda seemed to understand that I was now officially off limits. Her advances stopped. She appeared to be more committed to working on her own marriage, which I was glad to see. They'd eventually pursue counseling and marital workshops. Much of the personal dramas temporarily subsided, and Mark and I were again able to focus on the work at hand.

Now, when Rhonda and I spoke, it would be about a case – Amber's or one of her own. When Bryan called, he would be respectful but reserved, usually asking a specific strategy question or offering a savvy tactical suggestion.

Through the entirety of the case, though, one behavior was a constant: Rhonda and Bryan voiced their strong appreciation for my work and what they knew was my genuine concern for Amber and her baby boy.

Rhonda showered me with praise from my first day on the case until well after the trial was over. Sometimes in person, sometimes over the phone, sometimes in texts.

"I don't tell you enough but I am grateful and appreciate everything you have and are doing for my baby girl," she texted one day.

"Really nice job," she texted me after one pretrial hearing. "Thank you."

"I trust you," she texted me another time. "I'm grateful. Really, really grateful. Thank you for trying to save her."

After another hearing, she texted me that we "were freaking awesome!!!! Thank you."

Another day: "Oh k baby. As a lay person, I personally think you all rocked!!!!!!! I am so proud!"

Another text: "Really, amazingly proud!"

After she read a motion I had drafted: "Brilliant brief I might add!"

Another day: "Thank you for everything."

Another: "I AM PROUD of you both. I know we have fought hard and we are ready for battle. My prayers are with you and Amber & Levi. I appreciate you so much!!"

Much later, though, Rhonda would tell an entirely different story.

Loudly.

30

One hundred and forty one days after Josh's death, it was finally time for us to see the prosecution play some of its cards.

At 9 a.m. sharp, another packed courtroom awaiting, the Honorable Deborah Ludi-Leitch called the case to order for its preliminary hearing.

It's a routine stage of a felony case, where the prosecution sets out to prove to the court that it has enough evidence to move the case forward to a trial. The burden of proof at the hearing isn't high; the state merely has to show it has "probable cause" to go forward. If the prosecution fails to meet that low burden, the court can throw the case out on the spot.

We knew that wouldn't happen in our case. Amber had openly admitted to pushing Josh, and he had fallen to his death. Those two facts alone were enough to move the case forward.

Further, there was no way a judge was going to risk looking soft on crime by letting a high-profile walk without a trial. Oklahoma is among the most conservative states in the country. Going easy on the state's most notorious defendant could end a judge's career.

We had the option to waive the hearing and push for a quicker trial date, but chose not to. For one, Amber was out, free, raising her baby. We weren't in a hurry to risk her freedom. And the longer she was out, being a productive member of society and raising her son, I thought the harder it would be for a jury to send her to prison.

Also, we wanted to see what the prosecution had. We wanted to watch the state present what it thought was its strongest pieces of the case. We wanted to hear how the prosecutor would characterize the evidence, their themes, their strategies. We wanted to hear the state's witnesses. Even the way witnesses word things — having been coached up, fed key words and phrases to say — can give a lot of insight into the other side's trial strategies.

I also wanted to see Keely, the prosecutor, in action. Attorneys had privately warned me about her, characterizing her as someone not to trust. I thought they were ridiculous, maybe even sexist. To that point she had struck me as professional, diligent, polite, and fair. On a personal level, I quickly picked up in our conversations that she was a devoted mother. As a dedicated dad myself, I admired that about her. I had seen plenty of questionable tactics from attorneys in civil litigation. So far, Keely hadn't once given me pause.

The preliminary hearing, though, would start to pull back the curtain.

Mark and I had agreed, without debate, that he would handle the hearing. He had handled countless preliminary hearings while

I had been upstairs in the civil courtrooms fighting about money. As second chair, my job was to pay attention, take notes, watch for the state's strengths and weaknesses, and help Mark as necessary.

(I'd remain second chair throughout the case, including the entire trial. Like most of what the media has reported, they often got that detail wrong too.)

Mark said he had two primary goals: (1) digging as far into the evidence as we could to find out exactly what the prosecution had; and (2) pinning down the witnesses' testimony on key points, so we knew how they would have to answer questions at trial.

We were in one of the building's largest courtrooms to accommodate the unusually large crowd. Families and friends of both sides filled the first few rows. In the rows behind them were local and national media, interested attorneys and police officers, staffers from other courtrooms, and interested spectators who had arrived early to jockey for a spot. More reporters and cameras filled the hallway outside the room.

A wooden bar ran across the courtroom, separating the public gallery from the front section of the courtroom reserved for the practice. The judge's elevated bench overlooked two large attorneys' tables and the jury box. At the state's table to the right sat Keely and lead detective Jeff Felton. Mark and I sat at the far left side of the Defendant's table, with Amber just to my right, her back to the gallery.

She appeared calm, confident, and attentive, taking notes on a legal pad, behaving respectfully, and sharing sharp observations with me and Mark throughout the hearing. The Internet commenters, her family told me later, had a field day with lurid comments about her physical appearance that day, specifically how her white shirt appeared "tight-fitting" on her chest.

She had given birth 11 weeks earlier.

———

The state called Armando Rosales, the window repairman, as its first witness.

Rosales repeated much of what he had told police on June 7. Things we already knew, details from the scene and its aftermath. Why he was in their bedroom, what he saw, what he heard in the living room, what he witnessed after Josh fell.

He testified that when he was working in the couple's bedroom, he heard sounds in the living room he described multiple times as "fighting." From what he was able to hear, he thought Josh was in the living room "hitting" Amber.

He testified that when he had first walked into the apartment, Josh "was pretty upset" and had asked how much it would cost to repair the window. He said Josh wanted to do the repair himself to lower the cost. Rosales said he explained to Josh why that wouldn't work, at which point Josh turned to Amber and "asked her if her mother was going to pay for the window."

Rosales described Josh as having been "not real nice to me." By comparison, he testified, Amber had been quiet.

I was surprised to hear him begin his testimony in this manner, describing the sounds of the "fighting" in the living room, and casting Josh as "upset" and "not nice" and Amber as "quiet." The observations themselves weren't a surprise; by this point I had talked to numerous witnesses and Rosales's testimony was consistent with everything I'd heard. But I was surprised the prosecution had its first witness making these points so quickly. I thought it helped our defense.

I suspected the prosecutor herself was surprised as well.

Rosales was clearly nervous. I got the impression he was too nervous to remember to follow his instructions. It appeared he was simply trying to tell the truth.

But Keely was skilled and experienced, and soon she got her witness back under control. Rosales suddenly, and awkwardly, took the cues she fed him and began trying to fix the mistakes he seemed to have made at the start. He pointedly clarified that while Josh may have been the "upset" one in Apartment 2509, as he had already revealed, Amber had what he now diagnosed as a "bottled-up anger."

He kept interjecting that exact phrase, multiple times in a short stretch.

"She had bottled-up anger." And again a few moments after: "bottled-up anger." And again: "bottled-up anger." And then again: "bottled-up anger."

It was a phrase Rosales had never once used when he had given his detailed written observations on June 7. Nor had he ever used it when he gave his verbal statements to police at the scene, according to the full police report.

But now here he was, suddenly trying to force the specific phrase into his brief testimony wherever he could. It was obvious why. When an inexperienced trial witness tries to remember how he was coached, the results can be awkward. Rosales's efforts to insert the prearranged phrase into his answers were veering close to satire, a *Saturday Night Live* courtroom skit gone bad.

Did I mention she had bottled-up anger?

When it was Mark's turn to cross-examine Rosales, he wisely ignored the rehearsed bit and zeroed in on the sequence of the sounds Rosales had heard. Rosales testified that he had heard the sounds of fighting, then momentarily turned his attention back to the job when the sounds briefly stopped, and "then that's when the wall shook and a huge crash."

This was consistent with what Amber had described: a heated confrontation, pushing and grabbing back and forth, then Josh losing his balance and falling into the wall. And it was wholly inconsistent with Nathan McGowan's dramatic account of a "left to right" death march in which Amber intentionally shoved an unsuspecting Josh up and out the elevated window.

Rosales also testified that having just observed the couple's interactions, when he heard the sounds of the fighting he assumed Josh was in the living room "hitting" Amber. It was the same thing he had told police at the scene.

Then, he testified, after he saw the body on the ground outside and the empty living room, he thought for an instant that Amber was somewhere "knocked out" from Josh beating her.

But then he heard her out in the hallway, screaming: "My husband fell out the window!" She was crying hysterically and appeared stunned, Rosales testified.

"Obviously she did not want that to happen," he testified. "She couldn't believe that this was happening."

———

With her next two witnesses, the prosecutor tried to start constructing a narrative about how Josh had actually gone through the window glass.

Antonio De Paz, another window repairman who was at the building with Rosales, and Robert Baker, a resident of a nearby apartment complex, both took the stand for the same purpose: to testify that Josh had been facing forward as he came through the window.

De Paz went first. He had been down on the ground getting tools from a pickup truck when Josh fell, and had given three statements in the hours after: first a verbal statement to the police at the scene; then a second verbal statement downtown; then a handwritten statement. His three statements had been detailed, specific, and consistent.

At no point in those three original statements had he ever mentioned what direction Josh had been facing as he first came through the glass.

But that was before he met with the prosecutor.

Having now met with Keely to prepare his testimony, DePaz was now apparently able to recall a crucial detail he had not mentioned in any of his first three statements: Josh, he now testified, had actually gone through the window glass in a "face first" direction.

DePaz insisted that Josh hadn't just been "face first" while falling in the air — he had been "face first" *before he ever went into the window*.

"I saw this guy coming through the window," he testified.

It was a miracle.

When Josh fell, DePaz had been down on the ground retrieving supplies from a parked pickup truck, then walking back to the building with the tools in his hands. Apartment 2509 was more than 300 feet almost directly above him. Illustrating how close to the building DePaz was at that moment, he said some of the falling glass had almost hit him.

From this position, DePaz would had to have been looking almost straight up into the bright afternoon sun to have been looking anywhere near Apartment 2509. His head would have been tilted so far back his chin would have been pointed up in the air, all while walking through a parking lot carrying construction supplies. And had he been walking in this manner, he would have looked up and seen hundreds of identical windows across the building's 32 floors. There were no markings or features of the one particular window, or anything signifying the 25th floor, that would have drawn his focus.

Had he still managed to somehow pinpoint the one window Josh was about to go through, from his distance the window would have appeared about the size of one of his fingernails.

It was all but impossible that DePaz happened to be looking straight up and focusing on that precise piece of glass, from that angle, in the moments just before Josh impacted it.

And it was *completely* impossible to have also seen *inside* that window from straight below. His line of sight wouldn't have allowed it. Even if he had been farther away from the building to allow for such a line of sight, the window blinds had been fully closed. No one could have seen inside, from any angle.

He could not have seen Josh impact the window face first.

It was like claiming to have seen a raindrop form inside a cloud.

Yet the prosecution's miracles kept coming.

Baker lived in an apartment complex a few blocks away. He testified that he had been outside his own complex smoking a cigarette when, like DePaz, he just happened to also be focusing his vision on the exact same piece of window glass just before it shattered. Of the several hundred identical windows exposed on that side of the University Club Tower building, Baker testified he had happened to select that precise piece of glass for careful scrutiny just before Josh had fallen through it.

He testified he literally watched Josh as he broke through the glass, watched it happen in "mid" glass break, and could even see the "shattered glass" at first impact.

Having been zeroed in on this piece of glass, he told the prosecutor he was certain Josh had been in a "face first" position as he first made contact with that living room window.

I later went and stood in the spot where Baker had been smoking his cigarette. We measured the distance. He would have been standing more than 700 feet away from that 25th-floor window, a distance of more than two full football fields.

From that spot, the window appeared smaller than an M&M. Baker would have needed to have been using binoculars, maybe even a telescope, to have been able to see with the detail he claimed.

And even more troubling, from Baker's spot the subject window was on the far right edge of the round building. Even if he had been staring at the window through the lens of a powerful telescope, he couldn't have seen inside the window from his angle. It wasn't in his line of sight.

Mr. Baker, what would have possibly caused you to have been looking at that tiny frame of glass, out of the hundreds visible to you, that far away, up high in the bright sky, at that precise millisecond, sir?

He tried to explain that oddity, nervously stuttering: "I was looking at — I always stare at that building. I wonder what it looks like inside."

I was incredulous. I had seen witnesses lie in civil cases, but their motive was obvious: money. This case was about something far more important. Part of me wanted to stand up and walk across the courtroom, grab the witness by the ear, point at Amber and shout: "*You see that girl? Her life is on the line. She's got a baby at home. Think maybe you can quit the bullshit, quit trying to get yourself in the big story, and just be honest?*"

Instead I took a few breaths and tried to understand.

There was zero chance DePaz and Baker were both staring at that precise window before Josh came through. Why were they on the stand giving this story?

Were their minds playing tricks on them? Did they honestly believe what they were saying?

Was the prosecution helping them out in some way? Dropping some charge? Were they caught up in the public fury against Amber, wanting to help lock her up? Were they in it for the thrill of being part of a high-profile case?

I thought through all the possibilities.

Only later, when potential jurors from the Tulsa community took their turns answering questions during jury selection, did their zealous behavior make sense.

––––––

The apartment manager, Brad Blake, testified next. He testified that Amber had called him about the broken small window in the bedroom, and that the window repairmen happened to already be in the building on another job.

Blake didn't hide his contempt for Amber. His tone and his body language spoke volumes.

He testified about the scene on June 7. He heard there was a fall and walked from his office to the elevator to go up to the eighth-floor parking level. Then a pregnant, bloodied, distraught young woman rushed into the same elevator wailing about her dead husband.

Blake testified that he looked at her and immediately told her to "shut up."

Amber immediately responded to his aggression by slumping to the floor of the elevator.

Mark worked his way into some questions about the building's windows. Blake, who admitted he was already aware of the wrongful death claim pending against the University Club and its management, denied that the building had any history of window issues. He said there were only "two, maybe" window breaks a year at the University Club.

We were already aware of three on June 7 alone.

———

The state called its final three witnesses — a firefighter and two police officers — to establish that Amber had confessed to pushing Josh.

Tulsa Fire Captain Robert Peters, Officer Holloway, and Detective Felton all testified that Amber had admitted she "pushed" Josh. They testified that she was upset, crying, and appeared in disbelief that Josh had gone through the glass.

"I didn't mean to push him out the window," Captain Peters quoted Amber as having said.

Officer Holloway, who had been assigned to stay with Amber at the scene, spent more time with her than any other witness. He testified that the first time he heard Amber describe what had happened, she used the term "fall."

"She said that he fell," Holloway testified. "He fell back into the window. She reached out to try to grab him. She grabbed his foot but he fell and she watched him fall."

Holloway then testified about watching Amber and her grandmother talk in the interview room. He testified that Amber told her grandmother that the two were having an "argument" in "the living room" when Josh fell.

"She said that, quote, she pushed Joshua into the wall and he fell."

Holloway's account — a living-room altercation; a push into the wall as opposed to the window; Josh then "falling" — was consistent with everything Amber had ever told us.

But it was inconsistent with the version of events the prosecutor was seemingly trying to construct.

The lead detective, Jeff Felton, took the stand next. He and the prosecutor immediately set out to undo Holloway's testimony about Amber having described the living-room confrontation to her grandmother soon after Josh's death. Keely asked him about the partial recording the state had produced.

Q: And sir, as part of your duties as a detective, did you review that recording?

A: Yes, ma'am.

Q: And did Ms. Hilberling make statements?"

A: Yes, ma'am.

Q: And in those statements, did Ms. Hilberling say how Joshua fell – how Joshua came out of the window?

A: Yes, ma'am.

Q: And what did she say?

A: She said that she pushed him.

Q: And at another point did she talk about how he went out of the window?

A: Yes, ma'am.

Q: And what did she say at that point?

A: She said that — that he was messing with the TV and that she pushed him and he went into the window and fell.

Detective Felton's focus on that one specific excerpt was revealing.

In the video, Amber had repeatedly expressed her confusion about how Josh went through the window. Even in the one excerpt Felton chose to single out, Amber's words were rambling and incoherent: she spoke of candlesticks, Josh fixing the television, divorce, wanting to talk to him on the phone, and words indecipherable through her crying.

But prior to that, Amber had in fact given a much more clear account of the couple's fateful living-room fight, as reflected in

Officer Holloway's notes. That part of the conversation was missing from the video.

By the time the detective left the stand, the omission was starting to look like more than a coincidence.

————

The closing arguments were just for show. As soon as they concluded, the court ruled as expected: "The state has met its burden to show probable cause," the judge announced, binding the matter over for district court arraignment.

But for our purposes, the prosecutor's closing argument was an eye opener.

Keely argued that the excerpt from the video in which Amber referenced Josh "messing with the TV" was evidence she had taken him by surprise and pushed him "face first, feet first, standing straight up" through the window.

Face first, feet first, standing straight up?

Mark looked at me incredulously the first time Keely used the description. I thought she had misspoken. She hadn't. She kept repeating the description.

Josh went "out the window as though he was standing, remember, feet first?," she said. "It was as though he was standing as he went out the window."

"He was going out feet first, Judge," she said again.

"He is going straight out the window, as though he's been pushed," she said again.

"He's not merely falling out the window," she said. "He's not tumbling out the window, Judge, as somebody might be if they were being pushed against something else and they bounced. He is going straight out the window, Judge, as though he's being pushed."

"He fell out feet first, facing away from the building, and then he went straight down, and that's what the evidence says."

"There are two independent witnesses who saw this man go out the window feet first as though he was standing up."

"What the fuck is she talking about?" Mark finally whispered. "Feet first? That's not even physically possible, is it?"

We were about to find out.

31

Face first. Feet first. Standing straight up as he went through the glass.

Keely told the judge that "witnesses" had testified in the hearing that Josh had gone out the elevated window "feet first." I didn't recall anyone giving that testimony. Days later, when we received the transcript of the hearing, I scoured it. It confirmed my memory: no witness had ever said Josh had gone out the window "feet first."

Only the prosecutor had.

Further, none of the witness statements in the thick police report had ever included such a description.

Feet first. Standing straight up.

After Keely had given this description in her closing argument, I pulled out my photographs and measurements of the window.

The bottom edge of the window was more than 26 inches above the floor. It started somewhere near Josh's knee.

To have gone through the glass feet first, as the prosecutor had kept insisting, Josh would have had to first elevate more than two feet into the air while still inside the apartment. He'd also have to have been tilted at a significant angle, as he could not physically fit through the window space in an "upright" position as the prosecutor had alleged. The window was only 51 inches tall. Josh stood 76 inches tall, and on top of that had been wearing thick tennis shoes. He couldn't have gone through "standing upright."

The prosecutor's theory wasn't physically possible.

It was just math.

But I understood why the prosecutor liked this image.

There hadn't been any living room confrontation, folks. She took him by surprise, shoving him from behind, straight through the glass. He dropped straight down, still standing upright, feet going down first. He never knew what hit him.

It was a powerful and incriminating picture.

It just wasn't physically possible.

We assumed the prosecutor would realize her mistake before trial. But if she did try to pitch this story to the jury, we were confident the jury would see the truth.

They'd have to.

32

After the preliminary hearing, Mark and I were more confident than ever. The prosecution's theory — Josh went out *feet first, face first, standing upright*, through a window both elevated and shorter than him — was physically impossible, and the eyewitnesses eagerly claiming bionic powers of perception lacked credibility.

We felt things were headed in the right direction.

We were wrong.

Something in Amber seemed to change after the preliminary hearing. Our prep sessions had been going well for months, but when we met in early November I started to sense that something wasn't right.

She seemed distant. Emotionless. Lethargic.

I'd ask her a question and she would just look at me blankly, with no discernible expression. When she did speak, the warmth I had known was just… gone.

I decided to shut down the case talk and switch the conversation to life, Levi, the holidays. I was trying to find Amber, somewhere in there. I only found glimpses.

We rescheduled the prep session for later that month. But when I came back, she was again distant, distracted, detached.

It worried me. I didn't know this Amber. If this Amber, this stranger, testified in front of a jury, she'd be going to prison.

One afternoon, as I sat in her parents' den and talked to her, trying to reach her, she said something I'll never forget.

"I always dream that I'm looking for Josh and can't find him."

She spoke the words as if she was in a daze. A dream.

She soon got worse.

One afternoon, her grandmother said, Amber started hallucinating. First she seemed to be talking to herself.

Then she was talking to Josh.

Gloria tried to talk to her, to snap her out of it.

"You're not talking to Josh, Amber!" she said. "He's dead. Amber, wake up!"

Amber looked at her grandmother, confused.

"Josh is right here," Amber said. "Don't you see?"

———

Hallucinations. Lethargy. Bizarre thoughts and dreams. Energy loss. Reduced ability to focus and concentrate.

All telltale symptoms of postpartum depression, according to the medical websites I perused later. The condition occurs in 10 to 15 percent of all deliveries - but the frequency nearly triples in adolescent deliveries such as Amber's. And on top of that, the website listed five stressors that predispose mothers to postpartum depression. One was "stressful marital, family, or financial conditions."

Based on everything I read, it fit.

I couldn't help but wonder whether the preliminary hearing had also had played a part in knocking Amber off balance. The timing couldn't have been a coincidence, I suspected. We had told her not to expect dismissal, but maybe she had held out hope for a miracle.

Or maybe it was the impact of seeing the actual testimony in person, the officers on the stand, a line of people testifying against her. The prosecutor's theories. The state of Oklahoma calling for her head. The media frenzy.

Maybe, I thought, she had been living in some sort of denial about the case, and the preliminary hearing was when it all hit home.

Whatever the reason, Amber was in trouble.

She needed help.

She didn't get it.

Instead, her family left the state for a Thanksgiving vacation and took Levi with them, leaving Amber home alone. She couldn't travel due to her bond restrictions.

Left alone, Amber fell apart.

"That [preliminary] hearing, it made her feel like she didn't deserve her son," her close friend Sylvia Treat remembers. "Like she was a terrible mother, even though what she did was an accident."

Treat was with Amber often in the days after that hearing, and watched first-hand as her friend deteriorated. Feeling separated from her baby, Treat says, was more than Amber could handle.

Right or wrong, Treat recalls, Amber "felt like her parents were taking Levi away from her. She was very upset about it. I don't know if she wanted to keep living. I don't think she cared if she lived or died any longer."

Amber's parents had left her with a stack of cash. A few days after Thanksgiving, Amber made a telephone call to a friend of a friend, who came to her house with pills.

Amber took too many.

On November 29, 2011, Amber Hilberling was rushed by ambulance to Hillcrest Hospital.

33

The hospital nurses made Amber remove her ankle monitor as a safety precaution. Amber was under court order to notify the Court Services staff, who monitored her ankle unit's GPS surveillance, anytime she removed the monitor.

She didn't call them.

She had also let the monitor battery temporarily die on four recent occasions, having failed to charge it. Those instances coincided with the behavior changes I had noticed. She hadn't let the battery die once in her first four months wearing the monitor.

On Wednesday, November 30, while Amber was in the hospital, the Court Services office notified the judge of the ankle monitor battery failures. The judge called us and told us to bring Amber before him in the morning.

She went almost directly from the hospital to the courtroom.

And then to jail.

The judge revoked her bond on the spot for the ankle monitor failures. He ordered the bailiff to take her into custody. With

Amber's family sobbing in the front row of the courtroom gallery, the bailiff handcuffed her and led her out the courtroom, back to the Tulsa County jail. Her baby boy was home with a nanny.

We argued and asked for a hearing, and the judge set it for two weeks out. Amber would be behind bars for at least that long.

I researched and drafted a motion arguing for her release. I wanted her home with her son for Christmas. I knew she had been falling apart. I worried that being separated from her baby just before Christmas might send her over the edge.

On December 13, in front of another packed courtroom, we gave evidence that Amber had been nearly perfect in her compliance with her many bond conditions. We argued that her recent hospital stay was an unplanned emergency that shouldn't send her to jail.

And then we simply asked for mercy.

The state did its usual thing, casting Amber as a public menace.

We won. The judge released Amber, though this time under even tighter restrictions.

I was thrilled. She'd be home with her baby for Christmas after all. The family was elated with me and Mark. Twice now, we had managed to get Amber out of jail against some serious odds.

I warned Amber that there wouldn't be a third chance.

After being released from jail later that day, she had to return to the Court Services office in the basement of the courthouse to have an ankle monitor put back on. I was her ride, and I used the drive time for a little talk I felt she needed.

With the media all over the case, I said, there was no way the judge would show her mercy again. Toe the line, I warned her. Follow every rule, don't speed by one mile per hour, don't let that monitor battery get anywhere close to dying. And don't be anywhere near someone drinking, smoking pot, or doing anything stupid or illegal. Don't even jaywalk.

Do anything wrong, I told her, and you're going in until trial.

She had one friend in particular I was worried about, a girl who had been hanging around more often in recent weeks. I knew this girl liked to smoke pot. I also sensed she was drawn to the drama of the case. My litigation experience had taught me to trust my instincts, especially about people's character and motives. I told Amber I didn't want this friend around.

I finished my speech as I parked at a curb near the courthouse.

"You understand all this?"

I had expected her to agree. To be scared to go back in.

I shifted into park and looked over at her, sitting in the passenger seat. She was smiling. She started to chuckle.

"Don't worry about [my friend]," she said. "I'm not going to get in any trouble. And you know, I can beat a test anytime."

I couldn't believe what I had just heard.

"Wait. What? A drug test?"

"I'm serious, don't worry. If I wanna smoke a little with her I'll still pass the test. It's easy. Josh told me how. I know lots of people who have done it."

I snapped.

"Amber! What the fuck are you talking about?! Are you fucking kidding me right now?"

"It's OK," she said. "I'm not saying I'm going to. But I just, I might want to, after everything lately. But don't worry. If I do I'll still pass the test. I promise."

For the first time, and only time, I lost my cool with Amber Hilberling. I turned in my seat, facing her almost completely now, and yelled at her. Loudly.

"That is the stupidest fucking thing I have ever heard!" I yelled. "Do you know how lucky you are to be out? To be walking around? You wanna go back into that shithole? You will lose this case if you're in! Do not be fucking stupid, Amber!"

"Jesus, calm down," she said. She started to cry. She was clearly taken aback by my anger. "It's fine. I'll be fine."

I felt bad about coming down so hard on her, but I also felt some tough love might be just what she needed.

"No, it's not fine, Amber. Do not fuck this up. We have a plan. I want you working, in school, raising Levi, when you get in front of that jury. You are not going to trial as a fucking inmate. You got that? I'm serious, Amber. Do not fuck this up. Promise me you will not fuck this up."

"I promise."

But fuck it up she did.

34

On December 15, Amber's regular urinalysis came back diluted.

A "diluted" result means that the tested party had an unusually high amount of water in her system, which can render the test inconclusive. Water dilution is a strategy commonly used in an attempt to mask the presence of drugs in one's system.

Court Services called her back down for another test the next day. That also was diluted.

On December 22, she tested positive for THC, the active ingredient in marijuana. Her urinalysis on December 28 also tested positive for THC.

A few days later, Court Services called us to let us know the results.

We knew what it meant. She was going back in. This time there was nothing we could do.

I was on a Christmas vacation in Paris, walking a picturesque street with my family, when I heard about her test results. I had the urge to throw my phone into the Seine. I sat down on a bench and stared into the water, taking deep breaths. It was a struggle to not let the disappointing news ruin my day.

On January 4, the state filed a motion to revoke Amber's bond. The court set it for a hearing two days later. There was nothing we could do. The prosecution knew it, Mark and I knew it, Amber knew it.

Rhonda insisted that we use new strategies at the hearing. Mark rejected her ideas. They argued. Their relationship was becoming more tense.

The hearing was perfunctory, the arguments brief and just for show. The judge ruled as expected, and in front of another packed house Amber was again led away in handcuffs. She didn't cry. She knew it was coming.

She'd stay in jail until trial, which was more than a year away. My plan to present the jury with a law-abiding, college-attending, job-holding single mom was in ashes. Until the trial was over, or for perhaps much longer, Rhonda and Bryan would now raise Amber's baby.

35

My prep sessions with Amber would now take place in jail.

I went in to see her soon after her she was hauled out of the courtroom in handcuffs.

As usual, she didn't make any excuses.

"This is on me," she said. We were back in the same small visiting room on the perimeter of the women's detention center, where we had first met seven months before. "I screwed up. I was stupid."

I was glad to see her take accountability. And she was right: she had no one to blame but herself.

Her mother, though, found somebody else to blame: Mark Collier.

Rhonda complained several times over the next few months about the January 6 hearing, criticizing Mark's courtroom performance and his decisions that day. *If we'd have just handled the hearing my way,* she seemed to believe, *Amber would still be out.* I told her Johnnie Cochran wasn't going to win that hearing. Amber had been given a chance and blew it, period.

Rhonda wasn't having it. She started to complain more about Mark. *He doesn't return our calls. He doesn't come see us. He doesn't go see Amber.*

In one text message, Rhonda told me Amber "tells me you are the one she sees putting the work into" the case.

But Mark wasn't to blame for Amber's bond revocation. Amber was. Even she knew it.

Criticizing him for not working on the case was also unfair. Trial was months away. There are lulls in the action in criminal cases; there isn't the steady stream of discovery exchanges that fill the months, and sometimes years, in civil lawsuits. There wasn't always a lot for Mark to do. Further, I was completely immersed in the trial preparation, almost obsessively so. Mark told me he had "never seen a case as well prepared" as I had it.

Mark may not have been answering all of Rhonda's calls and texts or meeting with Amber, but he knew I was, just as he knew everything that was going on in the case. He would be more than ready for trial. We discussed things regularly, sometimes at his office, other times over a drink. He was excited about what I had put together, particularly the detailed evidence of Josh's history of physically abusing Amber. He knew what to do with it.

He'd be ready for trial. He liked our chances. So did I.

What he didn't like, though, was the increasing behind-the-scenes drama. He started to vent to me about what he saw as Rhonda's demanding nature.

"She really thinks this case is about her," he told me one night over drinks. "She wants the attention. She wants to be famous."

He responded to her calls and texts less often. Rhonda grew more upset with him. Finally, in the spring of 2012, Rhonda announced she had made a decision.

She was firing Mark.

"That's not how it works," I told her. "You're not the client. You can't fire him."

"Then Amber will," she said. "Or I'll stop paying."

Rhonda talked to Amber, and it was settled. They told me they wanted to replace Mark with a female attorney, which they felt would help the dynamic of the domestic violence case. I wasn't happy, but eventually recommended a talented young attorney named April Seibert. Like Mark, April had served at the district attorney's office before opening her own criminal defense practice. She was still in her 30s but already had years of criminal trials under her belt. She had built a sterling reputation as a savvy, no-nonsense attorney. Before I recommended her, I did some homework, asked around for references. All were glowing. A couple attorneys told me they predicted April would be a judge someday.

I called April. She was interested. Go on in and meet Amber, I said. This decision's between the two of you.

Rhonda and Bryan also met with April. "April really knew her stuff," Rhonda texted me after the meeting. "We were pleased with her."

"We are just waiting on Amber's blessing," she texted later. "The decision is up to her."

Amber quickly approved, and our criminal defense team had a new captain.

36

April and I got right to work.

It would be the same arrangement I had with Mark: April would be the lead, and I'd defer to her. It didn't take her long to learn the case inside and out. Just as Mark had, she liked our chances.

We met regularly, working and fine-tuning our plans for trial, which we expected to start in March. We developed strategies for how we'd handle each of the witnesses the state might call in its case, and game plans for whom we might call to testify for the defense.

Our options for relevant defense witnesses, though, were limited.

As to what had happened on June 7, the only witnesses other than Amber who claimed to have heard or seen anything from Apartment 2509 that afternoon would already be testifying as prosecution witnesses; we could elicit helpful evidence on cross-examination. We decided early on that Amber's grandmother Gloria was a vital witness, given her presence on the scene. None of Amber's friends or relatives could add much in the way of factual testimony about what had happened on June 7.

The first-hand witnesses to the worst of the previous domestic incidents were in Alaska. But we couldn't force them to fly in to testify, and Amber's family had put the clamps on case expenses. The spending limitations affected other plans. We had discussed hiring a mental health expert to explain Amber's behavior and statements in the hours after Josh's death, particularly her jumbled statements in the partial video recording.

"We simply are broke," Rhonda emailed on September 4, 2012. "Beyond broke."

They did pay April. She wasn't about to work the case without compensation as I was still doing. But I wasn't helping Amber for money; I just couldn't turn my back on her.

"I don't tell you enough," Rhonda texted one day, "but I am grateful and appreciate everything you have and are doing for my baby girl."

"I trust you," she said in another text. "I'm grateful. Really, really grateful. Thank you for trying to save her."

Rhonda often promised they would pay me when they could. "Just to let you know, I'm keeping cash back for you," she texted one morning. "No one knows but you need to be paid somehow, some way. I appreciate the work in the case."

A few weeks later: "I promise I will pay you more, hopefully get to where April is."

Those promises weren't kept. Yet at the same time, April and I would see glamorous photographs posted on their social media pages, showing luxurious vacations and a high-dollar lifestyle. We marveled at the inconsistency, but opted to hold our tongues. Maybe they needed those escapes, given the stress of the ordeal, I reasoned. I felt for them.

We wouldn't have everything and everyone we wanted for trial, but few defendants ever did.

We'd try the case we had. A case we believed was more than strong enough.

———

April and I worked well together, and we were eye to eye in our opinions of the case's strengths and weaknesses. We agreed on how to split up most of the trial duties. April would handle the opening statement and the police witnesses. We'd split the other witnesses from the scene, including the first responders and those nearby who claimed to have heard or seen things. I'd handle the witnesses and evidence related to the window problems, which veered close to my world of civil litigation. Amber asked that I handle her testimony if she took the stand, as she was more comfortable with me given our time working together.

But there was one role we didn't agree on: the closing argument. We both wanted it.

On paper, it made more sense for April to handle it. She had the edge in criminal experience, and if trial went as planned she'd already have played the lead role throughout. I had no doubt she would do a good job – as trial attorneys go, she was and is in the top tier. She was very confident in her courtroom abilities, having won more than her share of verdicts, and was clearly comfortable asserting herself.

I had no reason to not trust her. In our pretrial court appearances, I found her courtroom style to be clinical, organized, thorough, confident, and aggressive when necessary. Perfect for most cases.

But this case was unique, I felt. I wanted the closing argument. I thought it would need a certain... pathos, a je ne sais quoi, that innate ability to feel a jury in your gut, to make a juror cry or laugh or get angry on cue. We needed to be in both the jurors' heads and their hearts when they went back to deliberate. I knew April could reach their heads. But I wasn't sure her businesslike approach would reach their hearts.

I was confident I could. The closing argument was my single favorite part of the practice of law. They had always been my strength, an almost preternatural gift I knew I was blessed to have. I had always been able to connect in closing. I had won all sorts of awards for my closing argument skills, taught closing argument workshops, and had never lost a trial after delivering the closing. And I had long known the buttons I was going to push on this one: that Josh Hilberling had no business ever laying a finger on his wife, his pregnant wife, and you're damn right it was OK for Amber to push back.

I wanted to fire them up. I wanted a jury filled with moms and dads with daughters, and I wanted them thinking about their own baby girls, feeling angry and protective as I did. I wanted all 12 of them thinking about what Amber had gone through up in Alaska. The bruises, the welts, the jumping over a fence and running – pregnant and in the cold – to the neighbors in fear. The thrown plates and glasses and phones, the pushing and grabbing and shoving and tossing. The arrest, the protective order against Josh. Her fear.

For more than a year I had been delivering parts of Amber's closing argument in my head, in my sleep, in the car as I drove, as I sat in other courtrooms waiting for my case to be called. I knew it would connect. With two daughters and two stepdaughters of my own, I'd believe every damn word I said.

They'd be with me. All 12 of them. I knew it.

April and I debated it several times, always finally tabling it and agreeing to come back to it later. Eventually, I deferred. In every rational analysis, it made more sense for April, the lead trial attorney, the one with all the experience trying criminal cases, to take the finishing role at trial.

The dramatic closing argument I had been playing with for more than a year, the tearjerker I had longed to deliver as the final act of my legal career, would be left on the cutting room floor.

37

My jail sessions with Amber were becoming hit or miss.

We'd sit in the same little room and work through parts of her testimony. It wasn't an ideal place to prepare for trial. Other inmates would come stand by the room's window and peer in at us, often smiling and waving at me.

"They think you're hot," Amber would say with a laugh.

"That's because I'm the only man they've seen in months," I'd tell her.

We could laugh like this on the good days. On those days, Warm Amber was across the table from me. She was an ace. She understood the nuances of the testimony, gave vivid accounts of her and Josh's past troubles, her injuries, the neighbors, the police. She understood what the prosecutor would try to do to her on cross-examination, kept her composure as I played the role, stayed respectful and sympathetic.

But then there were the bad days, when Warm Amber was gone.

In her place I'd get Cold Amber, shell-shocked, lifeless, a girl struggling with depression. She'd stare blankly, answer questions robotically, appear aloof. It was the way she had behaved just after the preliminary hearing, in the weeks leading up to her hospitalization and the failed drug test.

It got to where I could tell which Amber I was getting the second she stepped into the room.

Cold Amber was now a major concern. If that person took the stand and testified, we'd be in trouble.

Her inconsistent demeanor wasn't my only concern. Her time in jail was also changing her physical appearance.

She was putting on pounds.

I urged her to make the most of their short break times, to exercise and burn calories whenever she could. To watch what she ate. But the menu in jail was carbs, followed by more carbs, followed by something fried.

As we got closer to trial, she continued to look bigger, thicker, and stronger.

My concern about her weight was entirely case-related. She was starting to looked less like a vulnerable young girl. Less like the scared teenager I had met the previous June. Less like the beautiful young bride I had seen in all the photos. Less like a victim of domestic abuse.

She was looking more like... an inmate.

38

Armando Rosales opened his front door and looked surprised. He hadn't expected to see me standing there.

He was clearly a bit nervous, uncertain, his little dog yapping wildly by his feet. I said hello, then bent down and sweet-talked the dog, petting him and calming him down. Calming them both down, in truth. I was trying to put Rosales at ease as well, to build a little trust before I even told him why I was there. It worked. I could feel him soften as he watched me play with his dog.

He invited me in.

We knew he was going to be an important witness at trial. The state had called him as its very first witness at the preliminary hearing, and he was the one person who had also been inside Apartment 2509 when Amber and Josh had their fateful living room encounter. I wanted some one-on-one time with him, to try to understand him and his testimony better before he took the stand.

I told him I just had a few questions, needed to go over his statements to make sure we had everything accurate. We sat at his dining room table, his dog now a constant by my side.

I asked him about his family, small talking and building some rapport. When I thought the temperature was right, I started asking him about his statements. He opened up and shared what he remembered about that day at the University Club Tower. What he told me was consistent with the accounts he had already given at least three previous times: verbally to the police, then in a written statement to the police, then on the stand at the preliminary hearing (with the exception of the "bottled-up anger" description he'd awkwardly added).

As soon as he had entered the apartment, he told me, he saw how upset Josh was about the broken bedroom window.

He went into the bedroom to fix that small window, he recalled, then heard the altercation in the living room. Based on everything he had already seen of the couple, he assumed Josh was in there beating up Amber.

When Antonio DePaz then called from the ground below to say he saw a body fall, Rosales assumed that Josh had just committed suicide.

Then, when he went into the living room and saw that Amber wasn't there, he figured Josh had knocked her out in another room.

It was obvious, he told me, that Amber hadn't tried or meant to push Josh through that window.

"I don't think she meant to do it on purpose," he said.

These were the same things he had said three times before, almost verbatim.

But when he testified later at trial, Armando Rosales would change his entire story.

––––––––

Still sitting at Rosales's living room table, I moved into the new subject I was eager to finally discuss with him.

The windows at the University Club Tower.

Rosales told me he had owned Budget Glass since 1997, and had been handling the University Club Tower's window maintenance, replacements, installations, repairs, and cleaning ever since. He had a wealth of knowledge about window glass, about the different strengths of different types of glass, about what exactly should be in high rises, and about what safety precautions should have been in place at the building.

I had arrived at his house hoping he would say something, anything, to help build my theory about the windows being dangerously thin.

He gave me more than I could have hoped.

He told me that glass in high-rise windows should be safe, and that high-rise buildings use "safety glass" that is usually at least one inch thick.

But, he told me, the University Club Tower had made the unusual choice to not use safety glass.

It was already my belief that this choice of glass was partly responsible for Josh Hilberling's death. Rosales appeared to share my belief.

"If it was a one-inch unit, which some buildings have that, the newer buildings, he wouldn't have went through," Rosales said.

He said he "wished" the building would have at least used "tempered" glass, which is stronger than the cheaper plate glass the building's management elected to use.

He said he had also been concerned about the building's lack of secondary safety measures for the large living room windows.

"I wish they would have put a bar across," he said. "That would have saved him."

"If they'd have put a bar across the middle of those big windows and screwed it into the frame it would have saved him. But you know the problem with that is the buildings like that, they're looking for the view. They don't want the bar obstructing the beautiful view."

"But I'd like to see it done."

He told me he had warned the building's owners that they need to change many of its windows to "safety-tempered glass."

He also confirmed something I had suspected: the University Club Tower had a history of window glass problems.

The University Club windows break easily, he explained. They can break if someone just "drops something on" one. They can break if someone is moving a chair or table around and it touches the glass, he said. They break when kicked, and when people fall into them. Once an elderly tenant just tripped near a window, Rosales recalled, and reached his arm out. His arm went right through the glass, requiring stitches.

And yes, Rosales said, they sometimes break when people inside the University Club Tower have fights.

"I usually don't ask how they broke it," he said. But he can often tell.

He couldn't give me a precise count on how many breaks there are each year. But "one year," he said, "it was quite often." "In the summertime," he said, there is usually "more activity" with window breaks. There was a scientific reason for that, which our window expert would later explain.

Even on the afternoon of Josh's death, the building's window glass problem was the reason he and Antonio were already inside the building. They had been there repairing another window, just before two more windows were broken in Apartment 2509.

His words were damning.

The civil litigator in me knew they carried immense value in a negligence lawsuit against the building. But more importantly, his admissions were great news for Amber's defense.

For the state to convict her of murder, it would essentially have to prove Amber knew this window glass could give way as easily as it did.

From what Rosales was telling me, there was no way anyone could have known.

Now we just had to make sure the jury would understand.

39

"I've put in more than a million square feet of high-rise windows, and I've never once seen window with glass this thin. Not once."

Those were the words of Mark Meshulam, a window expert out of Chicago. Meshulam had spent more than 30 years working in the window glass business, studied in window-testing laboratories around the country, and had testified as an expert witness in other court cases involving window safety issues.

We brought him in to examine the window glass at the University Club Tower and potentially testify as an expert witness in our cases. Amber's parents met with Meshulam, liked him, and agreed to hire him.

Meshulam flew into Tulsa and visited Apartment 2509, studying the subject window and other windows in the building. He told me that when he was inside Apartment 2509, even with his decades of experience, he had no reason to suspect the living room window glass was as thin and fragile as it was.

I took him from the high-rise to an office across town, where a custodian was keeping the glass pieces I had plucked from the broken window just after Josh's death. We emptied them out onto a table, and Meshulam held the pieces in his fingers.

"Wow," he said, shaking his head. "This is picture frame glass."

He opened up his kit of window tools and took precise measurements.

The glass was only .092 inches thick.

Said differently, the glass was about 9/100ths of an inch thick, or less than one-tenth of one-inch. In other words, the glass was more than 10 times thinner than what is in most high-rise windows, according to both Meshulam and Rosales.

"Unbelievable," Meshulam said after the precise measurement appeared on the screen of his electronic measuring tool.

Glass of that thinness is considered "single-strength glass" in the industry, he said. It wasn't safety glass, which is typically used in high rises.

Meshulam would continue to analyze the building, its windows, and our pieces of glass. He studied the police reports, photographs, witness statements, and autopsy report. He examined the local and national building codes, the weather conditions from the date of the death, and put together computer reenactments of the incident.

Then he issued his report. His ultimate conclusion was that the glass was "too dangerous" to be in a high-rise living room. It was "thin, brittle glass" which, "once broken, disintegrated into hundreds of small pieces almost instantaneously."

Had the building used safety glass, Meshulam said, it was "doubtful" Josh would have gone through. Tempered glass, the kind of glass Rosales had told me he wished the building used, would have been four or five times stronger, Meshulam said.

But it was more than just thin glass that had made that particular window dangerous on the afternoon of June 7, Meshulam explained after analyzing the data.

The window was old, Meshulam informed us. It had been an original, installed when the building was built in 1966. Neither the metal frame or the glass had ever been replaced. They should have been, he said.

The window gaskets, or what lay people might recognize as the rubbery cushions inserted between the edges of the glass and the window frame, were also old, deteriorating, and in some places around the window even completely missing. Those conditions, Meshulam said, made the window less sturdy, and more prone to failure. They were poorly maintained, he said.

Another risk, he said, was the low positioning of the window on the wall. The windowsill – the bottom edge of the window – was dangerously close to the floor for a high rise living room, particularly when coupled with the building's choice of extremely thin glass, he said.

Also contributing to the window's unusual vulnerability was the building's unorthodox design and location. The circular University Club Tower sits on a slight hill near the western perimeter of downtown Tulsa. Its western side, which faces the Arkansas River, is nakedly exposed to the strong Oklahoma winds that blow unchecked into that side of the building, a force of nature that over time builds pressure against the window glass. Apartment 2509 sits on that western side of the building. His report concluded that the subject window did not have sufficient windforce resistance.

He also explained the "chimney effect," or "stack effect," of air pressure in tall buildings, in which the air rises inside and looks to escape out through the highest floors. This effect, he added, increases dramatically in the heat. As the local newspaper had reported that morning, Tulsa was in the midst of a heat wave. "Look at all the pictures from the news that day," he explained, "the blinds are blowing out. That's air pressure. That's what happens, it sucks things out like a vacuum."

The heat and windy conditions of June 7 had made the glass even more susceptible. The windows would be most vulnerable, he explained via a detailed PowerPoint: (1) during a heat wave; (2) during times of high wind; (3) on the highest floors; (4) on the west side of the building; and (5) during afternoons, when the pressure is the highest.

All five of those conditions had been in effect when Josh went into the window blinds.

Meshulam's explanations gave reason to something Rosales had told me: the building has more window breaks in the summertime.

They also took me back to the confusion Amber had felt in the hours after Josh's death, as she sat in custody and spoke to her grandmother, and then to me the next morning.

How did he go through the window? It doesn't make sense. Why did this happen?

Now, finally, we had a much better understanding. Amber's confusion after her husband's death made more sense. Science had given us the explanation.

Josh's movement into the living room blinds, Meshulam would later write, was just one factor contributing to his death. It was "made worse by ... thin and weak glass, low sill height, and strong wind pressures from inside and outside the building."

Based on what the expert had explained, Amber's disbelief was justified. Josh never should have been able to go through that window.

40

filed the wrongful death lawsuit against the University Club Towers on September 19, 2012. Amber Hilberling, as the surviving spouse of Josh, was the plaintiff. So long as she wasn't convicted in the murder trial, she would remain the plaintiff.

The murder trial was still about six months away.

Mark Collier had wanted me to hold off on filing. But April had agreed with me. There were strategic benefits to filing it before the murder trial.

One benefit, I hoped, was to start changing the public narrative. I already worried that the one-sided media coverage was contaminating our jury pool. At least now, with the window lawsuit filed in the public record, people would start talking about another possible explanation.

Sure enough, the media jumped on the story. One night, flipping through channels, I saw two talking heads on Fox News debating the lawsuit I had just drafted and filed. One lampooned it, calling it ridiculous. But another, an attorney, called it a "brilliant" strategic move. Time would tell, I thought as I watched.

Another purpose was to make it clear that the window theory was more than a distraction tactic or a red herring. Having the lawsuit on file gave our theory credibility; it was a legitimate wrongful death action, not just a desperate excuse.

And further, we could now use the civil lawsuit as a means to engage in discovery against the building's ownership, something we couldn't do through the criminal case. In the civil case, they'd have to answer our questions and produce records. We wanted to get our expert inside the building to help draft his report, and we succeeded

But perhaps the most important reason to file the civil lawsuit before the murder trial, though, was to beat the statute of limitations. Under the law, the lawsuit had to be filed by June 7, 2013, the two-year anniversary of Josh's death. We expected the murder trial would start some time in the spring of 2013, not long before that two-year mark. If Amber was convicted, she'd lose the right to bring the civil lawsuit. That right would shift to whomever the probate court appointed as personal representative of Josh's estate. That's where I saw a potential problem.

I was concerned there wouldn't be enough time after the murder trial for a new person to be appointed in probate, evaluate the wrongful death claim, find a lawyer, and get it filed by June 7. Anything involving lawyers takes too much time. The probate appointment alone could take months. So I wanted to protect the case, for whoever would have it, by making sure it was filed before the deadline.

I named the building's owners and management company as the defendants. I also named a "John Doe 1" and "John Doe 2" as additional defendants, a legal maneuver allowing for the easy addition of parties should I or any other attorney on the case later want to do so. After filing it, I obtained the discovery we wanted in the short-term for the criminal case, then agreed to a "stay" that put the civil case on hold until after the murder trial.

The civil case could wait. The potential monetary payoff in that case, surely enough money to give Amber and Levi a fresh start, was a nice thought. But that was a thought for another day. A potential payday wasn't a pressing concern for any of us.

Or so I thought.

41

"**H**ow much money are you talking?" Bryan asked me.

It wasn't their lawsuit, but Rhonda and Bryan had some questions about the window lawsuit I had just filed for Amber.

I agreed to talk to them about it. After all, they had agreed to hire and pay our window expert, Mark Meshulam, whose work would potentially help both cases. We needed their continued support. And I could answer their factual questions without disclosing my attorney-client communications with Amber. Truth was, there wasn't much of that in the first place. Amber didn't care a whole lot about the window case, and we rarely talked about it.

Her focus was on something much more important.

I met with Rhonda and Bryan one afternoon and walked them through the entire history of the window lawsuit. I started with my first day on the job, when a hunch sent me hustling over to the broken window, to my calls to find a building inspector, and everything I had now learned from those pieces of glass. I told them what I had learned about the University Club Tower itself and its history, governing safety codes, other incidents in the building, and interviews I had conducted with Tower residents.

How much could they settle for, they asked me, *and how soon could they pay?*

I didn't make predictions, I told them, but I thought the case could generate a significant settlement or jury verdict if everything went our way. But that would be a lot of ifs. I was usually pretty good about sizing up case potential. I had just landed a seven-figure settlement on another case while working on Amber's defense, and I thought this one might have that kind of future.

But if Amber were to be convicted, I told them, the civil case would no longer be hers.

Bryan asked a question that surprised me: if Amber was convicted, could *they* get the wrongful death case?

No, I said. I wasn't a probate expert, but it was Josh Hilberling who died, and it would be Josh's heirs who would bring a wrongful death claim on behalf of Josh's estate. If his wife was stripped of her right to represent his estate, then his relatives would be next up in line. Not them.

Bryan and Rhonda bristled. By now the animosity between the two families was bordering on vicious. The idea of Josh's parents taking over the civil lawsuit, the one they were helping fund, didn't sit well with them.

We're the ones paying for the expert, not them, Bryan argued. It was a fair point. I told him they'd have the right to be reimbursed out of any recovery.

And we're the ones raising Levi, Rhonda said. *And isn't he the heir?* She had another good point. But as a minor, the court would likely insist that Levi have his own independent attorney, and any money going his way would be set up in a trust, protected and monitored independently. It wouldn't belong to Rhonda or Bryan.

They didn't like my answers.

So they soon came up with their own plan.

On November 26, 2012, without telling me or Amber, Rhonda and Bryan Whitlock filed a petition in probate court seeking to be appointed as the personal representatives of the estate of Joshua Hilberling. They also filed an objection to Amber representing her husband's estate, arguing that she was "incompetent" to serve.

Their filing blindsided both Amber and me.

Just weeks after I had filed the window lawsuit, Rhonda and Bryan were already trying to wrestle it away. The window lawsuit was the only potential asset of value in Josh's estate, the only reason for their sudden interest in taking over his estate.

Amber was stunned and disgusted.

I was offended and embarrassed.

I couldn't imagine the reaction of Josh's father, learning that Amber's parents, of all the people in the world, were moving to take over his son's probate estate and control his son's belongings, assets, and post-death affairs. And even worse, if they were appointed Rhonda and Bryan would have to then engage in direct communications with Josh's family about the estate matters.

As ideas go, this one was a dumpster fire. I wanted to call Josh's family and personally apologize.

Josh's father and stepmother quickly filed an objection to the Whitlocks' petition, arguing first that Rhonda and Bryan were unfit to be entrusted with the job. Their pleading cited the Whitlocks' record of bankruptcies, a recent foreclosure, a lien filed against them, and a judgment entered against Bryan for more than $200,000. It also cited the "irreconcilable conflict" between the Whitlocks and the Hilberlings, which I felt was obvious given the facts.

The Whitlocks' counterargument was that the window lawsuit should be theirs because they had been appointed Levi's temporary guardians during Amber's criminal case.

From where I sat, though, there was simply no reason for this fight. Neither the probate case nor the civil lawsuit were going anywhere until the criminal case was resolved. The filing was a horrific miscalculation, in my opinion, and a distraction to our efforts. Now, while we were trying to prepare for Amber's murder trial, her own parents were in court launching a separate legal battle against both their own daughter and Josh's grieving family.

About money.

Their surprise attack was not only devastating on a personal level to Amber, who felt betrayed, it was a burden to our defense team. I was now dragged into another of the family's legal proceedings: a probate fight in which I would now have to represent Amber against her own mother and stepfather. She had no money to go find another attorney. But even worse, it changed the dynamic between our defense team and Amber's parents.

I entered the probate case on behalf of Amber and argued against the Whitlocks' requested appointment. I urged the court to simply maintain the status quo: Amber retaining her position in the driver's seat pending the resolution of the criminal case.

Thankfully, the judge agreed.

But the damage had been done.

Amber was confused and upset. In turn, Bryan was angry that we had moved to block their bid.

It was an ugly, ill-advised, completely unnecessary mess. Like most court cases.

After the judge ruled against them, Bryan began harassing me with angry text messages, usually sent late at night. He demanded to know everything Amber and I had discussed about the probate and civil cases, which was confidential information I could not and would not share with him. My refusal only appeared to make him angrier.

Finally, I instructed him to quit texting me altogether.

"We can set up an appointment in either my or my co-counsel's office to discuss any questions you have with our cases, to the extent we can answer them without breaching attorney-client privilege," I texted. "Let us know what time & date works. Until then, please refrain from text messaging me. Thanks."

"DID YOU ADVISE AMBER TO NOT SPEAK TO HER PARENTS?" Bryan responded, escalating his text-message tirade to all-caps.

"I have never told any client that. Please stop texting. Thanks."

His response: "GTH!"

It took me a moment to understand his acronym: Go to hell.

It was all sickening. Physically sickening. All of it just reinforced my previous career decision.

I couldn't wait to get the hell out of law.

42

The latest drama – *her own parents* now filing against her in court — hit Amber hard.

She was frustrated, confused, and despondent.

On one visit to the jail, I noticed Amber acting strangely as soon as she entered the room. Very strangely. She started looking around the room, seemingly paranoid, oscillating between laughter and fear, speaking incoherently.

Holy shit, I realized. *She's high.*

The meeting was pointless. I rang the buzzer and sent her back in. I left disgusted.

She apologized at our next meeting, and took full accountability as she always had. She said drugs sometimes floated around the jail, and inmates would get together and get high. After everything that had been going on, she just wanted to put her head in the sand and escape. Laugh. Be gone from reality.

I understood what had pushed her, I told her. I understood her wanting to escape. But I didn't approve the method.

Don't do it again, I said. She promised she wouldn't.

But it was too late. Getting high with other inmates, we'd find out later, had already birthed a disaster that Amber never could have imagined: something that would be the biggest shock of her upcoming murder trial.

43

Everywhere I went, people wanted to talk to me about one thing: the Amber Hilberling case.

My neighbors would ask me about it. Friends. Relatives. Exes. I'd hear about it at restaurants. At the golf course. While getting a haircut. If I was in court on another case, attorneys would stop me to talk about it. My teenage kids followed it closely and often complained about the media's coverage, as they knew some of the facts that weren't being reported. Their friends, hanging out at the house, would ask me questions about the case.

The comments I'd hear around town ran the gamut.

"I think it was just an accident," more than a few people said. "She didn't know he was going out that window. No way."

"I heard she's crazy," a friend at the golf club once said, echoing similar comments I'd heard from others. "You talk to her, right? Is she fucking nuts?"

"Where'd you hear she's crazy?" I asked.

"I think I read it on the Internet or whatever. Isn't she? You ever afraid of her?"

One evening I met a friend for a drink downtown. A local TV reporter approached me at the bar and tried to talk about the case. I wouldn't. Later she cornered me in a hallway, trying again to convince me to give her an exclusive interview. I said no. She started to flirt, which I took as a compliment until I realized her real intentions. She was just playing me, trying to get me to agree to the interview.

Other clients, both past and present, would ask me about the case.

"So you're helping the whore?" one extremely difficult client, who later ended up in a mental hospital, gloated over the phone soon after seeing the case on the news. "The little slut who killed her husband? Make sure you're not standing by a window when she's around!"

It didn't matter who it was. Every day, I knew someone would bring up Amber's case.

Local and national media still regularly called, texted, and emailed about the case. We still regularly declined their requests. April and I agreed to make one exception: for Dateline NBC, whose producer showed a level of integrity and professionalism we hadn't seen elsewhere, not to mention the first real commitment to accuracy I had seen from a journalist on the case. Dateline's two-part special on the case, "Shattered," ran after the trial. It was fair and well done. In terms of accuracy and fairness, every other report I watched paled in comparison.

It was like this for more than two years: friends, relatives, neighbors, golf partners, attorneys, strangers, local reporters, national media... everyone wanted to talk to me about the same thing.

Amber Hilberling.

44

Amber's cases were taking a toll on me, emotionally, financially, and physically.

I had always slept soundly, like a baby, a trait my wife had envied. I'd often be asleep within a minute of hitting the pillow.

Now, for the first time I could remember, I couldn't fall sleep at night.

I'd lie awake thinking about Amber and Levi, feeling the pressure to reunite them. I'd think about our trial strategies, often reaching for my iPhone on the nightstand to write some notes. The behind-the-scenes ugliness in the probate and civil cases, the angry harassment from Amber's stepfather, bothered me. I wrestled with my decision to not try the case by myself, wondering if I had done the right thing.

These reactions were foreign to me. I had never let worries about a lawsuit keep me up at night, not even on the eve of tough trials. Not after good days or bad days or gruesome days.

I understood, though, that it wasn't the case itself that bothered me. I had worked death cases before, seen the unpleasant, the graphic. Before detouring into law, I had been at death scenes as a journalist, near the bodies, even inside prison watching the state execute the convicted.

What kept me up at night was Amber.

I cared about her. I had to save her.

I needed to.

The public saw a monster. I saw a girl who had been mistreated from all directions, horribly at times. I saw a girl who was holding more unfair cards than I had ever seen dealt to one person.

I wanted to save her because I knew her life hadn't been easy. She had been dealt an unfair deck of cards, growing up around more turmoil than she deserved.

I wanted to save her because I knew what her first love had put her through.

I wanted to save her because I believed Josh's death was an accident, not a murder.

I wanted to save her because of how horribly the media and public had treated her.

I wanted to save her because I was starting to suspect the prosecution wasn't playing fairly.

I probably wanted to save her for my own psyche, too. I wanted to feel that my law career — all the studying, toiling, law school, the bar exam, years spent litigating, the long hours, the fighting, the stress — had actually made a damn bit of difference other than determining what insurance checks were written to what parties.

And in retrospect, I think I felt compelled to save her because she was a scared young woman. Because she was female.

Though I wasn't consciously self-aware of it for years, I later realized the tendency I had to treat clients differently based on their gender. Right or wrong, and I'm not sure if it was chivalrous or sexist, I became more emotionally invested in cases with female clients, particularly where I felt the woman had been victimized. I often waived my fees, working cases for free, when the client was a woman in need. I wasn't that way with male clients.

If it was a divorce, and my female client was about to become a single mom without financial support from a good-for-nothing ex, I'd usually feel too guilty to add legal fees to her worries. I'd handle it for free, figuring I'd make some good money on a pending civil case.

In one wrongful death case, I represented a widow whose husband was killed on the job. Her recovery was capped by a workers compensation statute, which I felt was too low. It took me about two phone calls and one letter to get her the maximum settlement, a check that wasn't going to last her anywhere near as long as she'd need it to. I waived my fee, which seemed like the obvious move. *Who wouldn't*, I thought. Apparently most. In a conversation I'll never forget, the Zurich Insurance Group officer cutting the check said it was the first time in her long career she had ever seen an attorney do that. Her comment saddened me.

While I was an aggressive litigator not afraid to ruffle feathers, my fighting style masked an altruism I didn't advertise, but which those closest to me have long known.

So when Amber's parents would tell me they were "broke," that they'd pay me later, they'd get me "caught up" after the case, I didn't really care. I just wanted to help Amber.

But financially, professionally, and even ethically, I look back and view this approach as a mistake. If Amber would have been a man, I asked myself years later, would I have stayed on the case without compensation? I don't think I would have. And that's wrong.

For years I thought I was doing the right thing, that serving selflessly was living out the ideals my old Catholic school in Omaha had instilled in me. But I was misguided. Being too emotionally connected to a case or a client changes the dynamic of the attorney-client relationship. And it created problems for me numerous times.

Female clients often came to see me as something more than their attorney. I was a caregiver, a friend, someone they trusted and could count on. We'd form close bonds. They'd hug me, confide in me, text me after business hours, cry to me. I'd be there for them. I'd listen.

It wasn't uncommon for female clients to eventually want me to be more than their attorney. Clients would ask me out, make advances, show up to my office unannounced. A few even showed up at my home. Some would come back and try again, months after their cases had ended. One client, a young woman in her 20's, started showing up at my home and putting handwritten notes and drawings in my mailbox claiming she was "in love" with me. My firm worked 10 to 20 hours a week for one private family group controlled by an eccentric woman old enough to be my grandmother; despite her age, she eventually professed her desire for me and pursued me so aggressively we had to fire them as clients. Another client showed up at my law office the same evening we had finalized her divorce, closed and locked my door, and tried to have me on the spot.

For the record, Amber never behaved in this manner. But she may have been in the minority.

I used to write off this behavior as women being "emotional," whatever that really meant, and I ignorantly assumed it happened all the time in the practice. Now I look back and see it differently. I was to blame, not them. The common denominator with them all was my failure to set the boundaries I should have set.

I knew how to win cases. I enjoyed the intellectual challenge of the law, and always knew I could outlawyer the other side. But I had underappreciated the psychological challenge of immersing myself in other people's problems. And when I rushed to open my own law practice, still green, I wasn't emotionally ready to play the role of The Hero saving people in need. I let cases consume me. I let myself get too close.

It was no different with Amber.

On June 8, 2011, when I met this scared teenage girl hours after her husband died, my heart broke for her.

She needed me, and I wasn't going to let her down.

As her trial approached, Amber was no longer just a client, or hers just a case. She was like a little sister who needed me to protect her. I felt like it was us against the world.

I started to feel the physical symptoms of severe stress for the first time in my life. Tightness in my chest. Tension in my shoulders. Sometimes it felt like my upper body was frozen. I'd have a hard time taking deep breaths. In the weeks leading up to the trial, I'd think about it all day, every day, and even dream about it.

I knew what it was: the pressure had pushed me to the limit. We had to win. I had to get her out.

For her, and for me, I needed Amber back home with her little boy.

45

On Friday, March 8, three days before the start of trial, the prosecution called us with an offer.

An incredible one.

Amber could plead no-contest to manslaughter and receive just a five-year prison sentence, with credit for time served. And it would all be over.

It was the first time in his career, Judge Kurt Glassco told us in his chambers, that he had seen the prosecution offer a no-contest plea deal in a murder case. Typically the defendant would have to plead guilty in a plea deal.

Another coup was the offer to drop the case down from murder to manslaughter. Levi could grow up knowing his dad's death was an accident.

But more importantly, he could grow up with his mother.

The brevity of the offered sentence, just five years, was also nearly unheard of in a murder case.

Under the proposal, Amber, 21 at the time, could have been out as early as March 2016.

She'd be 23, her son just four.

April and I went down to jail that afternoon to take the offer to Amber in person.

We told her it was a hell of an offer. Yes, we were ready for trial, and yes, we were confident. But she needed to seriously consider taking the deal.

It was entirely her decision, we told her. April cautioned her in detail about the risks she was facing. She could get a sentence of life in prison. She could be a convicted murderer for the rest of her life. She could lose the chance to ever raise her child herself.

She had three options. Accept the deal, counter offer, or reject it completely.

She said she wanted to reject it.

"I want to go to trial," she said. "I want to clear my name. I want everyone to know the truth."

I wasn't surprised. I had spent enough time with Amber to know how driven she was to clear her name. I sensed April was surprised. April wanted her to think on it longer. She told her she'd wait until Monday morning to deliver the answer to the prosecutor. In the meantime, she wanted Amber to think about it more over the weekend, talk to her family, pray on it.

This is your life, April warned her.

On Monday morning, we met with Amber again. She said she had prayed on it and asked for guidance from above.

Amber said God had given her an answer: "He's got my back."

She was sure of her decision. She turned down the offer.

We were going to trial.

Part Three: Trial

46

The courthouse was abuzz. Media vans surrounded the block. Reporters and cameramen were stationed around the building. The lobby was full.

It wasn't yet 9 a.m.

Trial in the case of *State of Oklahoma vs. Amber Michelle Hilberling* was about to begin.

A pool of 60 potential jurors met in the courthouse basement. They received instructions and were brought up to our fourth-floor courtroom, one 20-person group at a time, to begin jury selection.

The process would start with written questions. On the judge's orders, the prosecutor, April, and I had worked together to draft questionnaires for each juror. The questions were designed to weed out anyone influenced by the publicity the case had generated. Only after that cleansing would we then move into traditional jury selection, known as voir dire, where the judge and attorneys talk directly to potential jurors to learn more about how they think and who they are.

April and I were concerned about the one-sided storyline the press had pushed since day one. The district attorney's office and Josh's family had waged a 21-month campaign for the hearts, minds, and votes of the jury. We hadn't responded in kind.

I had been worried their campaign was going to contaminate our jury pool.

I was right. And it was worse than I had feared.

When we received the initial questionnaires back from the jurors, I was alarmed.

It wasn't just a few potential jurors who had already formed opinions. It appeared to be most of them. Juror after juror said they were already familiar with the facts, having been educated by the media and Internet. Many had already discussed it with friends, family, and/or co-workers. Jurors talked of even watching the news coverage that very morning, before they got in their cars and left for jury duty. One said that after receiving notice of jury duty, she had set out to study the media's past reports to prepare for jury selection.

Studied the media's reports.

I could only imagine what she had read.

Amber was smiling at all the bystanders! She showed no remorse! She was mentally ill and used her "insanity strength" to intentionally shove her husband to his death!

She had "viciously pounced" on the "gentle giant" who was proudly serving his nation in the military.

It had been these media stories, the jurors freely admitted, that had shaped the pre-formed opinions they brought to the courthouse for trial.

"I can't imagine how anyone could do such a thing as a Christian," one juror said early on, citing "the TV coverage" as the source of his judgment.

Another said he was "stunned and appalled" by what Amber had done.

"I know there was a crime," said another, guilt already determined.

Josh was afraid of Amber, another juror proclaimed. The newspaper had said so.

"What led up to the fight?" another asked from the outset.

The media reports never said anything about self-defense, another explained.

"It's probably just a disagreement and, you know... people get into disagreements and they do get physical," said another.

Neither the judge nor any of the attorneys had told the jurors a single thing about any facts of the case. Yet they presumed to know the facts, crucially important ones, before the trial had started. They had formed strong opinions. They had formed conclusions.

At one point, the prosecutor asked a juror if she would consider only the evidence presented in the courtroom, or if she would also be influenced by what she had heard from the media.

"I would probably compare both," the juror said.

It kept getting worse.

"You form an opinion by listening to what's on TV," another explained.

Another said he already knew Amber "had acted out of anger." He said he was already "having a hard time" with Amber's defense strategies, before we had even started.

"It is hard to kind of, you know, be open-minded about it at times when you hear things, so, just being honest. It is hard... I do feel a little bit leaning one way at this point," one said.

Another potential juror openly glared at Amber. I noticed it immediately. Amber later expressed her own concern about him, his contempt that obvious.

Another openly warned: "Ms. Hilberling may not appreciate the bias she may see."

Another pointed out that his pre-formed opinions were all about Amber. Not Josh. "I haven't read anything about him," he said. "Nothing. So all I read about is her. So that's all I based it on."

April and I would consistently move to strike jurors who already appeared to have convicted Amber based on the media coverage alone. We weren't sure we could find 12 who hadn't.

The district attorney would fight to keep jurors regardless of their preformed opinions.

One juror talked openly about his belief, based on media reports, that Amber had been abusive of Josh "other times" in the past. We moved to strike him. Keely argued. Her words were telling:

"When he talks about 'I'm aware of other times,'" Keely argued, "honestly I think if most of the people are honest about what they've read or heard, we haven't asked them in front of everybody else, what they've read or heard because of concerns about contamination of the jury, but a lot of them are going to say they've heard that. It's been in the paper at least twice and on the news media."

I was taken aback. Keely's argument seemed to be that all of the jurors likely had such pre-formed opinions about Amber, so we just needed to accept it.

———

The jurors had a keen awareness of specific facts – both real ones and fake ones.

One talked about how Amber had just "turned down five years," which was true.

Another admitted she liked following high-profile cases. Another said friends with information about the case had already educated her. Another talked about his own phobia of falling from heights as Josh had.

The case was "sensational," opined another.

Several were already debating our window theory, despite the fact that we had not yet mentioned it.

One said he already knew the defense was going to call a window expert to testify that the building had "defective glass." It was "hard to believe" the glass broke, he said. He also asked about the building's inspections.

One asked "why a window that high up wouldn't be able to hold or be able to support a push, or whatever it may be."

Another expressed his skepticism about us using the window's thinness as a defense.

Courthouse staff was under orders to not discuss the case openly in the courthouse, given the possibility that jurors would be nearby. Yet one juror, while in a hallway on a break after testimony had started, heard two courthouse security guards openly discussing the facts of the case.

Another said he heard other potential jurors downstairs already debating the window issue, even though they were under strict orders to not be discussing the case.

It appeared obvious that a few jurors were doing more than discussing the case. They were actively trying to get onto the jury.

None more so than one man.

47

Late Monday afternoon during jury selection, a bailiff brought a handwritten note into the courtroom. It was from a potential juror down in the basement jury room. It read:

> *"I would like to speak with Judge Glassco or one of his bailiffs regarding a juror's biased comments in the criminal case he is hearing and presiding over. The juror is in the courtroom now."*

The judge called the note's author upstairs to the courtroom, then cleared the room of all observers. The author was a non-practicing attorney, a soft-spoken, middle-aged man who carried himself professionally. He testified that another potential juror, whom this book will refer to as "Peter" in the interest of privacy, had been downstairs telling the other jurors that he had personal knowledge of the case and was certain of Amber's guilt.

Peter had reportedly said he wanted to get onto the jury to "make sure" Amber was convicted like she deserved. He had boasted of having created an Internet blog called "Justice For Josh," and bragged that his blog had received "national hits," according to the witness.

I pulled up Peter's questionnaire. Nothing about his answers had stood out: he managed a local fast-food restaurant, said he knew little about the case, and denied having ever engaged in any Internet activity related to the case.

If the allegations were even remotely true, Peter had repeatedly lied under oath in his questionnaire answers.

The judge excused the witness from the room and asked us how we wished to proceed. We immediately moved to excuse Peter for cause. The reasons were self-evident. Given the allegations, his involvement would risk tainting the entire trial with the appearance of impropriety.

It was Fair Trial 101. His removal was a fait accompli.

Or so we thought.

Keely stood and objected to Peter's removal.

She argued that there was no real proof Peter had "actually started that website" and urged the judge to give Peter a chance.

Judge Glassco deferred to Keely. Instead of excusing Peter for cause, the judge called him in for a closed-courtroom voir dire Tuesday morning.

Peter took the stand, unaware of what we had all just heard the afternoon before.

"I remind you, you're still under oath from yesterday," the judge began. "Have you overheard, or have you been or participated in, any conversation about this case with your fellow jurors?"

"Not to my knowledge," Peter said.

A strange answer right off the bat, I noted. *To his knowledge?* Surely he would know if he had just conversed about the case downstairs.

The judge asked a series of questions following up on the account we heard, under the guise of traditional voir dire. Peter continued to testify that he had not been involved in any such dialogue downstairs, and that he had not been on any websites related to the case.

Judge Glassco then brought up the allegations. "I have been given information that you have been on a site 'Justice for [Josh],'" he said.

Peter instantly appeared anxious. He shifted in his seat and started to stammer.

"My mom's a — was a — participating in that site. She 'liked' the Facebook page. Me personally... I have not."

"OK," the judge said.

Though he had already answered the question, he awkwardly continued.

"She was — she 'liked' the Facebook page," he repeated nervously. "She's been following the case quite closely. For what, I have no idea."

"All right," the judge said.

Once more, Peter continued to stretch out his awkward protest.

"Me personally, I have not," he repeated.

"OK. And you have discussed this with your mother and your immediate family?"

"Whenever the case first — whenever it first got aired on the news, my mom kinda conversated about it. Whoever you're at dinner, it's kinda hard not to conversate about it, whenever that's the topic of discussion."

"OK," the judge said. "Right."

By now it was indisputable that Peter had contradicted his own questionnaire answers. There was no reason to continue with the charade. The man was not a good liar. Yet the judge continued. He asked the prosecutor if she wanted to ask him any questions.

Keely stood and tried to rehabilitate him, but his inconsistencies continued. The more he talked, the more rambling and nonsensical be sounded.

"Well the only mention of [the blog] was before I got here, whenever we were sitting in there waiting to be called for the jury selection, I guess you could say. I was talking because Fox 23 popped up on the thing saying that the jury selection reading the case today and that's whenever my mom brought that to my attention. That she was like, oh, I like Justice for Josh. I'm was like, oh, OK, I don't know what that is.

"She said, oh, well, you're in jury selection for a case and that's a part of what it was. And I was like, oh, OK. And that's as far as I went with it."

Keely nodded her head in a show of understanding, as if his answer had just explained things. She then asked if he had mentioned anything about a blog while he was downstairs. He continued his stream of incoherence.

"Well, I was talking about the fact that they were doing selection of this trial today. And that just happened to pop up in the conversation because I was like yeah, they've got Facebook pages dedicated to this site. We were conversating a little bit about it, but it was before I knew I was gonna be here."

Keely: "Yeah. And do you remember who you were talking to?"

"It was a little group of people that I was sitting with. Nobody that's on the jury selection with me today."

He wouldn't have known that, as there were three separated groups of potential jurors. The guy was clearly trying to lie and cheat his way onto our jury, for the sole purpose of throwing my client in prison. Everyone in the room understood what was going on. I could feel my blood starting to boil. Had he and I been in an alley at that precise moment, I'm not sure what I'd have done.

I had no idea why he was still in the courtroom. We felt the judge should have sent him packing long ago.

But Keely pushed against his removal. He was, after all, a guaranteed guilty vote. She adopted Peter's defense – *my mom did it* – as established fact, then asked 14 separate questions attempting to convince the judge that Peter could serve on the jury without any pressure from his mom.

Oh yes, he eagerly assured, he could still do the job. Most definitely.

Keely finished her questioning, and the judge had another opportunity to strike Peter from the pool. Once again, he elected not to.

Instead, he asked if we had any questions for Peter. I stood up immediately. Knowing the district attorney was lobbying for the guy, I had to make damn sure he wouldn't make it, even if it meant chucking the normal rules of jury selection decorum.

"Mr. Peter, isn't it true that yesterday morning you were talking in front of a group of five or six people about how this young lady was guilty of the crimes of which she had been charged?" I began.

"No, sir."

"You didn't use the word 'guilty' once?"

"No, sir."

This was cross-examination now, not jury selection, and I was in impeachment mode. I didn't like Peter. I didn't trust him. I didn't try to hide it. My tone was aggressive.

"How would you explain people reporting otherwise, that you have in fact made comments about her guilt in this courthouse this week?"

"I have not made any comments about her being guilty. The only conversation I had regarding the case prior to me being selected for the jury was the fact that there was jury selection for this case today and the Justice for Josh, and that was all.

"Isn't it true, Mr. Peter, that you bragged downstairs that this Justice for Josh blog or website has been getting national hits?"

"No, sir."

"Did you know this blog has national hits?"

"No, sir."

"Did you ever bring that to anyone's attention?"

"No, sir. I brought the blog site - as I was talking to the group of people, four people I was sitting with, none of which are on the jury selection, I may note - but only thing I said about that was that the site existed. I was not a member of that site. I never 'liked' the page."

"You admit you brought it to people's attention?"

"The four people I was sitting with, yes."

"And how do you know who's on the jury?"

"How do I know who's on the jury selection? The pool that was pulled yesterday, nobody that was pulled I was talking to."

"Would it surprise you to learn that in fact someone who over-heard you is in this group?"

"If they overhead me then that's something they were talking about, but they heard incorrectly."

"You mentioned with Ms. Keely, the district attorney, just a few minutes ago you referred to multiple Facebook pages, plural. You said pages with an 's.' What are the other Facebook pages?"

"The only Facebook page I know regarding this case is the Justice For Josh."

"Did I hear you right, you said you just heard about it for the first time four days ago?"

"Monday."

"Monday. So if I did a search on the Internet, I wouldn't find your name?"

"More than welcome to."

"I asked you if I did a search, would I find your name anywhere on the Internet?"

"Yeah you would find me on the Internet, my Facebook page."

"Would I find your name making any comments or associated with any comments about this case?"

"No. The only comment you'll find regarding anything regarding this week is I updated my Facebook Monday before I was selected that said "jury duty, ugh."

"Mr. Peter, let me try this again. I didn't say 'this week.'"

Judge Glassco had heard enough.

"Excuse me for interrupting," the judge said, looking sternly at me for a moment before turning to the witness. "Mr. Peter, at this time I think it's probably best that I excuse you from being on this jury panel."

Finally.

Courtroom staff took care of his paperwork then led him out of the room.

Then the judge turned his attention to me. He wasn't pleased.

"I think you were too aggressive in your voir dire," he told me. "Jurors are citizens that are absolute gold to us. And I understand you're being a zealous advocate for your client, and I understand the issue completely. And I'm tracking with you on that, but I hope you see that I'm being sensitive to this issue. But you need to ratchet back your aggressiveness."

"I hear you," I said. I had expected the speech. Having been on the receiving end of dressing-downs since second grade, by now I knew when they were coming before they started. But I didn't care. I was going to be as aggressive as necessary to send the man packing.

"And even if he had been clean and pristine and ready for being a juror in this case," the judge continued, "it probably would not have bode well with the aggressive tactic that you took with him for being a juror."

"You're right, Your Honor," I said.

I returned to my seat, pleased that Peter had been removed but concerned about the judge's apparent willingness to let him remain in the jury pool. I was ready to move on.

Keely wasn't.

"I object to his excuse for cause," she insisted again. "I think that the way he explained it that certainly there is a huge opportunity for misunderstanding."

"Sure," the judge said.

"And I think that because the person who came in and testi-fied - I don't recall his name ... he wasn't in the conversation. Certainly anytime you overhear a conversation it's easy to mis-understand. It could have been one of this other four people the he was talking to who made the comment that it was a national website. And we just object."

"Yes, ma'am," the judge said. "I understand."

———

The entire ordeal disturbed me.

How many other Peters were hiding downstairs in that jury pool? How many people had Peter influenced already? How lucky were we that one gentleman who had been in the right place at the right time had the integrity to bring Peter's behavior to our at-tention? This man was that close to deceptively maneuvering his way onto our jury and tainting the entire trial.

He was so close. It was that easy.

I was just as troubled by the district attorney openly fighting to keep a guy like that on the jury. Amber had a right to a fair trial.

But we hadn't seen nothin' yet.

48

We started with 60 and finished with 12.

The court sent home 22 potential jurors in the first round of cuts, citing questionnaire answers, language barriers, and other extreme issues. One juror, for instance, alleged that she had a condition that caused her to vomit spontaneously. We happily sent her on her way at once.

After that first round, the prosecution and defense took turns striking potential jurors from the pool, a back-and-forth tactical battle, eventually whittling the pool down to a final 12.

I had wanted parents of girls. I wanted moms and dads who would be as sickened as I was by a teenage girl's testimony about being physically abused, the police visits, her fleeing on foot, her injuries, his arrest, the restraining order against him. I wanted dads who would think of their own daughters at home, moms who would cringe in sympathy, when Amber gave her detailed history of being abused. I got my wish. Nine of the 12 jurors had daughters.

But the prejudicial tone of the entire jury selection dialogue, from the questionnaires to the voir dire, still lingered.

This was our jury:

Juror 1: A single mom in her 30's who worked in the financial industry. She had actually been at a Halloween party I hosted at my house, through a mutual friend, a fact I incorrectly assumed would prompt the state to excuse her. We liked her.

Juror 2: A food and beverage manager in his 30s, married, one son. We were slightly comfortable with him.

Juror 3: Retired from the airline industry, married, sharp dresser, mother of one adult child and two adult stepchildren. We liked her.

Juror 4: Married, 40, four kids, tough to read, seemed unhappy to be there, maybe just unhappy, period. We hadn't wanted her on the jury.

Juror 5: Married stay-at-home dad in his 30's, two kids. Quiet, hard to read.

Juror 6: Postman, married, about 50, ruggedly handsome with a shaved head, four kids aged 16 to 28. He had caught my attention early in jury selection, but I struggled to put my finger on exactly why. I saw him as a wildcard. He seemed to look at us with purpose. I thought he either really liked us or really disliked us. I went back and forth on him through voir dire. He held his cards close, never volunteering to answer a question, and kept his answers brief and diplomatic when called upon. He struck me as the kind of guy you'd want to have a beer with. He had experience in construction before joining the postal service, which we thought would help him understand the significance of the window problem.

He would end up as the foreman.

Juror 7: A woman with two adult daughters, worked in sales, appeared sympathetic to Amber.

Juror 8: A homemaker, all smiles, four kids. She radiated compassion. I was confident she would be moved by Amber's story. We liked her.

Juror 9: A quiet, married realtor, married to another realtor, two sons. He was well dressed, all business. I always had the impression he wanted it to be over quickly so he could get to an appointment.

Juror 10: A retired educator, married to a retired chemist, with six adult children and some grandchildren. She struck me as classy, caring, and someone who would feel protective of Amber when she learned the truth about their history.

Juror 11: A white-haired, bearded manufacturing sales rep in his 60's, married to an attorney, two adult kids, a soft-spoken grandpa. He struck us as perceptive and intelligent, someone who would understand the state's failure to meet its high burden of proof.

Juror 12: A skinny 28-year old, video gamer, polite, no wife or kids. We weren't sure about him, but we pegged him as someone likely to follow the majority.

The 12 jurors were placed in what would be their seats for the entire trial, along with two alternates who would be excused before deliberations.

April, Amber, and I watched from our table as they were shuffled into their spots.

Juror 6, the postman, took his seat and looked straight at our table.

I wasn't sure how to read it, but he smiled at us.

49

Each side had filed pretrial motions asking Judge Glassco to bar certain evidence from trial. Some of the requests were standard. Some weren't. There were seven evidentiary rulings in particular that had the potential to alter the course of the trial.

1. ON THE PARTIAL RECORDINGS

Three months into the case, I had filed a Motion to Suppress the partial recordings of Amber talking with her grandmother while in police custody after she had invoked her constitutional right to counsel. The court had sided with the state, finding that Amber did not have any lawful expectation of privacy as she spoke with her grandmother at the police department. We renewed the argument before trial and, as expected, lost again.

2. ON DRUG USE

Both sides had asked the court to prohibit any evidence of Josh or Amber having done illegal drugs in the past. We certainly had significant evidence of Josh's history of drug use, manufacturing, and sales. It was now well known, having been widely reported, that Amber had tested positive for pot before trial. Opening the door to this topic could have hurt us or helped us. Ultimately, both sides agreed that past drug use by Josh or Amber was not relevant to what happened on June 7. The parties agreed to not introduce evidence of Josh or Amber using drugs unless first clearing it with the court.

Notably, the judge also ordered that all references to Josh's drug abuse be redacted from the video recording and his Air Force discharge record.

3. ON PHOTOGRAPHS OF JOSH'S BODY

The cause of Josh's death was not in dispute: severe blunt-force trauma from landing on the concrete parking garage. The findings in the medical examiner's autopsy report were not controversial. So there was no need, we argued, for the state to parade a series of gruesome photographs of Josh's body. There would only be one reason to engage in such a tactic, we said: shock value, to inflame the jury's emotions.

"A good portion of those pictures are the same picture over and over again," April argued. They included close-up shots of Josh's broken limbs, skin that had been split open on impact, bone fragments, blood, tissue. April argued that they offered "no purpose or probative value."

The prosecutor countered that she needed them to prove how Josh had gone through the window glass. At the preliminary hearing, the state had repeatedly made the point that Josh had gone out "face first, feet first, standing upright." Keely said the photographs would help prove that point.

The judge ruled in the state's favor. "Gruesome facts bring gruesome photographs," he said.

4. ON THE WINDOW GLASS EVIDENCE

The state moved to bar all evidence about the dangerous conditions of the window. The prosecutor called it a "clever ploy" to "divert" the jury's attention.

We explained that whether Amber could have known about the unusual risk of this particular glass was directly relevant to the elements of second-degree murder.

The court ruled in our favor, allowing the window glass evidence.

5. ON AMBER'S DISCUSSION OF THE LIVING-ROOM FIGHT

In a request that struck me as inexplicable, the state asked the court to prevent Amber's grandmother from testifying that Amber had told her about the living-room fight with Josh. Though it was missing from the video, even the attending police officer's own notes had confirmed that dialogue.

"If those statements were made in a place such as in the jail, or around other people that the state has the ability to get the recordings," Keely argued, "the state needs to know that, because the state should have the opportunity to get those recordings to see if that statement was actually made."

I thought I was hearing things. The state had been the party in complete control of this very recording. There was no logical argument for this request, nor any legal authority supporting it, but it was a harbinger of the kind of trial the prosecution had planned.

The court ruled against the state's request.

6. ON PAST DOMESTIC INCIDENTS
Both sides had evidence of past domestic violence.

We had numerous accounts of Josh having been physical with Amber in the past, the police visits, his arrest, her fleeing, the bruises and welts and throwing and hitting and pushing and shoving. But the state was ready to respond with their own accounts of Amber also having been physical in the past, the storyline the media had obsessively pushed.

Under the law, there was only one way Judge Glassco could handle this: neither side could go into any such past abuse unless the defense first brought up the subject.

Under the governing Rule Of Evidence, "evidence of a crime, wrong, or other act is not admissible to prove a person's character in order to show that on a particular occasion the person acted in accordance with the character." In other words, the state can't introduce evidence that someone ran a red light in January as a way of arguing the driver is guilty of a speeding ticket issued in August. There are some limited exceptions to the rule, none of which we believed applied. However, if we elected to introduce evidence of Josh's domestic violence, that would "open the door" and allow the prosecution to respond with evidence of Amber's past behavior.

So we'd either limit the evidence to what happened on the afternoon of June 7, or risk turning the trial into a back-and-forth excavation of sordid stories from the couple's tumultuous relationship. It'd be all or none. Amber's constitutional right to a fair trial ensured that the past wasn't a bullet only one side would be allowed to fire.

Then the judge got creative.

7. ON THE LAMP-INCIDENT PROTECTIVE ORDER

The public campaign against Amber had, since day one, prominently featured the short-lived "protective order" Josh had obtained with his parents just after his Air Force discharge.

Neither the media nor the public seemed aware of the actual facts cited in the court filing — Amber had leaned over a staircase and pushed a lamp, which fell over and landed on Josh. Nor had they paid any attention to the recent "no-contact" protective order entered against Josh for battering his pregnant wife with his bare hands.

Only the second of the couple's two recent orders, the one against Amber, had captured the attention of the media and public. It better fit the narrative.

We understood the prosecution desperately wanted to bring it up at trial. The jurors had already heard about it in the news, and likely expected to hear more. The two words alone — "protective order" — carried an incriminating stigma, which is exactly why the law prohibits the use of such things as evidence. The jury's job is to decide what happened at the moment in question, not who they like or dislike based on other allegations or wrongdoings.

The law was just one reason for the inadmissibility of the protective order. The facts were another.

The order itself, as April argued to the judge, had almost no actual significance. The prosecutor, the judge, April, and I all understood the reality of this type of temporary order. They are handed out almost as casually as burgers at a drive-through window. They are granted *ex parte*, meaning the accused isn't even present to defend. The party seeking the temporary order simply shows up, recites a few lines, and leaves with a piece of paper. The burden of proof is exceptionally low. They're often used as cheap weapons in divorce cases, with one spouse obtaining the easy order as a tactic to quickly gain full physical custody of the children (which can affect the child support calculation) while the slow-moving divorce process plays out for months or years. In one divorce case, I saw a woman pull that trick then taunt her husband with dollar-sign symbols in a text message immediately afterward.

The more significant court order would come next. When the court grants the quick temporary order, it also schedules an evidentiary hearing at which the defendant can appear and testify. It is that hearing when the court makes an informed decision, this time based on a more complete presentation of evidence, as to whether protection is actually required. If it isn't, the court dismisses the temporary order.

This order had never even seen the light of a hearing. Josh disregarded it immediately, reaching out to Amber minutes after he had obtained it. He was back in his wife's arms that same afternoon, living with her again that week. Accordingly, the court had promptly dismissed his temporary order.

So to simply tell a jury there had been a "protective order" issued, without the jury learning the actual facts, would be grossly misleading and unfair to Amber.

Still, the prosecutor urged the court to make an exception to the longstanding rule of law. "This shows an absence of mistake," Keely argued at the hearing. She said it "certainly shows the opportunity and intent in the past... that certainly is very strong evidence of her state of mind."

But under the law, that argument had no chance.

Eventually recognizing this, Keely shifted gears and tried a new approach.

She argued that because there had been a physical, paper copy of the dismissed protective order inside Apartment 2509, it should be admissible as "part of the crime scene."

In reality, the protective order had been folded up with several other papers inside a catch-all bowl on a table nowhere near the window. It wasn't a part of the crime scene any more than a roll of toilet paper in the hall bathroom had been.

Nevertheless, Judge Glassco rubbed his chin and appeared to mull over this new approach. The impression that he was even considering it surprised us.

Glassco then asked a question that seemed to almost make April laugh out loud. He asked if that particular piece of paper was "certified." A court document is "certified" if a clerk simply stamps it.

"It is a certified document of the court," Keely confirmed. "So it comes in."

"And it is certified?" the judge asked a second time. He continued to theatrically rub his chin and wrinkle his eyebrows, as if pondering whether a clerical act of pressing a stamp might outweigh the time-honored rules prohibiting this potentially game-changing type of character evidence.

"Yes!" Keely said.

The judge finally stopped rubbing his chin and nodded his head.

The ink from a stamp had turned the tide.

Judge Glassco announced that the dismissed temporary protective order against Amber "will be allowed" as evidence in her murder trial. April looked at me in disbelief. Her nostrils flared. She had always maintained an excellent poker face in the courtroom. Not this time.

From the moment the trial started, the prosecution aggressively, and wisely, seized on this shocking ruling. Keely would use the two words "protective order" dozens of times throughout the trial, the jury never once learning anything about its actual facts.

And despite having claimed that the document was admissible not as character evidence against Amber, but as "part of the crime scene," the prosecutor aggressively used it in trial as character evidence. At one point, while wielding the protective order in her argument, Keely would tell the jury: "circumstantial evidence shows that she has a temper and she gets angry."

Between the jury's pre-formed beliefs about Amber, the judge's surprise decision on one of the couple's two protective orders, the omissions from the video, and the redaction of all references of Josh's domestic abuse and drug use, it felt like we were marching up a steep hill before opening statements had even started.

50

The trial plans were fluid, as they always are. The prosecutor, April, and I were all experienced trial attorneys. We all knew to expect the unexpected. A judge's ruling here, a surprise twist in testimony there, and the best laid trial plans can be chucked on a moment's notice.

Still, we expected much of the state's case to be straightforward. After all, Amber, and now Judge Glassco, had handed the prosecution gifts on a silver platter.

This wasn't a whodunit mystery. Amber had pushed him. She had then admitted it at the scene. She then admitted it on video for the world to see. We couldn't hide from the push.

And now the judge had decided to let the state freely bring up just enough of the past to cast Amber as a serial abuser.

Though there were two strikes against us before the first pitch, we still saw a path to acquittal. Our defense rested on two primary strategies.

Our first was to cast doubt on the prosecutor's case. In a criminal trial, the prosecution has the highest burden of proof in the legal world: beyond a reasonable doubt. Other types of cases have lower burdens of proof, such as the "preponderance of the evidence" standard in many civil actions. To convict Amber, the state would have to do more than simply prove she pushed Josh. They'd have to prove beyond a reasonable doubt that Amber's push met the elements of second-degree murder or the state's lesser alternative charge, first-degree Manslaughter.

For second-degree murder, the state would have to prove that Amber had acted with a "depraved mind" that disregards human life. The "depraved mind" standard requires proof of willful, deliberate, and contemptuous disregard for human life. It's also been described as morally corrupt and extreme physical cruelty. The state would not have to prove intent, an element required of first-degree murder.

For a conviction on the lesser charge, first-degree manslaughter, the state would have to prove that Amber had acted in the "heat of passion, but in a cruel and unusual manner."

The jury could convict on either charge, or acquit.

If the jurors believed the death had surprised Amber, that it had been an accident, we believed that under the jury instructions they could not convict her of the "depraved mind" murder. To that end, we were confident we could elicit testimony from every single first responder, police officer, and eyewitness on the scene that Amber was shocked, confused, distraught, sobbing, clearly behaving like someone who had never expected her husband to have been elevated into the air, fit through that living room window frame, and for the glass to then immediately give way. Her behavior, we felt, was not consistent with someone operating with a "depraved mind."

We also thought the window glass evidence would support our position that Amber could not have known how easily this large window would give way. In my mind, it was similar to pushing someone against a wall and having the entire room collapse. Unpredictable, not a foreseeable risk, and not an act the law defines as murder.

We felt the evidence clearly showed it had been a sudden push with an unexpected result.

If the jury was going to convict her of anything, based on the actual evidence and not preformed opinions, we felt it would have to be the "heat of passion" manslaughter charge.

The second prong of our strategy was asserting self-defense. This was tricky. Under the rules of evidence, we had two options: (1) a limited self-defense strategy, focusing only on what happened at the scene of Josh's death, or (2) a battered woman's syndrome defense, going into the long history of Josh's physical abuse. But the judge had made it clear that if we elected the second option, we would open the door to similar evidence against Amber. It would be a significant risk. We wouldn't have to decide until later in the trial, when we put on our defense case after the prosecution had rested.

First, our job was to attack the state's case. We had to demonstrate to the jury that what happened on June 7, 2011, simply wasn't a "depraved mind" case.

Despite all of the drama and attention surrounding the case, the jury's job, we believed, was straightforward: ignore everything you've ever heard about the case, pay attention, then go back and deliberate thoroughly and thoughtfully.

If they'd do that, we liked our chances.

51

The prosecutor rose from her table and stepped slowly toward the podium. She turned and faced the jury, then began her opening statement with a soft-spoken, step-by-step, dry account of what she alleged to have occurred on June 7, 2011.

"Ladies and gentlemen, on June 7, 2011, Joshua Blaine Hilberling was at his apartment where he lived with his wife, Amber Michelle Hilberling," Keely began. "They lived at the University Club Tower apartments, which are located at 1722 South Carson Avenue, in Tulsa. It has a beautiful view of the river. On that morning, he was in 2509. But on that morning his bag was packed. He was ready to go. But there was no taxi waiting to take him away.

"He called his dad and asked his father, Patrick Hilberling, 'Hey, can you come get me?' His dad said, 'No, I'm at work right now. I can't come get you.' Joshua called some friends. He called Brandon Morris, he called Michael Lloyd, and he said, 'Hey I'm ready to go. Come get me.' Well, they were over at some friends' and they were doing some stuff and they said, 'OK, we'll come get you.'"

Keely continued in this manner, standing in place, eyeglasses on, walking the jury through the afternoon's events in an almost professorial tone. The broken small bedroom window. Amber calling the apartment manager. Armando Rosales arriving soon after.

Neighbors hearing the sounds of an argument. Then the window crash. Then the first responders rushing to the scene. Amber's statements to witnesses.

All leading up to the partial recording of Amber's conversation with her grandmother.

"The defendant tells her grandmother later, 'he was fixin' - he was messing with the TV right here. And the windows are right there. And I pushed him and he fell out the - and he fell."

"Ladies and gentlemen, that is the evidence that you will hear in this case. That is what the defendant told her grandmother after it happened on June 7 of 2011. Ladies and gentlemen, after you hear the evidence in this case, the state will come to you and the state will ask you to find the defendant, Amber Michelle Hilberling, guilty of murder in the second degree. Thank you."

———

April's tone was more assertive. She immediately put to rest my uncertainty about whether she would have a commanding courtroom presence. She did.

"Ladies and gentlemen, on June 7 of 2011 there is no doubt that Amber Hilberling pushed her husband Josh Hilberling. Let me just clear that up for you right now."

"But there is going to be a great deal of discussion in this case about why. And for two years Ms Hilberling has been silent. She hasn't spoken to the media. No one has heard her side. And ladies and gentlemen, you're going to hear her side. Because on June 7, 2011, Amber Hilberling pushed back. That's what she did."

She pushed back.

It was a phrase, a theme, we had settled on in our trial prep sessions. It would tie in with Amber's long, detailed upcoming testimony about Josh's history of abuse, what we expected to be a painful, emotional, riveting account of everything that led up to Amber finally pushing back on June 7.

April walked the jury through a preview of what they would hear from both sides. She said the evidence would show that Amber had acted in self-defense. That the witnesses at the scene would all admit she was surprised and devastated, a young, pregnant girl in shock, a mindset inconsistent with the elements required for a "depraved mind" murder conviction.

"I anticipate that you're going to hear from 20, 25 witnesses from the state. But there are two things, two things, I want you to look at, and I want you to keep in your mind while you're listening to these witnesses: One, has Ms Keely proven to me depraved mind? Willful, contemptuous, disregard for life? And has Ms. Keely offered me any evidence that Ms Hilberling was not acting in self-defense? Pay attention to those two points with every witness and every photograph and everything you see, because that is what this entire case comes down to. Thank you."

Sitting to my right, Amber nodded in approval as April returned to our seat. I thought April had been stronger and more engrossing than the prosecutor, a perfect setup to the show about to start.

It was time for the state of Oklahoma to call its first witness.

52

"The state may call its first witness," Judge Glassco announced.

"Thank you," Keely responded. "State calls Patrick Hilberling."

Josh's dad walked slowly down the middle aisle separating the two sides of the public seating, through the swinging door in the wooden bar that bordered the front of the gallery, then between the two attorneys' tables. He stepped up into the witness box, raised his right hand and swore to tell the truth.

He was tall, white-haired, handsome, his eyes sad. I knew those eyes, the emptiness of loss, eyes I had seen too many times in my own life. His pain was sincere. I ached for him.

So did the jury. A few jurors were showing signs of emotion before he answered his first question.

"Sir, do you know a person by the name of Joshua Hilberling?"

"Yes, ma'am."

"And how do you know Joshua?"

"He is my son."

His voice cracked.

April and I knew there was little we could do with him. Any signs of aggression or disrespect would turn the jury against us immediately. We understood why the state called him first: to elicit sympathy. It was the smart move; we'd have done the same thing.

We'd take a punch or two then quickly move on.

He didn't testify for long, offering a little biographical background and recounting that Josh had asked him for a ride that day.

But he did manage to volunteer two pieces of the previously-launched PR campaign against Amber, as we assumed the prosecutor had instructed him to do.

He testified that Josh had just decided that "he was finally going to leave her and get a divorce," an assertion clearly contradicted by the couple's numerous text messages during their last few days. But those text messages weren't admissible evidence. The purpose of this storyline was clear: to paint a picture of a woman scorned, angry, motivated to kill her departing lover.

And just before returning to his seat, he made sure to seize on the judge's surprise pretrial ruling. He looked at the sympathetic jurors and reminded them that there had been a "protective order" issued against Amber.

Understandably, he didn't mention the one issued against his son.

———

The state then called two of Josh's friends, both of whom were on and off the stand within minutes. Before testifying, one of them posted "JUSTICE 4 JOSH" on his Facebook page.

They testified that Josh had asked them for a ride on June 7, and they had told him no. "We were at the pool hanging out with some other friends," the first friend said he told Josh, "and we'd come scoop him up here in a bit."

The state was attempting to establish that Josh had wanted out of Apartment 2509 that day. Our counterpoint was simple: Josh obviously hadn't shown any urgency or sense of worry, otherwise his dad or good friends surely would have come to his help. We felt their testimony was consistent with Amber's account, more helpful than harmful.

———

Mary Chandler had lived in Apartment 2409, just beneath Amber and Josh. She took the stand next, offering her account of what she heard upstairs just before the sound of the window break.

Chandler had been in her own bathroom when she heard Amber just above her through the ceiling vent. It sounded "like she was throwing up," Chandler testified. "Then there was a man's voice. They were arguing over a broken window."

She said they were arguing in the bathroom for about two minutes. She couldn't make it all out, but she heard one exchange clearly:

"What do you want me to do?" Josh yelled.

"I want you to grow up!" Amber responded.

The two then went into the living room. After about five minutes, Chandler estimated, she heard the loud crash, then Amber screaming: "Josh!"

Chandler became emotional, needing a moment to collect herself as she shared her memory. She testified that she turned to look at her window when she heard the crash. She saw pieces of glass falling outside; Josh had already passed by. She went to the window, looked down, and saw Josh's body below. Soon after, she testified, she saw Amber running across the top of the parking garage to Josh. She saw Amber crouch down by her husband's body, then look up toward the sky, crying.

I had previously obtained a photograph taken by another resident that shows this horrific scene: Amber kneeling by Josh's body, looking up into the sky, wailing, her arms out, palms turned upward, as if asking God why. It captures Josh's horrible fate and Amber's absolute anguish. It was shown to the jury. Out of respect for Josh and his family, such images will not appear in these pages.

————

Four witnesses down, and the most incriminating evidence, we felt, had been the reference to the "protective order."

Keely hadn't been the wolf in sheep's clothing I had been warned about. Whether the jury found her likable or sincere wasn't a question for me to answer. From what I could see, she was just an attorney trying to do her job. The advice I had received about her cutthroat courtroom style appeared unfounded.

That was about to change.

53

We believed Amber and Josh had been fighting in the living room when she pushed him.

From the morning I first met her, her account of the fight had always been the same. Armando Rosales, the only other person in Apartment 2509 at the time of Josh's death, had already testified at the preliminary hearing that he had heard the fighting. Police records, if not the video, established that Amber talked about the fight with her grandmother. Police photographs taken about an hour after Josh's death show fresh marks of a fight all over Amber's shoulder.

Whether Amber and Josh had been in a fight when she pushed him was a crucial fact. If the jury believed Amber and Josh were in a fight, we felt a self-defense acquittal was likely.

We knew the prosecution had no witness who could offer direct evidence that the two had not been fighting, as the state would need to prove.

It was an evidentiary problem for the prosecution. A determined Keely set out to overcome it.

She called three witnesses – Antonio DePaz, Nathan McGowan, and Robert Baker – to begin making the case that Amber had actually pushed an unsuspecting Josh from behind, rather than during a fight.

DePaz and Baker repeated some of the same testimony they had volunteered at the preliminary hearing almost 16 months earlier. Evidence we believed was not credible.

DePaz testified he was at the University Club Tower with Armando Rosales, repairing another broken window elsewhere in the building, when they received word about the small bedroom window Josh had broken upstairs in Apartment 2509. He testified that he had been down on the ground outside when he saw Josh break through the glass of the 25th-floor living room window above him.

Despite having been more than 300 feet directly below the window, and so close to the building he feared the falling glass would hit him, DePaz swore to the jury that he could make out Josh breaking through the window glass *face first, feet first, like he was jumping into a pool.*

Robert Baker testified that he had been standing outside a nearby apartment complex, smoking a cigarette, and watched as "the whole front of [Josh's] body came out first at the same time." He said Amber then went to the window, screaming. Baker said he then walked over to the University Club Tower, where he saw Amber at Josh's body, rolling him over onto her lap, crying: "He's dead! He's dead!"

Nathan McGowan, the neighbor who had been surfing the Internet before volunteering his story nine days later, testified that he had heard Amber yelling, followed by the sounds of footsteps moving "left to right" on the living room carpet toward the window before the glass break.

"Like it sounded like, just a like, just, stomp, stomp, stomp, stomp, stomp," he testified. "And it was from left to right facing that way." He reiterated that the stomps "started from the left, so it would have been in the hallway" then "traveled from left to right toward the exterior of the building."

While McGowan was busy repeating his "left to right footsteps" story, he let slip other details we felt actually helped our defense. He now said that in the moments before the window break, he heard the fighting between Josh and Amber. Their fighting was so loud and dramatic, he testified, he "was about to call security on my cell phone if it didn't stop."

A push during a fight. Exactly what Amber had said from day one.

———

Point out the window to the jury, April instructed DePaz on cross-examination.

He had repeatedly sworn he saw Josh's body come through the window. We knew the claim was bull. April handed him an enlarged photograph of the building, showing the hundreds of windows that would have been visible to him if he had in fact been looking straight up into the sun as he walked on the ground carrying construction supplies, as he had described under oath.

Show the jury where you claim you saw Josh come out the glass.

DePaz pointed to a spot about halfway up the building, nowhere near the 25th floor, nowhere near the actual window. Unlike his colorful previous testimony, the spot to which he pointed actually made sense. It was much more likely that he had first heard the sounds from above, and then looked up in reaction and saw Josh about where he pointed: after Josh had already been falling, not before.

By that point, as Amber had described in painful detail, Josh had been twisting and flailing trying to brace for impact, and may well have been in the position DePaz described.

On the next page is a photograph taken from the edge of the parking level, feet away from DePaz's position but eight stories higher, illustrating the angle from which DePaz would have seen the building as he looked up.

Apartment 2509's window is seven rows below the roof over-hang. DePaz claims he actually saw into that window, from this angle, and watched Josh come through the glass face first. What he claimed is not physically possible.

Neither is Baker's testimony.

Baker testified that he actually "saw the glass break" at impact and could pinpoint which of Josh's body parts had hit the glass first. This photograph is taken from the spot where Baker was standing when he allegedly saw this detail:

He was more than 700 feet from the window. The window is the furthest window on the far right edge, seven floors down from the top.

Baker couldn't have seen into Apartment 2509 from his angle. But for argument's sake, even if he had a much better angle and had been looking through a professional telescope, his alleged view into the apartment would have been blocked by the closed white blinds.

Even without the blinds, from that distance Josh's body would have appeared too small to make out any of the details he professed to have seen. Yet Baker insisted. He boasted that his eyesight wasn't just perfect, but was actually "better than perfect."

He even swore he "saw it before I heard it," having been zeroed in on that one tiny window frame in the distance just before Amber pushed Josh. Of the hundreds of windows, he had just happened to focus on that exact one.

Like DePaz, Baker had previously met with the prosecutor to rehearse his testimony. Like DePaz, Baker described Josh going out the window *face first, feet first, standing upright.*

On cross-examination, I showed Baker a large blowup of this same photograph and asked him to point out the window to the jury.

He admitted he couldn't.

Since he was so certain of the precise specifics of how Josh had gone through the glass, having zeroed in on these details with his "better than perfect" eyesight, I asked him to share some other simple details for the jury.

"When you saw Mr. Hilberling fall, could you tell what clothes he was wearing when he fell?"

"No, sir."

"Can you tell me if he had a hat on?"

"No, sir."

"Could you see if he had a beard?"

"No, sir."

"Could you tell me if he had glasses on?"

"No, sir."

"Could you tell if he was carrying anything in his hands?"

"No."

"Could you tell the jury which foot was in front of the other?"

"No."

"Did you see which way any blinds fell out of that window?"

"No."

Yet he swore he knew which part of Josh's body had first touched the inside of the glass.

Whether he and DePaz had been confused or were intentionally lying wasn't a question for April or I to answer. I wasn't sure we could. But we were confident the jury would share our view of their accounts.

We felt the same about the credibility of McGowan, who had waited nine days before voluntarily involving himself in the high-profile case he had been following, suddenly providing a dramatic and incriminating account he had notably failed to provide police at the scene. But aggressively attacking him on cross hadn't been necessary, as we felt his revelation that he heard a dramatic fight in Apartment 2509 just before the window crash had backfired on the prosecution and helped us.

What these three witnesses told us was that Keely had decided to stick with the "face first, feet first, standing upright" strategy she had suggested at the end of the preliminary hearing. She wanted the jury to believe there hadn't been any kind of living-room fight at all, that Amber had caught Josh off guard.

That strategy choice made us more optimistic. We knew the prosecution had no witnesses who could give any real corroboration to such a theory.

What we didn't know was that the prosecutor had an ace up her sleeve: an ace named Bonnie.

54

Armando Rosales had given four recorded statements before trial. They were nearly identical. I had studied them all closely, and knew exactly how he was going to testify.

I was wrong.

Rosales took the stand, raised his right hand, swore to tell the truth, then stunned us by dramatically reversing the key parts of his previous accounts.

His reversals started almost immediately.

Before trial, he had described Josh as having been "angry," "upset," and "not real nice to me" when he entered Apartment 2509.

On the witness stand, Rosales looked at the jury and testified Josh actually "seemed to be nice."

His words jolted me.

Josh seemed to be nice?

Is Rosales really going to...

I didn't have to wait long for my answer.

Before trial, Rosales had repeatedly described Amber as "quiet" inside the apartment.

On the witness stand, Rosales told the jury Amber was "really, really angry" and "very, very upset."

He even swore that Amber was, specifically, "very angry at [Josh]."

He now claimed that even when had been outside on the exterior bedroom balcony starting his repair work, he managed to see Amber inside the apartment and "it looks like she got angry" in there.

I couldn't believe what I was hearing.

Before trial, he had clearly described hearing the living room "fighting," believing Josh was in there "hitting Amber." He had even described mentally preparing himself to go confront Josh to protect Amber.

He changed that one too.

On the witness stand, he told the jury he was actually going in the other room to "confront *the situation*" generally, no longer Josh.

Before trial, he had described Amber as devastated, shocked, and traumatized at the scene. Matching every other account from the scene, Rosales had always given vivid, sympathetic accounts of Amber's hysterical crying and wailing.

He changed that one, too.

On the witness stand, he looked at the jury and described a cold-blooded killer. He suggestively told the jury he had even "wonder[ed] why she wasn't screaming when he fell out," implying he had immediately questioned her lack of remorse. A complete change of his earlier accounts.

Before trial, he had already testified that a sobbing Amber had cried: "My husband *fell* out the window! *Is he dead? Is he dead? Is he dead?*"

On the witness stand, he told the jury that Amber had actually come to him and delivered a much colder, more incriminating line: "'I pushed my husband out the window. I killed him.'"

My blood pressure was rising. My client's freedom was on the line, and Armando Rosales had apparently sold out.

Nothing, though, could compare to what he said next.

Before trial, he had consistently said it was "obvious" to him Amber hadn't meant to hurt anybody. "She couldn't believe this was happening," he had said before. "Obviously she did not want that to happen." He had previously testified "I feel that she didn't" want to hurt Josh, and that "I don't think she tried to do it... I don't think she meant it on purpose."

Before trial, he had spoken warmly of her, expressed his sympathy and concern for her, and even happily told me a friend of his had been meeting Amber for Bible study sessions.

On the witness stand, Armando Rosales told the jury he feared Amber would kill him.

After he rushed into the living room, he now claimed, he "kind of got nervous myself because I was... you know... I didn't want her to..."

He looked at the jury and paused.

"For my safety, I kind of moved to the side."

My jaw dropped. *Did I hear that right?*

I had.

Keely pushed, making him say the words she knew were coming. The words they had obviously rehearsed.

"You didn't want her to what?" she pressed.

"To push me out the window."

What. The. Hell.

I looked at the jurors, expecting to see the same disbelief I felt. I didn't see it. Based on their body language, they appeared to believe him.

I stared at him. He had crossed the line. I wanted him to look me in the eyes, to look at Amber, to recover his moral compass and do the right thing.

But he didn't look our way once. I understood why.

Keely kept pushing this brand new account.

Rosales now said he was even afraid to get inside the elevator with Amber, "concerned about my safety." This was yet another complete reversal of his earlier testimony. At the preliminary hearing he had testified that he got on the elevator because Amber "was just so upset, you know, that she – that she didn't want to get on there alone," and that he tried to comfort her on the way down.

This was the same elevator in which, moments later, Amber would react to the apartment manager telling her to "shut up" by weakly crumbling to the floor.

I had seen witnesses lie before. But this was the first time in my career I thought someone truly deserved to go to jail for perjury.

But first I had to keep my cool and cross-examine him. The jury had no knowledge of his previous statements, or that he had just reversed himself completely.

I had to scrap my original plans for his cross and instead set out to undo the damage he had just inflicted. I'd have to walk the jury through his previous statements to show how completely, dramatically, and repeatedly Rosales had just contradicted himself.

"In 2011, your testimony was that Ms. Hilberling appeared 'surprised' and that this appeared to be an 'accident,'" I began. "Did I hear that correctly?"

"Yes, I guess."

I guess.

It was a word-for-word account he had given multiple times, including under oath at the preliminary hearing.

I asked him if he had met with Keely to prepare and rehearse this new testimony. He admitted he had.

Then the judge threw us for a loop.

He interrupted and called a lunch break.

During the heart of my cross-examination.

The timing was odd. Typically, the court waits until a break between witnesses to call for a lunch break, which is the longest break of the day. Not during a cross-examination, which, more than any other part of trial, relies on rhythm and tempo. My strategy was immediately obvious to anyone in the room, including the judge: I was setting out to impeach him for having given inconsistent statements. A lunch break would give Rosales time to get his bearings, to meet with Keely and strategize his approach for dealing with this line.

And moreover, as all trial lawyers know, the longer the break, the more the most-recent testimony lingers and takes hold in the jurors' minds. You never want to go home for the weekend just after the other side hits a home run. But here were, off to a long break, Rosales's stunning testimony — *I was afraid she would kill me too!* — still fresh in the jurors' minds.

I couldn't eat. I stayed in the courtroom during lunch and prepped. I pulled out an easel and a marker and drew a simple two-column table on the mounted paper. On the top of the left, I wrote "2011." On the right, "2013." I listed his previous statements in the left column, his brand new reversals in the right.

When he came back from lunch, I set the easel in front of the jury and took Rosales one-by-one through his previous statements, comparing each to his brand new story for trial.

Yes, I had said that before. But now I'm saying this.

Yes, that. Then this.

That, then this.

Over and over. He had no choice but to concede he had dramatically changed his testimony about each of these important observations. He gave no good explanation for the changes, and stood by his newer accounts.

After finishing that unexpected first phase of the cross-examination, I then shifted to a topic I had originally planned to explore with Rosales: the building's unusual window problems.

He had made damning revelations about the building's negligence during our in-person meeting. He had given me detailed observations about how the University Club Tower had failed to make its windows reasonably safe, about how easily other tenants had broken through the glass, about the safety precautions that should have been in place that would have prevented Josh's death, and about his warnings to building management.

It was, of course, vital to Amber's defense. This evidence went directly to the heart of the "depraved mind" element of second-degree murder: whether Amber had understood the unusual condition of the large glass pane hiding behind her closed living-room window blinds.

It was finally time to start educating the jury about an integral part of our defense.

The judge had other ideas.

"Isn't it true," I asked, "that you told Mr. Felton that you could simply reach out your hand and go through a window like the one that was broken?"

Keely: "Judge, I'm going to object to this."

Judge Glassco: "Sustained. Can't answer that."

"Is it true that recently an elderly man simply tripped and fell and his arm went through-"

"Objection, Your Honor. Objection, relevance."

"Objection is sustained."

Not relevant? I almost had to laugh. Within seconds, the judge had put up a "road closed" sign on this entire line of cross-examination.

In our opinion, the state had been given carte blanche to introduce anything and everything, even misleading the jury about an expired protective order that had been folded up with other junk. But we couldn't so much as ask the building's own window repairman about the very window Josh had gone through.

If I had any doubt we weren't trying the case on a level playing field, it was now gone.

For second-degree murder, the state had to show that Amber acted with willful, deliberate, and contemptuous disregard for human life when she pushed him near the window. The window's breakability was absolutely relevant. Rosales's testimony on the window problems was vital.

But we couldn't go there.

I rerouted the cross again, then wrapped it up with some safer points I knew the judge wouldn't stifle. As I walked back to my seat, April gave me a look that vividly expressed her shared exasperation without saying a word. I saw Rhonda in the front row, leaning forward. She looked angry. "Good job!" she whispered, giving me an emphatic head nod. I clearly wasn't the only one who had been troubled.

Cross-examining someone you believe is flagrantly lying is not easy. On the next break, an attorney watching the trial went out of his way to come over and compliment the cross. But the only opinions that mattered belonged to 12 strangers. I hoped like hell they were paying attention.

As I sat there and exhaled, the feeling was unmistakable. It was really us against the world.

We had come into the trial maligned, tried and convicted by the media and the public. Now the state was parading witnesses who we believed were either blatantly changing their own testimony or offering accounts that were not physically possible. And I felt the judge's rulings had been dramatically one-sided.

I had looked forward to trial, thinking it would be the day Amber Hilberling would finally be treated fairly. I was now starting to realize how naïve I had been.

55

Why did Armando Rosales do it?

I'll never know for sure, but there was one very logical explanation.

He was the owner of Budget Glass, which was one of the three initial defendants I had named to the civil lawsuit for Josh's wrongful death. His company had installed the glass that was only nine one-hundredths of an inch thick in a high-rise living room. And, according to our expert, Budget Glass's window maintenance had also been subpar.

Rosales's business faced the risk of being held partly liable in the pending civil lawsuit. A verdict there could have been financially devastating to his small business.

But there was one specific event that could best shield Rosales's business from financial liability in the civil case: a guilty verdict in Amber's criminal trial.

56

Next up were the first responders – the paramedics, firefighters, and police officers who had responded to the scene.

After the previous round of troubling testimony, the first responders were a breath of fresh air. They testified with the integrity we had expected. They were neutral, honest professionals, men and women who had just been out doing their job on June 7. They didn't have a financial incentive to change their testimony. And they weren't taking the stand to give surprise testimony.

This time, the attempt to surprise came from the prosecutor herself.

"State may call its next witness," Judge Glassco directed.

"Yes, sir," Keely responded. "Mr. Daniels."

April and I looked at each other in surprise. *Mr. Daniels?* We knew the state's witness list inside and out. There had been no one named Daniels on it.

The rules of trial require each side to exchange witness lists in advance, along with a summary of the expected testimony of each.

We quickly rose to our feet.

"Judge, may we approach?" April asked.

"Judge," April continued at the bench, "I do not know that I know of or have any information about who this witness is. If Ms. Keely can point me in discovery where this would be, I'll stand corrected, but…"

Keely retrieved her file, then pointed to some fine print at the very bottom of a single page deep inside the thick police file, listing three names of firefighters who had been on one of engines at the scene that day. "It's hard to read," Keely said.

It wasn't the witness list. She had never identified Daniels as a potential witness.

The judge asked what Daniels was going to testify to.

"Obviously he made observations," Keely responded, not revealing what she had in store.

Allowing a surprise witness to take the stand would be grounds for a reversal on appeal. The judge wouldn't allow it. He ruled that Daniels couldn't testify. I couldn't help but wonder what trick the prosecution had been about to pull.

Over a two-day period, the procession of first responders — those who were actually listed on the state's witness list — walked the jury through a detailed account of the scene at University Club Tower. Throughout their testimony, Keely skillfully found ways to drop in reminders of the unexplained "protective order" document that had been pulled from inside the apartment.

A paramedic testified about pronouncing Josh dead. Two police officers testified about guarding the apartment door, another about going to get the search warrant.

A firefighter gave a vivid account of Amber's behavior at the scene, testifying that Amber was so distraught on the parking garage that he was "actually afraid that she was going to jump off" of it. Amber, he said, kept asking him to fix her husband.

He told her "he had injuries that we couldn't fix."

He testified that Amber said "she didn't mean for this to happen." She said "she pushed him and he hit the desk and went out the window, and that it was an accident."

"'I can't believe this happened,'" he recounted her saying, "'I tried to grab him but he was too heavy.'"

A paramedic testified that Amber "was pretty upset, pretty distraught."

"I asked her what had happened," he said. "She said – all she would repeat over and over is, 'I didn't mean to push him.'"

April and I took turns on their cross-examinations, emphasizing that each of them made the same observations of Amber: she was distraught, sobbing, and shocked that Josh had somehow managed to go through that elevated living room window frame.

Officer Holloway, as he had done at the preliminary hearing, testified about being assigned to Amber and taking her and Gloria downtown. As Amber sat in the first-floor conference room crying and talking to her relatives, Holloway testified, he caught bits and pieces of what she said.

He heard her explain to her uncle that Josh "stepped back into it and he fell through the window." He heard her describe trying to catch him as he fell, how she "grabbed his foot, but then watched him fall to the ground."

He testified that he drove them downtown to the detective division and placed them in the small interview room, where Amber started to again talk about what had happened.

According to Holloway's description, Amber specifically described the fateful living-room confrontation between the two, their back-and-forth arguing, in the moments before he fell. He testified he heard Amber describe going into the "living room," where "the argument continued. And that she had pushed Josh and he fell into the wall, which she described as being a wall of windows. And that there was also a TV on one other — on the other wall. And that he fell into the wall, then fell into some candlestick things, and fell out the window."

Detective Justin Ritter testified about responding to the call and learning from fire personnel that there may have been a "domestic dispute" in the apartment before the fall.

On cross-examination, April skillfully forced Ritter to admit the police had observed tissue and blood on the window, yet failed to collect any of it as evidence. He also admitted to her that the police failed to collect a single piece of the broken glass, evidence we clearly believed to be relevant.

April also used Ritter to establish that Keely's "feet first, standing upright" theory was not physically possible. She took masking tape and marked the dimensions of the window on a wall in front of the jury: the opening was 51 inches in height. She demonstrated that Josh, at 76 inches tall and also wearing tennis shoes, could simply have not gone through the much-smaller opening while "standing upright."

The only way he could have fit through the opening is at an angle, falling in one direction, his body tilted or bent, which was a movement entirely consistent with what Amber had always described – Josh stumbling into things behind him, then falling over in the direction of the window blinds, his upper body going through the blinds first.

April then marked the distance between the floor and the bottom of the elevated window: 26 inches. The dimensions told this story as well. In order for Josh to have gone out "feet first" he'd have to have been first elevated more than two feet into the air, then launched out feet first while leaning backwards.

We showed the jury a large cardboard cutout reflecting the same window dimensions. The prosecutor's "standing upright, feet first, caught off guard, shoved straight out the window" scenario was not physically possible.

It was a visual we were confident would resonate with the jury.

But it was no match for the visuals the jurors would see next.

57

Judge Glassco warned the courtroom.

"The jury's going to be shown some exhibits that may be unsettling for some folks," he said. "I cannot have any outbursts in the courtroom. And if you believe that the exhibit might cause you to behave inappropriately or express emotions, I would invite you to leave the courtroom at this time."

The prosecutor stood smiling and ready. She had appeared eager to unveil her stack of gruesome photographs of Josh's body.

April approached the bench and once again strenuously objected to the parade of photographs, as she had in our pretrial motion and again in an earlier conference at the judge's bench. The graphic photos "serve absolutely no purpose," she insisted. They were "prejudicial, not probative... and cumulative." Nor were they relevant, April argued, as there was no dispute about how Josh died. The photographs could not help prove any element of any crime.

She singled out one of the blown-up photographs, a close-up of Josh's face, as exceptionally offensive. Keely argued that she needed to include that particular photo to show the jury that Josh's pupils were "fixated and dilated," a fact we believed neither relevant nor in dispute. Keely added that "it's not really a gruesome photo. We've had more gruesome photos."

The judge ruled in the prosecutor's favor, allowing the photos. He initially made one exception, disallowing the close-up of Josh's face. What Keely did next is an image I will remember as long as I live.

She pranced.

There is no other word to describe it. With a smile on her face, she turned away from the bench and pranced across the courtroom, almost hopping, seeming to bask in the ruling. For a smart, successful prosecutor, I was aghast at her apparent lack of awareness of her body language. April later shared the same observation. Josh's family was feet away. Everyone – the spectators, the jurors, the families – had to have been uneasy about the upcoming photographs. It was a time for somberness, not smiles.

Still smiling, Keely launched her slideshow. One by one, she projected 19 large, zoomed-in photographs of the broken body of a 23-year-old whose family sat feet away. Photographs showing Josh's skin burst open, tissue and bone exposed, from the impact with the ground. Blood. Limbs lifelessly bent in unnatural directions.

It was clear the photographs weren't simply evidence; they were part of the spectacle. Instead of discreetly handing the photographs to the witness and jury, out of respect for Josh and his family, the prosecutor opted to project large blow-ups of the gruesome images onto the courtroom wall so everyone else could see, the public following intently.

Keely went over the photographs with Tulsa Police Detective Darren Froemming, who had taken them at the scene, and then again with the Tulsa County Medical Examiner, Joshua Lanter, M.D.

Before long, Keely asked once again if she could use the close-up photo of Josh's lifeless face, the one even Judge Glassco had found too disturbing to be admitted into evidence. The first time around, Keely had claimed she needed to use the photo to show Josh's pupils. That hadn't worked. This time she claimed she needed the face close-up to prove Josh had landed on his feet. That detail, however, was not in dispute.

"This is absolutely unnecessary," April argued again. "They have about 20 photographs of his body, some of which already include a picture of his head with blood on it. A close-up shot to get this is not necessary. They've got the M.E.'s Report, they got into his description, and they have the full body pictures. It's just completely prejudicial and not probative of anything. It's not even the cause of death, your honor."

In a pattern that was now becoming predictable, the judge changed his ruling on the prosecutor's second request.

Keely introduced the close-up photograph of Josh's face.

The media later reported how disturbing and painful the scene was for the courtroom gallery.

What stunned me more than the photographs was the prosecutor's carefree tone. As I watched her in action, my heart was with Josh's family and friends in the first two rows. I thought about what my own family had gone through after losing my 22-year-old brother years before, and what I'd have done if Keely had treated him, all of us, this way.

And despite what the prosecutor had claimed was the reason for the photographs, April was proven correct. They were not used to demonstrate how Josh had gone through the window, fallen, or hit the ground. Cause of death was never at issue. The medical examiner's testimony was identical to what he had put in his report: Josh died as a result of "severe blunt-force trauma" suffered in his impact with the concrete below. The close-up of Josh's face added nothing to that determination. It was a way to inflame the passions of the jury.

In case the photographs weren't enough, Detective Christine Gardner also took the stand and played the jury a long video showing the same scene on the parking garage, with the same images. Josh's body again, bone fragments next to him again, his blood and tissue again.

The video also showed Amber's sunglasses on the ground near Josh's body.

Next to a puddle of her own vomit.

58

Just before trial started, the state had filed a petition for writ of habeas corpus, asking the court to order an Oklahoma prison inmate named Bonnie Lambdin to testify.

April and I had never heard of her.

The state identified her as a "material witness" who was so important to the prosecution that "the state cannot proceed with the presentation of evidence in the Jury Trial without the presence of Bonnie Lambdin."

So important to the prosecution. They can't even try the case without her.

We had no idea why.

We asked Amber. She recognized the name. She said Bonnie had briefly been in the Tulsa County jail at the same time as her. But she couldn't hazard a guess as to what Bonnie could bring to the trial.

But April could. She had been around the criminal block enough to know what the prosecutor was going to try.

"She's going to try to say you confessed to something," April said. Amber assured us she had done nothing of the sort. *Besides,*

Amber said, *what could I even confess? A million people already heard me say I pushed him.*

It'll be something worse than that, April promised.

She was right.

Late on the fourth day of trial, Bonnie Lambdin took the stand.

She was an oft-convicted felon in her mid 40's who went by several aliases. She wore an orange jail suit and spoke with the husky voice of a longtime smoker. She looked older than her age, weathered by the lifestyle her long rap sheet described.

She raised her right hand, swore to tell the truth, the whole truth, and nothing but the truth. I took a deep breath and braced myself for whatever surprise was coming.

I didn't have to wait long. Bonnie testified she had met Amber in jail back in January, 2012, just after Amber's bond was revoked for the positive drug test. They had lived in the same pod and occasionally talked, Bonnie said.

Then, about 90 seconds into her testimony, on Keely's cue, Bonnie delivered the rehearsed line that had earned her the ticket to the trial:

"She told me that she and her husband, Josh, had gotten into an argument and that **she had caught him off guard** — he was going to leave her, and that **she caught him off guard**, and she shoved him, and her words were she 'killed the bastard.'"

There was a visceral reaction in the courtroom. I heard at least one gasp from the gallery behind me. I saw jurors' heads jolt back, their eyebrows raised, clearly alarmed. A few immediately turned and glared at Amber, who looked at the witness incredulously.

It was the bombshell moment of the trial.

The accusation was damning. Finally, the prosecution had a witness to corroborate the "face first, feet first, standing upright" scenario, giving life to the idea that Amber had caught Josh off guard rather than pushed him back during a living-room fight.

The state's language in its writ now made perfect sense: *a witness so important to the prosecution they can't try the case without her.*

Sitting to my right, Amber wrote two words on the legal pad in front of her, then moved it in my direction.

"She's lying."

Bonnie had little else to say. She had been brought to the courtroom for the one purpose only. Just seconds after Bonnie delivered her well-rehearsed line, Keely finished with her star witness and sat down.

April practically jumped out of her seat for the cross, showing a palpable anger for the first time in the trial. She hammered the point that Bonnie was a convicted felon many times over, a jail-house snitch who didn't merit the jury's trust.

But the damage had been done.

On a brief redirect, Keely had Bonnie repeat her claim about Amber's alleged confession. Then, before sitting back down, Keely decided to elicit one last shot. There was something else the prosecutor wanted the jury to hear.

On cue, Bonnie turned to the jurors and delivered the news that Amber Hilberling had "breast implants."

The prosecutor smiled and nodded.

———

Neither April nor I believed Bonnie for a second. But we didn't get votes.

We knew the signs of sculpted testimony. We recognized that the way Bonnie had forced the key phrase "off guard" into her explosive statement – not just once, but twice – was a telltale sign she had been instructed to emphasize the two words.

But for Amber, it was another phrase that had stood out even more.

"Bastard?" Amber asked aloud, almost to herself, during the next restroom break. "Who even says that word? What am I, 40?

That's a word old people use. I don't think I've ever used that word in my life."

Her reaction struck me as authentic. I believed her. We'd find out later what the jury believed.

The state used Bonnie's testimony as the crux of its case. She was the only witness the prosecution called to the stand twice, testifying again later in the state's brief rebuttal phase. The prosecutor later began her first closing argument with Bonnie's testimony, then built her entire second closing around the version of events Bonnie, and only Bonnie, had given. Keely also told the jury that should they convict, it was Bonnie's testimony that mandated a stiff sentence.

Her testimony had cast a shadow that hovered over the rest of the trial.

But the trial wouldn't be the last time I would hear from Bonnie Lambdin. More than three years after she testified, she called me and delivered another bombshell.

59

With the aftershocks of Bonnie Lambdin's testimony still reverberating, the prosecution swiftly moved to seize the momentum.

It's a time-tested trial strategy, saving your most helpful evidence for last. The state would finish its case by playing its two biggest cards: Bonnie testifying that Amber had confessed to catching Josh off guard, then the partial video of Amber and her grandmother.

Lead Detective Jeff Felton took the stand after Bonnie. He quickly summarized his work on the case, listing the interviews he had conducted, what he had observed in the apartment, and made a point to insist there had been no evidence of self-defense in the living room, an opinion that matched what Bonnie had just claimed about Amber's alleged confession.

Then it was time for the video.

At about 3:20 in the afternoon, with the courtroom lights dimmed, Keely turned on a television and started to play the recording of the conversation between Amber and Gloria in the police station's interview room. The video began in mid-conversation, all previous dialogue between the two omitted.

For 62 minutes, the courtroom watched in a stunned, near frozen silence as Amber wailed on the screen, whispering, crying, talking with her grandmother, trying to make sense of it all. It was a raw, emotional gut punch for the audience, watching the teenage girl on the screen, seven months pregnant and bloodied, weaving in and out of shock, trauma, disbelief, grief, and self-blame.

Amber tried to watch herself, sometimes covering her face in her hands, wiping a steady stream of tears from her face. We had elected to not show her the video until trial, wanting the jury to see and understand her authentic first reaction. Amber's family watched behind us, Josh's family across the aisle, the public and media behind the families watching it for the first time.

For 62 minutes, it felt like time had stopped.

When it was over, Keely walked slowly to the wall and turned the courtroom lights back on. The room was still silent, the air sucked out of it. No one said anything for a few moments. Everyone needed time to recover. The jurors' faces were ashen, several eyes red. Some had clearly been crying.

Keely turned to the detective and resumed her direct examination. She went straight to one of her main points.

"Was it your understanding that the victim came or fell out of the window feet first out of the window?"

"Feet first out? No, ma'am."

We were taken aback. Even the prosecution's own lead detective now rejected Keely's theory that Josh had somehow gone "feet first" out of an elevated window. I respected Felton's honesty.

"Yes, OK," Keely said, clearly surprised herself. "What was your understanding?"

"Face first," Felton said.

"I'll pass the witness," she said quickly.

On cross, April immediately launched an attack on the detective's claim that there had been no evidence of self-defense. She handed him a police photograph, taken downtown on June 7, showing the fresh scratches across Amber's back. She asked Felton if he was aware of the neighbor having heard a loud living-room argument in the moments just before the window crash.

He said he was.

And if he had heard Armando Rosales testify about hearing a physical "scuffle" in the living room moment before the glass broke.

He said he had.

"And is it your testimony today that none of this evidence points to the fact that there was some sort of physical altercation?" April asked.

"Not taken individually, no ma'am."

"If you put it all together, it's pretty good evidence that there was a physical altercation, isn't that correct?"

"No, ma'am. I disagree with that."

There had been testimony from witnesses who had heard sounds of a loud argument, yelling, and a physical scuffle. There was photographic evidence of scratch marks on Amber's upper back.

Yet there was no evidence of a living room altercation?

I watched the jury as April made these crucial points. They were vital to our defense. Yet some jurors were looking down into their laps, while others appeared to be staring ahead in a daze. To me, their body language said everything.

Their minds were still in that video.

60

The prosecution wasn't going to be able to top its one-two punch of Bonnie's bombshell and the dramatic video. As Detective Felton left the stand and retook his seat, the state rested its case.

Before we began presenting our defense case, we made the customary oral motion for the court to acquit Amber on the spot on the basis of the state not meeting its burden of proof. It's a motion that rarely wins, and which had no chance with the bright public spotlight on our trial.

We argued the motion outside the presence of the jury, as is standard. The jurors wouldn't observe or be told of the motion or its arguments.

April argued that the prosecution had not presented sufficient evidence of a depraved mind to continue with the second-degree murder charge. The state had not demonstrated extreme disregard for human life, she said, as every witness on the scene confirmed that Amber had been shocked, surprised, and distraught, that all testimony (other than Bonnie's) pointed to an accident. Nor had the state made a first-degree manslaughter case, having failed to prove cruel and unusual behavior.

In her argument, Keely finally acknowledged what we had said all along, and what we felt the evidence clearly demonstrated: Amber and Josh were having a heated confrontation in the living room when he died.

"They had an argument and she pushed him, judge," Keely said.

But the jurors would never hear the prosecutor acknowledge this. When she later talked directly to them, she would say something completely different.

61

April called me about 10:30 that night.

I was at a hotel bar sitting with Mark Meshulam, our window expert, who had flown in from Chicago to testify. We were reviewing his testimony for the next morning, when we would open our defense case. April's name appeared on my phone screen, and I stepped away from the table to take the call.

"Listen, I've been thinking," she said, "and I think we shouldn't open the door tomorrow."

I knew what she meant. She wanted us to change our strategy and limit Amber's testimony to the events of June 7, not going into the history of Josh's physical abuse as we had planned. The change would remove most of what we had planned for Amber's testimony.

"I don't think they've made their case," she said, referring to the prosecution's high burden of proof to convict. "I think we've got them beat."

We both knew the risk of opening the door to the past incidents. Keely herself had said that if we opened the door a sliver, she was going to "bust it down." She may have been bluffing, but her pretrial witness list had included names of rebuttal witnesses she claimed were prepared to testify about instances of Amber's misconduct in the past — if we opened the door.

April and I were both uneasy about the risk, particularly given the prosecution's tactics so far. We had no reason to expect fair play. At jury selection we saw how effective the pre-trial P.R. campaign had been, how badly the jury pool was contaminated. We had witnessed the judge's laissez-faire deference to whatever tactics the prosecution chose, compared with the strict constraints placed on us. There was no telling what the prosecution was going to get away with in a rebuttal phase focused expressly on attacking Amber with new evidence. The rebuttal witnesses, we were concerned, could potentially be vicious – if, and only if, we opened the door and invited them into the trial.

Amber faced a maximum sentence of life in prison. If we opened the door and it backfired, Amber could conceivably get life.

I still wanted to roll the dice. If the jury believed the two had been physical with each other, back and forth, I liked our odds. There is never an excuse to put your hand on a woman in anger. I was confident the jury, filled with parents of daughters, would agree with me on that point. And if they did, I thought, they would want to acquit.

I also wanted to let Amber finally tell her story. The one she had been patiently, quietly waiting to tell for 21 months. To tell the jury, the world, about everything she had been through with Josh. How he had treated her. The abuse. Everything that happened in Alaska, and before. The horror stories.

I wanted them to understand why she finally pushed back.

But April was a better criminal defense mind than I was, by a longshot. I had deferred to her on strategy decisions for a reason. And she had been performing well throughout trial, I felt, doing the best work of the three attorneys trying the case.

I told her I was on board. We'd deliver the news to Amber in the morning.

We were changing her entire game plan.

62

Amber took the news well. She was surprised, but understood.

I respected her poise. She had been waiting for 21 months to finally tell her side of story, and now she wasn't going to get to. She'd have to limit her self-defense testimony to what happened on the afternoon of June 7, 2011. If she brought up any of Josh's history of domestic abuse, she'd open the door to whatever rebuttal evidence the prosecutor had up her sleeve.

She had every right to complain, but she didn't. She shared our belief that the prosecution hadn't made its "depraved mind" murder case. She agreed we could win on the facts of June 7 alone.

To give her time to readjust, and to finish our case on a strong note, we decided to call her as our last witness. We'd instead start with the window evidence.

Several jurors had brought up the window issue in jury selection, clearly interested in the topic. We were confident the evidence would have an impact, particularly with the jurors with construction and mechanical science backgrounds. If they had a good understanding that the window shouldn't have given way like it did, we felt they'd be unable to find that Amber's push showed the "contemptuous disregard for human life" required for a "depraved mind" murder conviction.

To that end, our glass expert, Mark Meshulam, took the stand. He introduced himself as a "building envelope consultant," an expert with 32 years of being immersed in "the walls, the glass, the window, even the roof" of high-rise buildings. He told the jury about his vast experience, his time studying window glass in laboratories, and his role in the construction of more than 1,000 buildings and the installation of millions of square feet of window glass.

He told the jury he'd spent about 60 hours studying the case, visited the site, examined the glass, analyzed it with various devices, studied the governing safety codes, and conducted tests.

I guided Meshulam through a detailed PowerPoint presentation he had prepared, through which he explained the University Club Tower's myriad window glass problems. Meshulam appeared at ease on the witness stand, looking the jurors in the eyes and speaking in layman's terms. They appeared responsive, leaning forward, nodding their heads, and taking notes as he spoke.

He gave a brief explanation of the "curtainwall" window system the building uses, the aging condition of the windows, and what he said was subpar maintenance. He showed the jury his photographs from inside the apartment and outside.

Then we opened up a sealed envelope and pulled out pieces of the actual window glass. He showed the jury the electronic instrument he used to measure the glass thickness, then a photograph capturing what the tool had revealed: .092.

For context, he also created an image showing the window glass thickness in relation to an ordinary ruler:

"So you have ninety-two thousands of an inch," he said. "But that also equals fractions that we commonly use in construction. And in this case, this is three thirty-seconds of an inch. Now, three thirty-seconds of an inch is very small. It is – in the industry, this thickness of glass has a name. It's called single-strength glass."

In his experience, he testified, glass this thin is "used for small windows or picture frames," not large high-rise living-room windows.

"In your entire career, how many times have you used glass this thin for a high-rise building?" I asked.

"Zero."

"Why not?"

"It's not safe."

Meshulam also showed the jury, with photographs and measurements, the exact dimensions of the window. Its height, width, and location on the wall. He pointed out that there was "no real windowsill" on the window; the glass sat only one and five-eighths of an inch back from the slim metal strip serving as a windowsill. That meant the glass was "very, very close" while completely hidden behind the window's long vertical blinds. He showed photographic evidence from the scene showing that the blinds had been fully closed when Josh hit the elevated window.

His message was clear: the window was unusually dangerous, plagued by extreme characteristics and conditions. A standard high-rise window, with safety glass, would not have given way near as easily, he said. It was the same opinion the building's own window repairman, Armando Rosales, had confided to me in person.

He looked directly at the jurors as he delivered his expert opinion: "The window where the accident took place is not safe, and it's too weak for its application."

"Mr. Meshulam, when you went into apartment 2509, when you walked into the living room, did you have any reason to believe that any of these unusual window conditions existed?"

"No."

"Would you expect a teenage girl to know what you know about glass?"

"No."

Keely's cross was brief, focused more on trying to impeach Meshulam's work experience than his expert opinion. She would try to rebut Meshulam's scientific findings with an expert witness of her own, later calling an engineering consultant named William Lingnell to the stand.

Where Meshulam's style was amiable and conversational, Lingnell's was professorial and stern. Lingnell took the stand and gave long, technical explanations as to why the window was technically in compliance with certain codes. I saw jurors with eyes closed, not taking notes or appearing to listen, as he spoke. They either already had made up their minds about the window issue, I thought, or about the entire case.

Lingnell's main point was that the window was not legally required to have "safety glass" because of its exact location. The glass was thick enough, he argued.

I began my cross with an old trick.

Isn't it true, I asked him, that "building owners want thicker glass to make that glass more resistant to lateral forces?"

"Not necessarily," he argued, giving another long, scientific explanation as to why my statement wasn't accurate. He even alleged what I had asserted "could be a false statement if it's analyzed."

It was just what I had hoped he would do.

I pulled out the actual trade journal article I had taken those words from, verbatim, and handed it to him. I asked him to read the author's name to the jury.

It was none other than William Lingnell.

"Would you consider Mr. Lingnell, or yourself, to be a reliable authority?"

He squirmed.

"Yes," he said.

He walked into the same trap a second time. He had argued that because the window technically met one safety code – due to its location in the room – it was therefore safe. I pulled up another line he had written: "Code requirements are a starting point, but glass must often be designed to resist loads greater than the minimum requirements."

I kept pressing. He admitted that under most of the factors the industry uses, the window should have had safety glass. The window was, he finally conceded, "close to being dangerous."

I moved to enter the published articles into evidence. The state's own expert had now taken the stand and given the jury testimony that was, in fact, clearly contradicted by his own previous published words. I wanted the jury to be informed.

The prosecutor objected, asserting that the expert's previous inconsistent statements about window safety were not relevant.

The court ruled in her favor again.

63

Gloria hurt for her granddaughter. Nearly every time we spoke in person, her eyes were filled with tears. Her heartache was tangible.

Her pain still appeared fresh as she walked to the witness stand. She looked sick, sad, and afraid. When she raised her right hand to take the oath, it was shaking.

April made an effort to be tender. She asked Gloria to share her memories of the afternoon of June 7, 2011. Gloria tried. She testified that Amber had called her, hysterical, crying on the phone that "Josh is dead!" By the time Gloria arrived at the apartment building, it was already a madhouse of fire trucks, ambulances, media vans, and curious onlookers.

When she finally found her granddaughter, Gloria testified, she was "in shock. I mean, she was terrible."

She recalled that Amber kept repeating two words, over and over:

"His face! His face!"

Gloria asked her what had happened.

"He pushed me," Amber told her while the two were in the University Club Tower's downstairs conference room, Officer Holloway standing nearby and eavesdropping. "I pushed him back... I tried to catch him."

Holloway then took her and Amber downtown and placed them in the interview room, where they started talking again about what had happened. According to Holloway's notes, this was when Amber gave details about the final living-room fight — the dialogue omitted from the recording the state later produced.

April tried to reinforce this point with the jury.

"Now, have you watched that videotape of you and your granddaughter before today?"

"Yes."

"And to the best of your recollection, after you watched that video, do you think it contains your entire conversation with her?"

"No."

"OK. Where do you think there was additional conversation?"

"Right there in the beginning we were talking."

On cross, Keely immediately set out to paint Amber's grand-mother as a liar.

She questioned Gloria's claim that Amber had ever mentioned a living-room fight. If Amber had talked about a fight, Keely argued, Gloria would have immediately rushed to the police and reported it.

"You never turned around and told Officer Holloway, 'my granddaughter's a victim,' did you?" Keely asked.

"I never talked to him, no," Gloria admitted. She had in fact, as the video showed, repeatedly emphasized the importance of not making any statements to the police until an attorney arrived.

Keely then suggested that in their jailhouse conversation, Gloria was advising Amber to make up a fake self-defense story. Keely played an excerpt from the video in which Gloria referenced that Amber and Josh had been "struggling."

"You suggested to her that they were struggling, didn't you?"

"No, ma'am," Gloria answered.

Keely kept attacking, even insinuating that Gloria had personally concocted Amber's entire self-defense account. Her aggressiveness rattled the soft-spoken grandmother, who was not a sophisticated or educated witness, and who showed no interest in engaging the experienced prosecutor in courtroom combat.

"Would you agree that Amber really needs help today, doesn't she?"

"Yes."

"You could understand why these jurors might think that you were making that suggestion to Amber, couldn't you?"

"Yes."

When Gloria finally stepped down from the stand, her face was flushed red, with tears streaming down both cheeks. She looked down at Amber as she walked by our table, her lips trembling.

Amber looked up at her grandmother and tried not to cry herself. She didn't have time for that.

It was time for her to testify.

64

After 648 days of silence, the world would finally hear from Amber Hilberling. I got straight to the point on the very first question:

"On the afternoon of June 7, 2011, did you push your husband?"

"Yes."

"Why?"

"Because he was grabbing me."

"Did it hurt when he grabbed you?"

"Yes, it did."

"When you pushed him off you, Amber, were you trying to kill him?"

"No."

"Were you hoping that he would somehow die?"

"No."

"Were you trying to hurt him in any way, Amber?"

"No, I was not."

"What were you trying to do?"

"I just wanted him to stop. I just wanted him to stop."

I stopped to let her take a breath. She had said a lot already. I had chucked the traditional script, which would have had begun with Amber's background, her life story, her family, meeting Josh, all eventually leading up to that split-second moment on June 7, 2011.

But I wasn't interested in suspense. I didn't want the jury ignoring the background story while waiting for the moment of truth.

Hell yes, she pushed him.

He was grabbing and pushing her. It hurt. She pushed him back. She pushed him off her, and she wasn't taking the stand to deny or spin or make excuses. I wanted everyone in the jury box to understand that point right off the bat.

Hell yes, she pushed him.

That question answered immediately, I asked Amber to go ahead and tell the jury a little bit about herself.

But the prosecutor immediately objected.

"My name is Amber, I'm 21 years old, I have a son named Levi who is 18 months old and I love him so much. I grew up here in Tulsa--"

"Judge I'm going to object! Relevance!"

"Overruled."

"I grew up here in Tulsa. In high school, I wanted to—"

"Objection! This calls for a narrative."

Sustained.

Like clockwork, I had learned that if the prosecutor wanted her objection sustained she simply needed to voice it a second time.

Amber was on trial for murder. She faced a life sentence. She had been vilified in the local and national media for 21 straight months while she had sat silently, dutifully waiting until she was on the witness stand to finally say word one about who she really was. Yet just three sentences into introducing herself, the state of Oklahoma had decided she had already said enough.

Three sentences.

And just like that, Amber appeared off. Uncomfortable. Nervous. Maybe that was the prosecutor's intention. If so, to her credit, it worked.

"Cold Amber," the one I had occasionally seen in our prep sessions, reappeared. Amber looked scared, not confident. I tried to put her at ease, shifting into safe territory, guiding her conversationally through the basic facts and timeline of her relationship with Josh. How they met, when they started dating, getting married, the move to Alaska.

Alaska.

She tightened up more.

I could see the wheels spinning in her head. Their time in Alaska was a horror show, one trauma after another. But we had now instructed her to not open the door to their past fights, not to bring up Josh's physical abuse. And the subject of most of their arguments in Alaska, Josh's drug problems, was also off limits. The very reason Josh got kicked out of the Air Force, the reason they had to run back to Oklahoma, was something she was under orders to keep secret from the jury.

She was wrestling with what she was allowed to say, reminding herself to not bring up the wrong thing. She looked at me helplessly.

What can I even say about Alaska? About our marriage?

It was clear the overnight strategy change had thrown her. I was already second guessing the decision myself. Amber had been more than ready to tell her story, to tell the world what she had really gone through with Josh Hilberling. All the abuse, all the violence, all the police investigations, all the bruises and marks and grabbing and pushing and hitting and throwing things. Her pain. Her trauma. Her fear. Everything that had led up to her pushing back at 4 p.m. on June 7, 2011.

Instead, she took a breath and whittled that crucial, dramatic stretch of their marriage down to a few innocuous words: *we moved to Alaska on October 17, 2010, then moved back to Tulsa the next May.* Period, the end.

Her delivery became awkward, almost robotic, as she pushed herself to be careful with each word. I wasn't seeing the personable, smart, vulnerable girl I had talked to for 21 months. We weren't connecting. I was seeing a deer in the headlights, a terrified inmate, pale skin, eyes wide, almost frozen with fear.

Her words themselves were strong. She gave good, solid answers that hold up well on the written transcript.

But it was her nervous delivery, her stiff body language, that was off.

I should have found a way to pull her out of it, but I didn't. There's an old adage that the direct examination belongs to the witness, while the cross-examination belongs to the lawyer, but that saying didn't give me any comfort as I stood there in the courtroom and watched Amber clam up in the most important moment of her life. I felt like I was failing her. I felt stuck, unable to show the jury the Amber I knew, searching for rapport with a pallid imitator.

We eventually circled back to June 7, 2011, as planned.

"Tell the jury how that day began."

She started to come back to life.

"We woke up and showered and ate breakfast," she began. "And we had a talk, and I decided that I wanted a divorce, and told Josh to call his family, that I was gonna give the key back to my mom. She owns the apartment. I was gonna give her back the keys and go to my grandma's.

"So Josh's bags were already packed. And we were talking in the bedroom and I was separating our dirty laundry and an argument started, the [bedroom] window got broke, and then I went out onto the balcony to start sweeping up the glass.

"And Josh was saying some stuff and I went into the bathroom. I stayed there for probably 10 minutes crying and throwing up. And Josh came in there, and we continued talking. And that's when I came out and called the maintenance man to tell him that the window was broken."

She recounted the details of Armando Rosales coming up to the apartment, Josh asking if they could repair it themselves to keep Amber's parents from finding out. The same basic facts Rosales had given earlier.

Then, for the first time, Amber began to tell the public the details of what she remembered from the final moments of Josh's life.

"Josh was standing at the edge of the- at the farthest edge of the TV, and I was standing by this wall," she said, pinpointing, in a blown-up photograph of the living room, a spot near the TV stand. "We started arguing. I don't remember exactly what was said, but we were getting to each other and met in front of the TV. And Josh was really frustrated and grabbed my shoulders and I pushed him off of me, and I don't remember what happened after that. I remember... I remember watching him go through the glass. And I don't know how it happened."

I showed the jury a large photograph the police had taken of Amber just after Josh's death. I directed Amber's attention to the red scratch marks on her shoulder blade and asked her if that was where Josh had grabbed her.

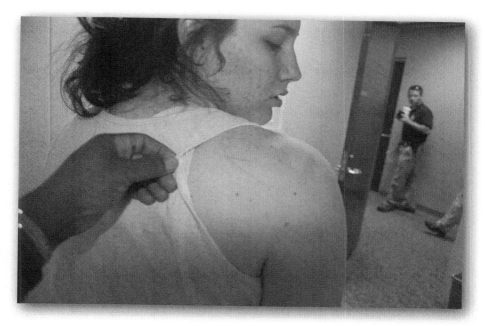

"Yeah," she said. "He had big hands."

For a moment I thought she seemed wistful, as if even the memory of Josh's big hands grabbing her had somehow made her miss her husband. She gathered herself and continued.

"His fingers are able to wrap around my actual shoulder."

"Amber, when he was grabbing you on June 7, 2011, were you pregnant?"

"Yes, I was."

"Did he know you were pregnant?"

"Yeah, it was obvious."

"How far along were you?"

"Seven months."

"Did that baby have a name?"

"He had a name from the very first time we found out we were pregnant."

Levi.

I asked her about the physical disparity between her and her husband. Josh was an athlete, a former high school and college football player, was taller than her by nearly a foot, and typically outweighed her by nearly 100 pounds.

I asked her if she felt scared when Josh grabbed her.

Yes, she said, and not just for herself.

She said she was "scared for Levi."

She was speaking softly now, clearly in pain again, struggling to find the right words.

"I want you to tell the jury what you remember about what happened after you pushed him."

"I just remember him going through the glass. We, we made eye contact the whole time. I mean, that's all I, and then I kind of looked for a second trying to understand it. And I ran to the window and I grabbed the edge and I looked over in time to see him hit the ground."

She was becoming more upset. I let her keep going.

"All, I mean all I remember is trying to get to him. I don't, I don't, I don't remember anything but that. That was all I could think about. I thought he had been knocked out. I mean I thought he was just hurt. I don't know."

She described her memories as "all squished together."

"I don't know how to explain something like that," she said.

She remembered going down the elevator after, running outside, looking up and seeing him on the parking garage, then going back inside and rushing up to him.

"I rolled him over and I tried to wake him up," she said. "That's all I remember."

Then someone pulled her away. "Next thing I know, I'm sitting on a wall with an oxygen tank around my face."

She remembered "the oxygen was burning my nostrils so I took it off."

I walked her through the earlier testimony of the first responders, to remind the jury of their consistent testimony that Amber was "surprised and shocked" at the scene, had been "crying and sobbing and wailing" and "distraught and hysterical."

Amber said she "absolutely" believed they had testified accurately. We thought that if the jury believed them too, on this point, they'd almost have to acquit Amber of the "depraved mind" murder. That evidence wasn't consistent with willful and deliberate behavior.

"Amber, did you want this moment to happen?"

"No. No."

"Did you expect that this moment would or could happen?"

"Not in a million years."

Before turning her over for Keely's cross-examination, I reiterated what we hoped was the main point the jury would take from her testimony.

"Amber, just so we're clear, in the fight with Josh on the afternoon of June 7, 2011, who got physical first?"

"Josh did."

"And why did you push your husband?"

"To get him to just stop."

"Was there anything else on your mind when you pushed him away from you?"

"No."

We were done, but there was something I felt I needed to do before handing Amber over to the prosecutor. I knew we had succeeded in not opening the door to their past incidents, thus preventing Keely from trying to bring up any such behavior as a way to further attack Amber's character.

But given the aggressiveness I had seen from her throughout trial, I suspected she would still try. So I paused and asked the judge for a private bench conference before officially giving the prosecutor the stage.

"Judge, just to be on the same page before I pass the witness, I want to go back to our agreement, our understanding that if we do not open the door to past incidents then they're not going to be able to go into them as well. And I wanted to get confirmation from Your Honor that we have not done it."

Keely confirmed my hunch. Though Amber had carefully avoided bringing up Josh's past — never mentioning any previous abuse, arrests, protective order, police investigations, drug problems, criminal behavior, or his Air Force discharge for misconduct — Keely tried to insist she was still allowed to now charge into Amber's past on her cross-examination.

"You said as long as all we talk about is June 7 of 2011, we won't open the door," Keely argued at the judge's bench. But Amber's testimony, Keely argued, "went way beyond that. We talked about when she *lived* in Alaska. That is not - that was not in June. We talked about them *getting married.* "

April and I looked at her in disbelief. Bringing up a marriage or an address was not the same as testifying about Josh's past wrongdoings.

"No, I disagree," Judge Glassco said. "She has not. I don't believe she's opened the door."

This time, Keely didn't repeat her objection.

With the judge's assurance in hand, I turned Amber over to cross-examination.

———

From the start, I felt the prosecutor showed deep contempt for Amber. She opened her cross-examination with what I saw as a taunt, then continued the approach throughout.

"Now you talked some about your own family and that they're here, is that right?" Keely began.

"Yes."

"Josh's family is here too, aren't they?"

"Yes, they are."

"And in fact, is Josh's mom here?"

"I don't know her. His stepmom is, yes."

"And is she here?"

"Yes."

"OK. And Josh's dad, is he here?"

"Yes, he is."

"And Josh's sister. Is she here?"

"I assume. I haven't met them."

"Josh's brother Zach. Is he here?"

"Yes."

"So they're all here as well, aren't they?"

"Yes, they are."

It was all a set-up for the next question, her first punch:

"But... *Josh* isn't here, is he?" she asked, in a raised pitch feigning wonder.

"No," Amber said, stating the obvious. "He's not."

Keely's opening barb thrilled at least one person in the crowd behind her.

"Go girl!" a woman cried out from the gallery.

I turned and looked into the crowd, then back at the judge. I expected him to admonish the gallery, perhaps throw the woman out of the courtroom. But instead he opted to let the comment pass. The lynch mob had been waiting for 21 months. They were hungry.

The unsettling remark rattled Amber even more. She was visibly shaken.

"Now, I notice that when you talk about Josh in the courtroom, that your voice gets" – Keely lowered her own voice to deliver the next two words in an exaggerated, mocking whisper — "very quiet. Is that correct?"

Amber appeared taken aback. "I guess," she said, "I mean sure, yeah."

"Well, sometimes when you talk about Josh or about the instance of throwing him out the window, sometimes you aren't so sad."

Throwing him out the window.

I objected. Overruled. This was going to be the prosecutor's approach, aggressively scornful, and we were going to have to sit back and take it. We hoped it would backfire with the jury. But it clearly took its toll on Amber.

Keely brought up the "protective order" on two dozen separate occasions during her cross, knowing Amber was constrained from revealing its real facts. I sensed Amber was frustrated, wishing she could tell the jury the whole truth, her testimony limited by rulings and decisions made by other people.

The prosecutor carefully played the partial video card. She asserted that Amber's testimony on direct about "some kind of fight that happened in the living room" was "different" from what was shown in the video. Amber chose not to argue that point, though it was easily rebuttable. I took it as a sign she was already feeling overwhelmed.

Then, in an exchange so dramatic that at least one spectator could not physically tolerate it, Keely ordered Amber to "come on down" from the witness chair, stand on the courtroom floor, and physically reenact her husband's traumatic death.

Amber stepped down nervously. Keely placed her a few feet from the jury box, then directed Detective Felton to stand by Amber and pretend to be Josh. The detective obliged, standing and walking directly to Amber, then remaining inches in front of her.

Amber was visibly shaken. She looked confused and afraid.

I objected to the physical reenactment. Overruled again.

"Detective Felton," Keely continued, "now can you put your arm on her shoulder?"

Amber was stunned and scared. She looked over at our table again, imploring. There was nothing we could do. I thought she might collapse to the ground. Keely didn't skip a beat.

"Put your other arm on her shoulder," she directed Felton.

Felton towered over Amber. Both of his hands were now clenching her shoulders, inches from being around her neck. Amber was literally being manhandled, in front of an emotionally charged crowd that had been shouting out against her, now being forced to relive the death of her husband.

"Now," Keely said, turning her direction back to Amber, whose eyes were still wide in disbelief. "I want you to extend your arm—"

A loud commotion from the gallery again interrupted the show.

A spectator had literally passed out and fallen to the floor.

I wasn't that surprised; the scene was so disturbing I had started to feel the room temperature was getting warmer. Courthouse staff rushed to tend to the fallen woman, helping her up and guiding her out of the courtroom. As soon as the door closed, Keely ordered Felton to put his hands right back on Amber's body.

"Detective Felton, can you grab her with your arms?" she instructed.

The detective followed orders and physically grabbed Amber.

"All right," Keely said. She turned to Amber. "And you pushed him. Is that right?"

Amber was still too stunned to speak. She looked over at us, the man's hands nearly around her neck, then back at the prosecutor.

She couldn't form a word. She only managed a head nod.

"You have to say yes or no," Keely commanded.

"Yes," Amber said in a near whisper.

"OK. Now, when you were standing there, did you just stand there and push him?"

"I didn't- I don't know what you mean."

"Did you move toward him?"

Amber looked at her in confusion.

"I just pushed him off of me."

"You just pushed him off of you?? And how did you do that?"

Amber lifted her hands up in front of her own chest and barely motioned them forward into the direction of the chest of the detective, who still stood in front of her. "Like that," she said.

"Like that?!" Keely responded, sarcastically imitating the hand motion Amber had just made. Keely put her palms out in front of her and tilted her fingers downward, as if effeminately waving goodbye with two hands. "With your fingertips, you just pushed him back?! Is that right?"

Shellshocked, Amber once again couldn't find a single word. She managed another slight head nod. Keely didn't stop.

"After you pushed him," Keely pressed, "he went toward that wall. What happened when he went toward that wall?"

"I have— I don't— I don't know. I just—"

"Did you push him again?"

"No, I didn't."

"You didn't? Are you sure?"

"Yes."

"So he went toward the wall?"

"He— his arms extended and then I remember him going through the glass. It all, it happened so fast."

"When you say his arms extended, can you show me how his arms extended?"

"I mean out to— I mean to—"

"Show me. I'm sorry, I can't see."

"I don't know. I don't know. I don't remember details."

Amber was falling apart. Keely continued to hammer her like this, pressing repeatedly for the most minute details of the push and Josh's fall. Amber had already testified she couldn't remember the exact details. And she had never been able to explain exactly how Josh had managed to go up and out that elevated window.

Yet Keely pressed her over and over — 51 separate times — for the details of that exact split-second moment.

The repeated questions were a strategy; the prosecutor was clearly trying to trip up Amber into giving an inconsistency, at which point she could pounce and try to cast her as dishonest. With 51 different answers, surely two wouldn't be exactly alike. But Amber remained consistent. Keely kept trying.

Finally, Amber gave an answer Keely seemed to find inconsistent. She pounced.

Q: "Now, in your testimony you said that you didn't know if Josh fell through the blinds. Is that right?"

A: "I'm assuming that he did because they were closed. I don't remember the details. I mean, I don't know."

Q: "OK. Ma'am, when you were talking to your defense attorney on direct, you told your defense attorney that you didn't know if he fell through the blinds. Didn't you?"

A: "And I—"

Q: "Didn't you say that?"

A: "I stand by that statement."

Q: "OK. But now, just a minute ago when I said that, you just said 'I assumed he went through the blinds.' Didn't you?"

A: "Yes."

Q: "Would you agree *that's* a little bit of a change in testimony?"

Keely's attempt to find an inconsistent answer — somewhere, anywhere — elicited audible groans and laughter from the gallery. "Mr. Bailiff!" the judge barked. "If there is any more discussion or outbursts from anyone in the gallery, you are to remove them from the courtroom and they're not to come back!"

The "go girl!" cheering for the prosecutor was allowed. Sounds of disapproval were apparently not.

Keely repeated her point: "Would you agree that is a little bit of a difference in testimony, that you 'knew' and then you 'assume,' is that right?"

April shot me a raised eyebrow. Neither of us understood Keely's point. Amber hadn't said anything inconsistent. Still, Amber once again chose not to fight.

"Yes," Amber said. "Yes, I guess so, yeah."

Amber now appeared to be sweating, which was not an ideal visual for a testifying defendant.

When I had felt the room getting hotter during her cross-examination, I had first written the sensation off as a psychological reaction to the dramatics of the testimony. But I soon realized it wasn't just psychological. The room temperature did significantly increase during Amber's cross-examination. The judge even commented on the record about the unusual temperature spike, apologizing to the courtroom for the sudden problems with "the air conditioning."

This temperature increase, so severe it caused the witness to visibly sweat on the stand, just happened to occur only once throughout the entire trial: during the cross-examination of Amber Hilberling.

Just another coincidence.

I worried that Amber's physical discomfort would make her appear less believable to the jury. But I held out hope that it would engender their sympathy, especially in light of the prosecutor's behavior.

At times, the prosecutor's choice of words jolted me.

It wasn't enough for her to ask Amber about her husband falling. She opted for phrases such as: "when he fell and crunched his bones in his entire body."

It wasn't enough to say Amber had pushed him. She called it: "throwing him out the window."

At one point, Keely asked if Amber wanted her to play the dramatic video recording a second time.

"No, I don't," Amber answered.

"You feel bad about pushing Josh, don't you?"

"I feel bad about what happened."

"Ma'am, you feel bad that you pushed Josh, don't you?"

"Yes."

"You feel bad that because you pushed Josh, Josh is dead. Isn't he?"

"Yes," Amber answered, confirming once again that her husband was indeed dead.

At another point, Keely asked Amber if Josh was a "handsome looking guy?"

"Yes," Amber answered.

"And *that's* the guy you pushed out the window?" Keely asked.

The afternoon Josh died, Amber had been wearing a white tank top. The style of shirt is commonly referred to as a "wife beater" in pop culture parlance. Keely distorted that name: "You've seen the pictures that the state introduced of you in your red pants and your white *spouse beater*. You've seen that picture, haven't you?"

I jumped to my feet. "Objection, Your Honor!" I called out, louder than I had spoken in the entire trial. I was angry. It seemed obvious to me that Keely had made up the term "spouse beater" just to denigrate Amber. I called the remark "unnecessary, argumentative, that phrase - it's clearly intended to inflame the jury."

Keely gave the judge a look of innocence. "Judge, I think it's commonly what it's called."

"I've never heard it called that," I said.

"Well," the judge said, "I'm gonna overrule the objection."

The prosecutor looked back at Amber and grinned.

65

By the time the prosecutor finished with Amber, I suspected the verdict was in.

We were confident the jury had disliked Keely's aggressiveness on cross-examination, and hoped it had backfired. The unknown was whether the jurors liked or disliked Amber, and, more importantly, whether they believed her when she testified she had pushed back during a living-room fight.

After the cross-examination, I kept my redirect short. Amber was drained. So was the room. I went back through the accounts the neighboring witnesses had given in their testimony, having Amber again confirm that their descriptions had all matched hers: arguing, yelling, scuffling, pushing, crash, shock, confusion.

And I had her clarify one final time that she had never been able to exactly describe Josh's final movements or footwork, a point the prosecutor had attacked relentlessly.

"Last question, Amber. Did you mean for Josh Hilberling to fall through those blinds and that glass and out the window when you pushed him?"

"No, I did not."

We rested our case.

The prosecution then called Bonnie Lambdin back to the stand as a rebuttal witness, this time to say she had heard Amber joke in jail about pushing people out of windows. Keely called a second prison inmate to make the same charge about Amber joking.

Finally, the state called a friend of Josh's to testify simply that Josh was physically strong and often had to push opposing players while playing football. He was only on the stand for about two minutes, and we elected not to cross. It was an anticlimactic end to the testimony.

It was Friday afternoon. Closing arguments were all that remained. Judge Glassco sent everyone home for the weekend, with a reminder to the jurors before they left the courtroom.

"During this weekend, I do not want you to watch any news reports," he told them. "I don't want you to watch any national television. I don't want you to read the newspaper on anything that has to do with news. So stay out of the local — what do they call it — the local page, state and local page and the main page. I don't care if you read the classifieds and the sports page and Scene and things like that, but I don't want you reading anything else. And please do not discuss the case."

There was little chance, we felt, that all 12 jurors would follow this admonition.

"I want to thank all of y'all for a good job in this," the judge then told us attorneys. "It's great to have good lawyers trying a case.... Enjoy your weekend, and I'll see you at 8:30 on Monday."

I hugged Amber and saw her off for what I hoped would be her last weekend behind bars. Amber's mother Rhonda sent a text message to April and me: "I love both of you... we appreciate you both soooooo much."

We left the courthouse cautiously optimistic.

Others weren't so sure. One observer, a friend who had seen her share of trials over the years, said she had been watching the jury closely.

"They hate her," she said.

I had more confidence than her.

We felt the witness accounts of Amber's behavior at the scene, both in the moments just before and after her husband's death, didn't support the "willful, deliberate, and contemptuous disregard for human life" mindset the prosecution needed to prove for a "depraved mind" murder conviction.

We also knew the judge would give the 12 jurors a written jury instruction requiring them to acquit Amber unless the prosecution had proven beyond a reasonable doubt that there had been no self-defense. We felt there had been strong evidence corroborating Amber's account of the living-room altercation. Conversely, other than Bonnie Lambdin's testimony, the state had presented little evidence supporting its own theory that Amber had caught Josh "off guard."

We trusted the jury would read and discuss their written instructions, go back through the evidence showing self-defense, then realize what they had to do. That trust, though, rested on one assumption: that the jury hadn't already made up its mind long ago.

66

Michelle Keely stood up at 10:53 a.m. Monday and began the first of the prosecution's two closing arguments.

She clearly aimed for an eloquent start. Whether she delivered it was a question only the jury could answer.

"Ladies and gentlemen, I was honored to spend this Saturday at a regional speech contest judging debate and speech events," she began. "And it was in Claremore, on Rogers State University. And as I walked around the campus, I came upon a statue of General George Washington. And on this statue, like so many others, there was a quotation. And the quotation talked about the newness and the unfurling of flag of a new nation of freedom. And I contemplated the fact that our freedoms are not unfettered freedoms, ladies and gentlemen. Because one person's unfettered freedom can diminish another's. And so what we depend on are the laws of our nation, of our state, to bind us together. To bind us together as individuals in this society. Because each individual is important. And we each write on our own pages and we each help decide what our own future is gonna be. But not only do we write on the pages of ourselves, we write on the pages of each other. And today you will be writing on the page of the defendant, Amber Hilberling."

Her wording struck me as off — *writing on the pages of ourselves?* — and she appeared physically uncomfortable. I had watched her closely throughout jury selection, opening statements, 32 witnesses, and numerous evidentiary arguments. While she lacked the "it" factor – the captivating courtroom presence very few trial lawyers are blessed to have – she generally overcame her style shortcomings with a tactically strong and aggressive approach. She knew what she was doing in the courtroom.

But now she seemed out of gas. Rambling. She used the phrase "ladies and gentlemen" 119 different times during her closing, a verbal crutch she relied upon so frequently it was almost distracting.

She wasn't the only one who appeared exhausted. It had been a long case, and a draining trial, for all of us. Minutes into her closing argument, I saw jurors closing their eyes for extended stretches.

I wrote a note to Amber on a piece of paper: "April is going to look like a rock star compared to this."

But what the prosecutor lacked in pathos, she made up for in persistence.

She methodically walked the jury through the five elements required to prove a second-degree murder charge: "First, the death of a human; Second, caused by the conduct which was imminently dangerous to another person; Third, the conduct was that of the defendant; Fourth, the conduct evinced a depraved mind in extreme disregard for human life; Fifth, the conduct was not done with the intention of taking the life of any particular individual."

Then she recounted what she said was the evidence supporting each of the five elements.

As to the first element, death, she reminded the jurors of the details of Medical Examiner's testimony. As she had done earlier with the photographs, she opted for the graphic approach.

"You saw the bones that had been splintered out, placed onto the pavement. You see his arms. His arms the contusions, the contortions. The fact that they're broken." A while later: "you can see bone fragments on the pavement. You can see the deformed arms. You can see the legs."

As to the second element, imminently dangerous conduct, she told the jury that "each one of you has the ability to use common sense... How many of you would allow your children to play right next to a sliding glass door?"

"Glass breaks," she continued. "It's brittle. Everybody knows that."

The third element, the conduct was that of the defendant, was not in dispute. Neither was the fifth, that the conduct was not intentional murder.

The key was the fourth. The state had to prove that Amber had acted with the extreme "depraved mind" element. That meant,

Keely explained, that she had to have proven Amber showed "contemptuous and reckless disregard and total indifference to" Josh's life when she pushed him "toward a window."

Keely suggested that when Josh had broken the small, sliding bedroom-window with the clothes basket minutes before, Amber had suddenly realized that the large living-room window would also break if she pushed Josh into it.

"She knew that window would break," Keely told the jurors.

April and I thought that was an argument for a first-degree murder case, and thus improper here. But attorneys are given wide latitude in closing argument, where judges are loathe to interrupt. Having watched the prosecutor all trial, we knew she would hold nothing back now in her pursuit of a murder conviction.

She briefly touched on the elements of first-degree manslaughter, the alternative charge, but it was clear the state was focused on the murder case.

Then, one by one, the prosecutor went through each of the 32 witnesses who had taken the stand, listing each name on a simple PowerPoint presentation projected onto a large screen. It was a strength-in-numbers approach, suggesting the state had put on an overwhelming amount of evidence.

She painstakingly analyzed the "credibility" of each witness, arguing that the state's witnesses were all credible and trustworthy. We agreed with her on most counts, particularly the police and first responders.

But not all of the witnesses had been truthful, in our opinion. A few had stood out.

"Ladies and gentlemen," she argued, "when you look at Armando Rosales, what do you consider? What is the interest that he has? Does he really have an interest in this case? Probably not." I felt Rosales in fact had a significant financial interest in seeing Amber convicted.

The accounts from Antonio DePaz and Robert Baker, she argued, were clear proof that Josh and gone through the elevated window fame face forward, feet first, standing upright. April and I found neither witness credible.

Keely even urged the jury to believe Bonnie Lambdin, a witness she insisted was credible despite what she conceded was "lots of felony convictions" on her record. Bonnie "took responsibility" for those felonies, Keely said, and thus now deserved the jury's trust.

Plus, Keely argued in another notable choice of words, "if you don't like a witness, do you just *throw them out the window*?"

She wielded Bonnie's testimony aggressively, devoting 59 sentences of her first closing to Bonnie's incriminating accusation, then building her entire second closing around Bonnie's theory. Bonnie, Keely stressed to the jury, "told you that Defendant told her that she caught the victim, Joshua, her husband, unaware and pushed him out the window. That's what the physical evidence indicates, ladies and gentlemen, when you examine it. That's what it indicates."

While Bonnie was a person to be believed, Keely told the jury, Amber and her grandmother were not to be trusted.

"Gloria Bowers," Keely said, with a tone of disbelief. "Gloria Bowers is the Defendant's grandmother. That's something that you're gonna want to talk a lot about. And quite honestly, I'm gonna talk more about it in my second close."

She would, and a lot.

As for Amber, Keely argued that her inability to remember the specific details of how Josh went out the window proved she had been lying.

"How many times did I ask her a question that she said 'I don't know' or 'I don't remember?'" Keely asked the jury. "You can consider that."

She finished by attacking Amber's claim of self-defense.

"There is no person who is at the scene who ever, ever, ever reports that it was self-defense," she said. "She never, ever, ever tells that to any of those people. She doesn't tell that to any police officer. Her grandmother doesn't tell anybody at the scene. Her grandmother doesn't even ever tell police officers. There is no police report of self-defense. None."

"He was messing' with the TV and I pushed him," Keely said, again relying on the excerpt from the partial video. "Ladies and gentlemen, there is no self-defense. There is a man who was caught off guard who was pushed."

"I ask you to find the defendant guilty of murder in the second degree."

67

It was April's turn.

It was hard for me, sitting there and watching, not standing up to deliver what had always been my favorite, and strongest, part of trial work. For 21 months I had visualized delivering Amber's closing, one last win to cap off my legal career, then riding off into the sunset.

Didn't happen.

It had been April's trial. She had handled most of the witnesses, most of jury selection, and the opening statement, and through it all had lived up to her reputation as an excellent trial lawyer.

So it would be her closing.

A minute into it, I already regretted the decision.

"Ladies and gentlemen, I want to start off by thanking you," she began. "I know it's been a long week. You have had a lot of evidence to listen to. I appreciate you being here. This case is important to my client, so thank you. I also want to say that at any point in time that I've been less than eloquent, or fumbled the ball, or anything, or I've done something that's made you annoyed or dislike me, I'm sorry. And I ask that you not hold that against my client."

I tried not to visibly bristle. Thanking them, then apologizing, were two moves I strongly disagreed with, particularly as the way to start. Apologizing set a defeatist tone, I felt, as if we already expected to lose. And thanking the jury for their service, while a common move, was a gesture I had always found patronizing and misplaced. The jurors weren't there to do us a favor, they were there to do their duty. Their hardest and most important work, they needed to understand, was still ahead of them. We could thank them after the verdict, but not now.

My concerns, though, were short-lived. April soon found her footing and delivered a confident, well structured, and occasionally passionate argument.

She quickly focused on what we felt was the heart of our entire defense: the prosecution's failure to prove beyond a reasonable doubt that Amber had acted with a "depraved mind."

The prosecutor, April argued, had mischaracterized Josh's final moments as a "course of events that took place ... over a long period of time." But what the evidence actually revealed, April said, was that Amber had acted quickly, reflexively, in the middle of a heated altercation. Such a split-second act, April argued, was inconsistent with the deliberate cruelty required of a "depraved mind" murder.

"What evidence did they give you that the Defendant acted with a depraved mind?"

"That's a thought process the that to take place in your mind. OK? And what you've heard in the testimony from witnesses is that there was some altercation, that it happened quickly. In fact, you heard there was a grab. There was a shake. There was a 'no, no, no' and a push. That's what you heard. And you heard from witnesses that took seconds. Seconds is what we're talking about here."

"And the state of Oklahoma wants to brush over that with you and talk to you about what you think about with your children. Ladies and gentlemen, she's got to prove to you beyond a reasonable doubt that in that moment, in those seconds, that Amber Hilberling thought to herself, in that moment, she considered and had a contempt and a reckless disregard and extreme disregard for human life. Read that jury instruction and ask yourself with each witness: how did she prove that? Don't let her gloss that over."

That one question, April told the jurors, is the single most important one for them to answer.

She then went through the evidence corroborating Amber's version of events, that she had in fact pushed Josh during a physical altercation in the living room.

There were the photographs of Amber's back, clearly showing scratches and finger marks consistent with Amber's account.

There was the testimony of Armando Rosales from inside the same apartment: "I heard scuffling" in the living room.

There was testimony of the next-door neighbor: "'No, no, no, no!'" Stomp, stomp, stomp. Crash.

"We know there's a physical altercation going on during that moment," April asserted.

Later, she brought up a moment from the police-station video that hadn't received a lot of attention.

"You know what is the most important statement in that video, that you can hang your hat on when you're making this decision about whether this push was lawful? And I bet you missed it the first time you watched it, because I watched it five times and didn't see it until the fourth. Amber says: 'I wish Josh would come in and just tell me *he's sorry.*'"

"I wish Josh would come in and tell me *he's sorry.* And why do you say that, ladies and gentlemen? Unless *he's* grabbed a hold of you, and you've had to push *him* off of you. Listen to that video again."

Amber nodded her head next to me. I felt we had the momentum.

"These witnesses, all of them, tell you something physically is taking place in that apartment. It's the state of Oklahoma who has to prove to you, beyond a reasonable doubt, that Amber- that push is not her defending herself."

She told the jury to look at the clues from before and after the push that, when added up, establish that Amber wasn't the aggressor.

Josh's "angry" and "upset" demeanor when Rosales showed up. The neighbor below hearing Amber vomiting while Josh was yelling at her. Amber pleading to Josh: "I want you to grow up."

Amber's behavior in the moments after. Sobbing, crying, wailing.

When the apartment manager told her to shut up, April reminded the jury, "what does she do? She curls up in a ball on the floor of the elevator. That's the description of how Amber Hilberling is that day. She's not throwing punches. A man yells at her and she curls up in a ball on the floor of the elevator. That sound to you like an aggressor?"

She moved into what she described as "kind of an elephant in the room."

The video.

"Ms. Keely, the state, they like to bring up little pieces from that video. And Gloria Bowers said something interesting in that video I'd like to bring up because I think it's just so evident when you see this little clip: 'Amber, they're gonna twist your words. Amber, they are gonna twist your words.'"

Which is exactly what the state was trying to do, April argued, accusing the prosecutor of trying to prove her case "with bits and pieces of the video."

She urged the jurors to focus on the entire video when they watch it back in the deliberation room after closing arguments, as we all expected them to do at least once. "You have to watch that video from start to finish," April instructed.

She reminded the jury that the video did not show the entire conversation, a point she made diplomatically rather than directly accuse the state of impropriety: "That video does not capture the whole conversation, and it's not a secret to anybody. It starts mid-sentence. That's no proof of anything."

April soon transitioned into the issue of the window glass.

"I want to be very clear," she said, that we were not trying to "say somehow that this is this glass's fault. OK? Just forget that. The glass is not on trial here. That is not the issue." The purpose of the window glass evidence "is to talk to you about knowledge. You remember Ms. Keely talked to you about how any reasonable person would know that playing near glass is dangerous. But that is not a fact scenario in this case. OK?

"The reason this case has gotten such widespread attention or that anyone even cares about this case is because nobody expects somebody to fall out of a high-rise building. And that is the point! And that is the reason why this glass — take it back and look at it, and hold it in your hands — nobody expects this glass to be what's in a high-rise apartment building!

"Nobody thinks that you could simply trip and go through this. You don't expect that. And the reason that is important is that Ms. Keely has to prove to you that any reasonable person would contemplate and believe that this could happen. And that is why this glass is important.

"It is nine one hundredths of an inch! It's picture frame glass! It's not what you would expect. And you need to reason and you need to think about that."

I couldn't wait for the jurors to hold that thin glass in their hands back in the deliberation room. They'd need to feel it, to touch it, to fully comprehend just how flimsy it was.

April then picked up the large cardboard window replica we had made, showing the dimensions of the window and its elevated location on the wall. She set it in front of the jury and explained, one last time, that the prosecution's "face first, feet first, standing upright" theory was simply not possible.

The bottom of the window was two feet, two inches above the ground. The window opening was 51 inches in height. Josh was about 77 inches tall with his shoes on.

"We have Antonio DePaz and Robert Baker making statements that, frankly, it's not possible for them to make," she said.

DePaz, she argued, simply could not have seen what he claimed he saw. He couldn't have been looking straight up, focusing on this one nondescript rectangle 300-plus feet in the air and surrounded by hundreds of identical ones, in the very second just before Josh entered the frame.

She reminded the jury of where DePaz had pointed when she had challenged him to pinpoint the window in the photograph during his testimony. He had pointed to an area in the middle of the building, nowhere near the actual spot. Where he pointed had made more sense than his testimony: it was consistent with DePaz "seeing him after he's come down about ten stories," April said. "It's just not possible that he saw him come out that window face forward."

"Let's talk about Robert Baker," she continued, who "wants you to believe that as he's down on Riverside [a nearby street] in his apartment, looking up, smoking a cigarette, of all 400 windows he just happens to be starting at apartment 2509 on this particular moment.

"And he says - and this is why the window ledge is important - he says when he sees this person coming out, they're standing straight up, feet down, head up."

"This is the window ledge!" April said, pointing again at the bottom line of the rectangle on the cardboard.

"If Josh Hilberling comes out standing straight up and down, first of all, he's got to clear two feet, two inches, to get out that high! And he's too tall, because the rest of the window is four feet, four inches. He's six-four. It's not possible that Robert Baker saw him come out of the window face first. Robert Baker was too far away to tell which direction he was facing. Robert Baker couldn't tell you what clothes he was wearing. What he had in his hand. Whether he had facial hair. But none of that really matters, because we know it's not possible because of the window ledge."

"And the reason I'm making such a big deal about this is because Ms. Keely has to prove to you that Amber did not act in self-defense. And she's trying to do that with these two witnesses saying that she pushed him in the back and he came out face first. And that's just not possible with the evidence. It just doesn't work."

April had nailed that argument, I thought as I watched her. The jury had to get it. They'd go back, ask for the window replica, study the dimensions and understand.

She then attacked what she called the "non-evidence" the prosecution had flooded the jury with.

On Bonnie's testimony about Amber's alleged confession: "she's a liar."

On the gruesome photographs: "20 pictures of his broken body is meant to distract you, because there is no evidence about that push."

On the dozens of references to the unexplained protective order: "this constant talk about a protective order . . . Why do we talk about it? To distract you."

"What is this case about? At the end of the day, it's about a 19-year-old pregnant girl, her 23-year-old husband who obviously had problems, have fought all day, have fought all day long. Are getting ready to separate. And in the heat of the moment he grabs her, she pushes him, and bam, he's out the window. That's what this whole case is about."

"Ladies and gentlemen, it is time to end the circus. It is time for you to go back and look at the state's evidence, just like I asked you at day one, look at the state's evidence, or the lack thereof. It is time for you to send Amber Hilberling home to her baby and be done with it."

When "you consider all the real evidence in this case, you will find that Amber is not guilty. And you will send her home. Thank you."

April nodded confidently at the jury then walked back to our table. She sat down next to me, and we fist-bumped under the table. Amber gave her a confident nod and smile. "You did awesome," she whispered.

We were done. We had spoken our last words of the trial.

But the very last words would belong to the prosecutor, who, unlike the defense, was allowed to give a second closing under the state's trial rules.

All we could do is sit back and watch in disbelief.

68

"Ladies and gentlemen," Keely began, "the evidence shows this is not a case of self-defense."

Over the course of the next 40 minutes, Keely presented numerous different versions of what she said happened in the final moments of Josh's life. The versions often contradicted each other. We weren't sure if the approach was intentional.

But the one constant through them all was her assertion that Amber and Gloria were liars.

Amber's whole self-defense story, the prosecutor argued, was a fiction Gloria had concocted at the scene.

"Recall when she's asked by her grandmother in the video if they were struggling. She didn't know what her grandmother was talking about. Remember that. When her grandmother says, 'are you struggling,' and she says 'what do you mean?' It's not 'what do you mean' if she's already told her grandmother we were struggling, her grandmother already knows that. But that's not what she's saying."

"Her grandmother tries to suggest things to her on June 7 of 2011. But on June 7 of 2011, she was distraught. She was upset. She wasn't able to process that her grandmother is trying to help her out and her grandmother's trying to suggest some things to her."

"Look at the grandmother's testimony," Keely said moments later. "It isn't reasonable."

We didn't agree with the prosecutor's characterization of that exchange, and hoped the jurors would see it our way when they studied the video in deliberations. The actual exchange went as follows:

Amber: "How did this happen?! Why did he have to fall out a window? Fall out a window?! WHY? Why did mom put us in that apartment? Why were we there? Why didn't I just leave?"

Gloria: "Were you both struggling?"

Amber: "What do you mean? I can't get the image out of my head of him falling out the window. I keep trying to tell myself this isn't real, it's all going to be over soon. Josh is dead! His bones were sticking out all over his body. His whole body was broken. And I just held him and kissed his cheeks and screamed at him to wake up."

We saw it as Amber lost in her own train of thought, her grandmother's interruption barely registering. It was just one of many times in the video in which Amber appeared unable to finish a thought or comprehend words.

Keely ridiculed Gloria's testimony that Amber had spoken of a living-room confrontation. "It isn't reasonable," Keely said. "It doesn't make sense." Keely discounted such talk, telling the jury "you don't hear any of that" dialogue in the video. "None of that is on the videotape," she argued.

I hoped like hell the jury understood how brazen this argument was. That very dialogue did occur, but had been omitted from the video.

Gloria had also told Amber repeatedly, as the video reflects, that they shouldn't make any statement until consulting an attorney. But Keely pounced on that decision as evidence of guilt.

"Why in the world, if her granddaughter is gonna stay in custody, is she not beating feet to tell [Detective] Felton this is what she told me? You need to know this. Why is she not making a police statement, if that's what Amber really said? Why does she not make a police report? If Grandmother is upset, and Grandmother is talking to the Defendant on that day, why did she never, ever, ever, go back and make a police report? Why did she never tell police this was self-defense? Why did she never say, 'Amber told me while we were at the apartments that he pushed her?'"

I glanced at Gloria, sitting with her family, as Keely continued to hammer her. Her eyes were once again red.

"Mistake to attack Grandma," I wrote.

"I agree," April scribbled.

The prosecutor then turned her attention back to the dismissed protective order, as she had done dozens of times during the trial. The judge had allowed it as evidence as "part of the crime scene;" we felt the law barred Keely from using it as character evidence to imply Amber's guilt.

Yet that is exactly what she did.

Directly referring to the protective order, Keely told the jury: "circumstantial evidence shows that she has a temper and she gets angry."

April and I jumped to our feet in protest of what we thought was a blatant violation of the rules of evidence. The judge immediately halted the closing arguments —a highly unusual move — and summoned Keely to the bench for a private talk. He ordered the court reporter to go "off the record" for this particular bench conference, meaning there would be no transcript of what was said, though there had been a consistent record kept of previous bench conferences throughout the trial. When the written transcript resumes after this discussion, it first reflects Keely saying these three words:

"I'm sorry, Judge."

Nevertheless, after the apology Keely turned to the jury and resumed making the same prohibited argument, this time with just a shade more subtlety. In the midst of repeated references to the protective order, Keely reminded the jury about Amber's "demeanor" and described her as an "angry" woman.

Then, in a moment that shocked me perhaps more than any other, the prosecutor seemed to blame Amber's own anger as the reason Josh grabbed her shoulders in their living-room fight.

"He grabbed both shoulders at the same time and he held on to them," Keely said. "And remember she said that she was pregnant. And while she was pregnant, he held on to her and she said she was scared. When people grab somebody else by the shoulders, why do they do that? It's not generally to hurt somebody. We're gonna grab somebody to hurt somebody, we grab our arms, we grab our hair. But when we grab shoulders - what's the purpose of that? It's to get somebody's attention. Somebody's angry. You calm them down."

I couldn't believe my ears.

Yes, Josh violently grabbed his pregnant wife, the prosecutor now seemed to admit. *But she deserved it. He had to assault her to calm her down.*

Not only did the theory strike me as reprehensible — an attempt to rationalize domestic abuse — it was also a direct refutation of what Keely herself had always argued. She had repeatedly denied that any living-room altercation had occurred, even accusing Amber and Gloria of lying when talking about it.

But now she was admitting it... and blaming it on Amber?

April and I looked at each other, confused. Amber looked at me, just as confused, and scribbled on a piece of paper in front of her: "I TESTIFIED that he was grabbing!"

I couldn't follow the prosecutor's argument. She continued to contradict herself over the next several minutes.

"He was messin' with the TV," Keely soon said. "Ladies and gentlemen, that is not 'he was holding in to my shoulders.' That is not 'he was pushing me.' That is not 'I was scared of him.' That is 'he was messing' with the TV.' That is not self defense."

Now I wasn't sure which version she was asking the jury to believe: that Josh had grabbed his wife to calm her down, or that he hadn't grabbed her at all.

Then she pitched yet another new one.

After having long argued that Josh had been "face first" to the window when Amber shoved him, she now told the jury he was actually standing sideways. "She runs up on him. She screams 'no, no, no' because she's mad at him because he's leaving her. And she pushes him. And he's sideways and he's off balance and he goes right out the window. Ladies and gentlemen, the evidence shows that makes sense. Because she's already angry, he's sideways, he goes off balance."

And almost as soon as she finished that version, she seemed to test drive a brand new one.

"It's likely that Joshua had his phone in his hand when he was pushed. The evidence shows that Josh decided to leave. And ladies and gentlemen, she got the last word. It's likely that he was standing at the window waiting for his friend to come and she ran up from behind him and she pushed him, and she pushed him out the window."

By now, in a matter of minutes, Keely had told the jury that when Amber pushed Josh, he had been: (1) facing her, grabbing her to calm her down; and (2) sideways looking at the TV; and (3) facing the window, his back to Amber.

"This is brutal," April wrote on her note pad.

"She is fucking up big time," I wrote back.

The state had the burden to prove beyond a reasonable doubt what had happened. But if the prosecution couldn't even figure out which story to pitch, we were sure there was no way an attentive jury could convict. But throughout the prosecutor's second closing, we had again noticed multiple jurors closing their eyes.

We couldn't tell if they were listening. We hoped like hell they were.

"Ladies and gentlemen, the evidence shows that there is no self-defense," Keely said, beginning to wrap up. "I'm going to ask you when you go back there to mark your ballot guilty, because there is no self-defense, there is no accident."

She urged the jury to give Amber a stiff sentence, reminding them of Bonnie Lambdin's accusation.

"And many of you are going to look at each other and say, 'but she's been in jail for this period of time,'" Keely said. "OK. But ladies and gentlemen, consequences. Does she really understand the consequences of her actions? When she's in jail and she's laughing about pushing somebody out the window. Is that accepting the consequences? Ladies and gentlemen, I think the evidence speaks to you that it's not. What happens when somebody does not receive consequences for their actions?

"You, ladies and gentlemen, are the binder of the book. The book of people's lives. You will write peoples' pages and peoples' stories. This is your opportunity to speak the truth. To keep society together. You enforce the law. Thank you."

69

The case went to the jury at 1:21 p.m.

Back in his chambers, Judge Glassco predicted an acquittal on the murder charge and a conviction on manslaughter, the classic compromise verdict, along with a sentence of three to five years.

We held out hope for a full acquittal.

Waiting in the hallway outside the courtroom, Amber's family was confident. "You guys did fantastic," Rhonda texted. Other relatives echoed her praise and optimism.

Two experienced journalists who had watched the entire trial said that based on evidence alone, they expected a total acquittal.

The judge ordered us to stay within five minutes of the courtroom so we would be present when the jurors came back in to watch the video. "I anticipate that pretty soon we're going to have to show the video again," the judge said on the record. We anticipated the same, expecting the jury to watch the video within the first couple hours of deliberations. We visited with courthouse staff about the logistics of the video playback, wanting it ready as soon as the jury sent in the request.

The lobby area just outside the courtroom doors was filled with relatives, friends, and supporters of Amber. More approached us with compliments. I sat in the hallway visiting with Amber's father, Mike, and her grandmother. Mike was somber, concerned, and tense, yet appreciative of our efforts. Gloria was still overcome with sadness and anxiety. She just wanted her baby home.

"I'm throwing up," Rhonda texted me from a nearby restroom. "Tell Amber I love her and I believe in her and you both."

We expected the jury to deliberate into the evening, and very possibly the next day. Watching the video would take more than an hour, and we suspected they may watch it twice. Going through the jury instructions alone could take another hour. Then there were dozens of other items of evidence to review and discuss, along with the testimony of 32 witnesses.

I figured the jury would use the restrooms, eat lunch, sit down and review the 45 detailed jury instructions, then request the video about two hours into deliberations. The judge instructed the jurors that whenever they were ready to watch the video, they needed to "inform the bailiff and we'll bring you back into court" to watch it.

But they never did.

Less than two hours after closing arguments had ended, the jury sent its first note to the judge. The judge called us back into the courtroom to hear it. The note read: "Is the punishment suggested by us, the jury, stand or can it be modified by the judge, and does it include time served?"

The note meant one thing: it was over.

April turned to Amber with a somber expression.

"That note means you're already convicted," she said. "They've been back there debating the sentence."

They had never even watched the video. They hadn't studied it, hadn't examined the statements favorable to Amber, hadn't discussed the actual words and context of the language the prosecutor had alleged to be incriminating. They hadn't tried to pinpoint where the video had actually started, or gone through the steps to realize what Amber had said just before the recording.

They hadn't been back there long enough to talk about the 32 witnesses who had testified.

They hadn't asked for the glass to be sent back. They hadn't held those paper-thin pieces in their fingertips. There wasn't going to be that "a-ha" moment, with the glass in their hands, we had long envisioned.

They hadn't asked for the window replica to be sent back so they could examine the dimensions and consider if the "feet first, standing upright" allegation was even physically possible.

They hadn't been back there long enough to discuss the dozens of items of evidence. They hadn't asked to see a single one.

They hadn't even had time to read and discuss the 45 detailed jury instructions the attorneys had labored and argued over, instructions the jury needed to carefully read and understand in order to responsibly perform their duties.

They hadn't sent in a single question about the evidence, the elements of murder or manslaughter, any particular witness, or any jury instruction.

They had been back there long enough to have some lunch, use the restrooms, maybe crack a joke or two, take a quick vote, then start discussing how long they wanted the notorious Amber Hilberling to be in prison.

It was our worst fear: they had made up their minds a long time ago.

We broke the news to Amber's family. We knew the jury was going to convict. We weren't sure on which count, and we had no way of knowing the sentence. But they had found her guilty.

Less than 30 minutes later, the jury sent the judge a second note: "We, the jury, have reached a verdict."

It was signed by the jury foreman, the postman we had pegged as the "wildcard" back in jury selection. His designation as foreman meant he had led the deliberations, and had likely been the most influential juror. I remembered the confident looks he had shot our way during jury selection, him smiling at us after he was selected, my belief that he wasn't swayed by the facade of the pre-trial public narrative.

We had pegged him wrong.

Word spread, and the courtroom quickly filled up. According to the *Tulsa World*, "while waiting for the jury to enter, family members and friends of both Joshua and Amber Hilberling sat shaking in nervous silence, many dabbing at tears."

By now, though, both families understood what the jury's note had meant. A conviction was coming.

The bailiff led the jurors back in. I watched their faces as they walked back into the jury box and took their seats. Only one juror looked our way, a woman we had strongly wanted on the jury. Her eyes were red. She had been crying.

Judge Glassco addressed the jury.

"Ladies and gentlemen of the jury, it's my understanding you've reached a verdict," he began. "Is that correct?"

"Yes," the foreman answered. He stood proudly and appeared pleased.

The bailiff collected the verdict form from the foreman and handed it to the judge. who read it to himself then looked up at Amber.

"Ms. Hilberling," the judge said, "please rise and face the jury of your peers."

She, April, and I stood together.

"In the District Court In And For Tulsa County, State Of Oklahoma, plaintiff, versus Amber Michelle Hilberling, defendant, case number CF-2011-2444, CF-Docket C. Verdict: count 1, murder in the second degree: We, the jury, impaneled and sworn in the above-entitled cause, do upon our oaths find as follows:

"Defendant, Amber Michelle Hilberling, is guilty of the crime of murder in the second degree, and punishment is set at 25 years in prison and a $10,000.00 fine. Signed [name redacted], foreperson."

Amber cried out and collapsed back into her seat. I heard cries in the gallery. Out of the corner of my eye I saw Amber's sister Ariel being half-carried out of the room, sobbing loudly. The room started to spin. I looked down at the table and clutched its edge to stay on my feet. I tried to look calm, but the Dateline NBC producer told me later: "I thought you were going to pass out. You looked like you saw a ghost."

Amber sobbed in her seat. I reached out and put a hand on her shoulder, my other hand still holding onto the table, telling myself to breathe.

April and the judge engaged in some logistical small talk. I couldn't hear any of it. April leaned over to Amber and promised we would appeal. Amber nodded her head but didn't speak.

The judge turned his attention to the jury and asked each member, one by one, if the verdict was theirs.

"Yes, sir," he heard 12 times.

The jury's reasoning for the sentence was lost on nobody. The window was on the 25th floor. They gave Amber 25 years.

The judge announced formal sentencing would occur on April 23, then asked Amber about the whereabouts of her son, Levi. Amber still couldn't talk. We answered for her, telling the judge that Amber's mother had already been appointed as temporary guardian and that the child was in excellent care.

"At this time," the judge continued, "I will order Ms. Hilberling remanded to the custody of the sheriff, and that she be taken to a place of confinement and held without bond until sentencing on April 23, 2013, at 1:30 in the afternoon."

A deputy sheriff came to our table and escorted Amber out of the room, through the attorneys' side door. April and I followed. The deputy let her sit in a hallway chair to compose herself. She was still crying. Down the same hallway, Keely was crying as well. District Attorney Tim Harris embraced Keely in a long, emotional hug. Even for a seasoned prosecutor, it had been an unusually taxing case.

I stood in the hallway and watched both Amber and her prosecutor cry.

April then talked with Amber about the immediate post-trial procedures. I'm not sure she heard a word. We told her we'd see her soon, and the deputy led her away in handcuffs.

Judge Glassco and his clerk remained in the courtroom, visiting with the jury privately and off the record, a traditional post-trial event.

When he came back into the chambers area, the judge expressed his shock at the stiffness of the sentence. Even Josh's own family, we were soon told, had only wanted a sentence of three or four years. April and I shared his surprise. Not just at the jury's sentence, but at its lack of deliberation.

Then we heard something that explained it all.

During the judge's private chat with the jury, one juror had asked a question that would disturb us more than any single moment of the trial.

They had just convicted a young mother of the "depraved mind" murder. They had just sent her to prison for a quarter century. They had barely deliberated about her guilt or innocence, if at all. Having already returned the "depraved mind" murder conviction and the stiff sentence, the juror raised her hand and asked the judge one shocking question:

"So what does depraved mind mean anyway?"

Part Four: Post-Trial

70

I left the courthouse and drove straight home. I went into my closet and changed out of my suit, threw some clothes into a suitcase, and got back into my car within about 20 minutes. I hit the highway and headed south.

I drove by myself for 12 straight hours, telephone off most of the time, relying on the familiar comforts of Wilco, the National, and Springsteen to clear my head. About every couple towns I had to remind myself to take deep breaths. To breathe. I arrived at the beach in the middle of the night, to our family's vacation spot in the Florida panhandle, where my wife and kids were sleeping soundly on spring break.

For the next several days I did little but sit on the beach and stare at the ocean, the lapping water in front of me, the blue sky above, and try not to think about the case.

I failed.

71

Two days after the verdict, Rhonda texted me and asked me to join her for drinks.

I declined, telling her I needed to be around my family. I hadn't told her I had left town to recover.

She could tell from my texts alone that I was hurting.

"Don't beat yourself up," she texted. "We don't hold you accountable. You are a good man. Don't be down plz."

She was right, though. Beating myself up was exactly what I had been doing.

We had lost. We had failed. When that happens, whether it's a ballgame, a marriage, or a high-profile murder trial, it's natural to look back and rue what went wrong. And wonder.

I wasn't ready to heal. I sat on my beach chair and began the audit that would replay in my head for years. Reliving every decision, every objection, every witness, the pivotal moments in the trial. The judge's rulings that tied our hands while giving the prosecution extra bullets to fire. The misleading use of the protective order. The strange omission from the video. The game-changing Bonnie bombshell.

Mostly, though, I dwelled on what I could have done differently.

I blamed myself for not winning the battle with Mark Collier and waging our own media war from day one. In retrospect I think Rhonda was right to push for it, even if she wasn't the right person for the job. Mark was educated and trained in a day before the age of the Internet and social media, when the smart course was to lay low and save your evidence for trial. I suspect those days are long gone. Today a powerful and damaging narrative can be created overnight, and attorneys in high-profile cases need to be fully prepared to address that challenge head-on. In that area, we failed Amber.

I also blamed myself for our mid-trial decision to scrap our prepared strategy of going into the long history between Josh and Amber. I regretted not giving our closing argument, even though April had done a good job. I blamed myself for not being able to erase the frozen, scared look on Amber's face as she testified. I lamented that we hadn't been hard enough on the two eyewitnesses who had given those impossible accounts of seeing Josh come through the glass. I wondered if we underemphasized the importance of the video omission, if maybe the jury had missed the significance. We had lost, so we hadn't done enough things well enough.

Rationally, though, I knew the bigger truth. Like most trials, ours was likely won or lost before opening statements.

We had lost it at jury selection.

It hadn't taken long, once jury selection started, to realize how badly 21 months of one-sided media coverage had contaminated the jury pool. They all knew about the case. They had opinions, often strong ones. Some admitted to it. Some hid it. We had caught and booted many because of their pre-formed opinions, but had clearly not caught them all.

We sat a jury that was in a hurry to convict first, then explore the material questions after.

Amber and her family saw it the same way.

"It's the media all the way," Rhonda texted me. "We know damn well that they [the jurors] went home and looked up all that garbage. Cases like this prove why most countries do not allow [the media to] talk about a crime until afterwards. Our media laws fucking suck. I hope they are happy - I Lost my daughter and Levi lost his mommie."

"You guys did your best," she said in another text. "We will appeal it. We hold nothing against you and April. This is the media's fault."

The family's support and encouragement helped. They had been just as positive throughout the case and even during the trial, both verbally and via text messages. In one text during the trial, Rhonda wrote: "We have never felt more confident than today with you both. Thank you." In another: "Great job so far!" Another: "I love both of you."

All that was about to change.

72

Sentencing was scheduled for Tuesday, April 23, where the judge would formally impose the 25-year term the jury recommended.

On the Sunday before the sentencing, as I waited for a table at a local brunch spot, I picked up a copy of the *Tulsa World* newspaper from a nearby chair. There was, of course, a long, detailed article looking back at the case. Against my better judgment, I opted to give it a look.

In the article, the *Tulsa World* made a point to report that "Hilberling started showing up to court hearings in fitted jackets, full makeup and a mane of blown-out blonde tresses."

I interpreted *fitted* jackets as code for *tight. Full makeup? Blown-out blonde tresses?*

The local newspaper was openly deriding Amber for her bust, her makeup, and her hair.

Having stopped paying attention to the news coverage early in the case, I had apparently missed the media's progression from inaccurate sensationalism to outright sexism. I felt certain that if I searched years' worth of the *Tulsa World's* coverage of murder trials, I wouldn't find a single such report of a male defendant's hair, grooming techniques, or how his attire fit his torso.

Later in the same article, the paper did accurately report one thing: "After Tuesday, there is prison, a messy behind-the-scenes probate battle and a pending lawsuit over the strength of the glass windows in the apartment tower."

In truth, that probate battle had already started. And "messy" didn't even begin to describe it.

73

The shocks kept coming.

It was about 3:20 p.m. on the day of the verdict when the jury had sent the judge their note asking about sentencing. About 10 minutes later, we had gone to Amber's family and explained that the note meant a conviction was forthcoming.

Most of Amber's family had reacted to the news with anguish. Her grandmother and sister cried. Her father Mike was stone-faced in disbelief. I felt like I had been kicked in the stomach.

Rhonda and Bryan Whitlock reacted much differently.

At 3:59 p.m., according to court records, Rhonda and Bryan formally entered the wrongful-death civil lawsuit I had filed. Less than a half-hour after learning their daughter was going to be convicted.

They had long known that if Amber was convicted in the criminal case, she would lose her legal right to serve as plaintiff in the window lawsuit. The case would then have to shift to a new plaintiff.

But from a legal perspective, there was no rational reason for their urgency to file that same day. It wasn't a race; there wasn't a reward awaiting the first one to file. The civil case would eventually go to whomever the probate court would appoint as personal representative of Josh's estate. That process alone would take weeks, if not months. In the meantime, the window lawsuit would remain in its court-ordered standstill.

If only for appearances' sake, I felt they could have at least waited until the next morning to file. There is no way to sugarcoat it. The timing looked bad.

Amber and I would learn days later about what they had done, and how quickly they had done it. We were... not pleased. But not only was their aggressive pursuit of the civil case tacky, it had the ironic effect of badly hurting that very lawsuit.

With Amber's conviction, any subsequent pursuit of the window lawsuit would be extremely complicated. The case wasn't necessarily dead; a jury could still find that the negligence of the building's ownership and management, as well as that of Armando Rosales's business, were partially liable for Josh's death. But moving that case forward would now require a cooperative effort on the plaintiff's side, where the situation was, to say the least, highly delicate.

While the window lawsuit would legally belong to Josh's estate, there were potentially several parties with various interests in its outcome: Amber, Josh's parents, Josh's stepmother, Josh's siblings, Levi, and now apparently even the mother and stepfather of the person convicted of Josh's murder. With that many parties on the same side of the ledger, infighting and divisiveness could easily derail the effort. Such conflict would be a gift to the defendants, who were already well represented by a sharp Tulsa attorney. They didn't need any extra help.

Further, whoever ended up personally holding the reins of the civil lawsuit would need both me and Amber. I had been the one to conceive of the case, to hustle to build it with my own hands and mind, and had studied it inside and out. I knew more about its history and particulars than anybody. The new plaintiff's legal team would want my work product, knowledge, research, and strategies. Therein was just one of the problems: I couldn't help anybody who had a position adverse to Amber. It would be a conflict of interest. My legal duty was to Amber.

Similarly, the new plaintiff would likely want Amber's help, cooperation, and potentially even her testimony.

And above all, we felt there was still a real chance her appeal would win. If it did, Amber would be restored as the plaintiff in the civil case.

So we all needed to get along and be helpful partners on the playing field, not adversaries. It was no time for a brawl.

———

On May 7, 2013, on Amber's behalf, I filed a motion in the probate case urging the judge to appoint an independent party, rather than relatives of either side, to represent Josh's estate.

Rhonda and Bryan appeared irate. On the day she received her copy of my filing, Rhonda published a post on her Facebook page directing, without any explanation, that her social media followers "write the bar association" about me and "stop horrible, unethical attorneys!!!"

On the same day, she sent me the following text: "I could of destroyed you on Dateline. I didn't. You got my daughter 25 years."

You got my daughter 25 years.

It was a vicious shot. For me, that one line outweighed the dozens of compliments she had already given me. It haunted me for a long time. The verdict was already keeping me up at night. Her text didn't help.

Just like that, from that day forward their behavior toward me changed dramatically. Their two years' worth of consistent praise and gratitude gave way to anger, insults, and defamation. Bryan angrily disparaged me to numerous others, his words often leaking back to me. It wasn't Amber's case that had turned them against me, or any of the other cases I had worked on for them.

It was a fight about money.

I felt their anger was misplaced. It was clear to me, and everyone else in the probate case, that they were going to lose their bid to take over Josh's estate. It was also clear that what I had requested – the appointment of an independent personal representative – was in the best interest of both Josh's estate and his young son. It was the obvious course. To have expected either set of parents to work well with the other was unrealistic.

Further, if there ever was a payout, Amber had already told me in writing she wanted independent professionals handling every penny to protect Levi's interests.

The court agreed. The judge eventually ruled that she would appoint a neutral party – a local attorney – to represent the estate.

I stepped back and waited for the new representative to take over, hoping she would elect to go forward with the window lawsuit.

The unnecessary infighting, though, had already caused a delay that now threatened the future of that civil case. The two-year anniversary of Josh's death was around the corner. That date would be the statutory deadline to add new defendants or claims to the existing civil lawsuit, moves I anticipated the new attorney may demand. But the probate court hadn't formally appointed the estate representative, which meant the wrongful death case still was lingering in limbo without a proper plaintiff or an attorney.

So while there was work to do quickly, there was no one appointed to do it.

Though it was no longer my role, I worked behind the scenes to try to protect the case. Amber hoped it would still generate a payday to help Levi's future.

I reached out from the sideline to some of the state's top plaintiff's attorneys. I finally convinced one, Clark Brewster, to take the window case on the blind faith that whomever was appointed to represent the probate estate would want to keep him on board. And sure enough, Brewster wanted to amend the existing lawsuit. But he couldn't, because he wasn't yet on the case. Though I wasn't sure I still had the status to act, I made the changes for him and filed the amended version on the two-year deadline. I then worked with his firm to guide them through the strategies and evidence I had developed for the civil case over the previous two years.

Once again, I was working for free. Between the murder case, the civil case, the probate case, and the defamation case, I had now worked four cases for the family, over two full years, all the while collecting a grand total of one cash payment of $3,000. I'd never collect another penny.

After I turned the case over to Brewster, another problem arose. He got a taste of the behind-the-scenes drama: the families fighting about Josh's probate estate and the rights to the wrongful death case, the legal conflict of interest within Amber's own family, the ugliness and animosity.

Wisely, he ran.

He texted me that he was now "unwilling" to enter the case "in the face of acrimony and cross shooting."

"Frankly," he added, "the case will be doomed by the past course of events."

He was right.

The infighting brought the entire civil case to a near halt. I had started putting it together in 2011, filed it in 2012, and handed it off in 2013. But according to the case docket, the appointed estate representative didn't even enter the civil case as the new plaintiff until April 29, 2014. Then it was July 25, 2015, before an attorney dared enter the contentious window lawsuit – only to quit three months later. Another attorney then took the case, then also soon quit. Yet another new attorney took over in 2016.

But as of 2016, Rhonda and Bryan apparently still hadn't given up their own hopes of taking control of the case. They filed their own new wrongful death lawsuit that March, essentially a copy of the petition I had drafted some four years earlier. It was changed to name themselves as the new plaintiffs acting on behalf of Levi.

So more than five years after Josh's death, the window lawsuit was still derailed by what I viewed as greed, infighting, and bad decisions. Had I known how it would all play out, I'm not sure I'd have hustled to Apartment 2509 the morning after the tragedy and pulled those brittle pieces of glass out of the window frame.

As it turns out, it hadn't done a damn bit of good.

74

On April 23, 2013, in front of another packed courtroom, Judge Glassco officially imposed the 25-year prison sentence the jury had recommended.

From a legal perspective, the hearing was a formality. Though we could, and did, ask for mercy, there was no chance the judge was going to reduce the sentence in the high-profile case.

It was also an opportunity for Amber, and supporters on either side, to make their own statements about the sentence.

Josh's relatives chose to submit their statements in writing rather than make them in open court. The prosecutor introduced letters from Josh's father, stepmother, grandmother, brother, and sister. Josh's mother, now struggling with serious health issues, elected not to provide one.

The five shared their grief, their recollections of Josh's relationship with Amber, and restated their belief that Amber had hit and thrown things at Josh while the two had been in Alaska. They went out of their way to share their criticisms of what they called Amber's "dysfunctional family," her "crazy" mother, and her "toxic home environment."

Josh's father Patrick wrote that the night of the verdict, March 18, 2013, was "the first night I have slept a full night since Josh's death." He wrote of his feelings for Josh, and how he was "sickened" that Amber's "mother and stepfather want to sue the apartment building to get a financial reward." He also wrote: "my hope is that one day I will be able to forgive Amber, her mom, and stepfather."

Josh's stepmother began her statement on a completely different note, expressing her anger at Amber for something unrelated to the case, Josh's death, or the sentencing. She focused on Amber having once referred to Josh's actual mother during her testimony. "Amber said when on the witness stand that I am not Josh's mother?" Jeanne began her statement. "Josh would argue that fact. Since Josh was five years old, I am the person that Josh called his mommy/mom." She then wrote about how the case had affected her own life professionally, physically, and emotionally.

Josh's grandmother wrote affectionately about Josh's smile, his kindness, mowing her lawn in exchange for vanilla pudding, and other fond memories of her grandson.

Rhonda opted to make her statement in open court. She took the stand, pulled out a piece of a paper, and read it aloud while fighting back tears: "On behalf of my family, Amber's five siblings, sister-in-law, grandmother, Dad, we know the truth in this case, and I will never stop fighting for you baby. This was nothing more than a tragic accident that has affected all of us. Amber misses Josh so much and every morning that baby looks at me in the morning, he misses his mommy, too. And I will always raise that baby until you are home, knowing that his dad and his mom loved him so much and this was nothing more than a mere tragedy, nothing more. We love you and we will always support you and the truth always."

Amber took the stand next. She was composed. She said she was "grateful for the opportunity to speak today" and began by thanking the court "for every attempt at revealing truth for the families who have persevered."

"To the Hilberlings," she said next, looking up briefly at Josh's family, then down at her notes. "By my own painful, sometimes all-consuming loss of Josh, I measure yours and I send my condolences. You have my most genuine apology that we find ourselves here, and for the grief we all battle.

"For my own family, I would give the world if I could make each of you closer to me. I am so sorry for sometimes allowing you to fight harder than I myself had the strength to. I could not go on without the love I feel is behind me through this, and anything we face. I owe you all more than is ever possible.

"In regard to the immense amount of support I have received from the public, every single effort made in reaching out and standing behind me gives me courage when I need it the most. You answered my prayers and I thank you for everything.

"My baby, Levi. Though I understand you are not here, I could not avoid mentioning you. You are the keepsake I endure toward. Near and far, I promise you with everything my heart can muster that you are always with me, even while I dream. Mommy loves you infinity, Squirt.

"My final and most desirable acknowledgement is for my God. I trust you to pick up the broken pieces left in each one of us who is hurting. Whatever sentence given me in this room, I will use it to follow you into the next. For everyone involved in this tragedy, I pray for. Nobody can begin to see or estimate what I have been through in more places than only this courtroom. Aside from my sentencing today, I will live with this for the rest of my existence.

"I miss my husband just as much and I know my family misses me, but I put my faith in so much more than anything happening here and now. I never intended for this accident to happen, and I am so sorry that it did. I still cannot believe it.

"Again, I am appreciative for the court's gracious decision in allowing me to disclose some of the things in my heart, as well as the consideration and mercy shown me and my family by the Honorable Judge Glassco. Thank you."

Keely, April, and I each made brief statements about the sentence.

Keely called the sentence "reasonable," criticized Amber's trial testimony as inconsistent, and cited Bonnie Lambdin's testimony as proof that Amber had no remorse. She gave an eloquent defense of jury verdicts as "anchors" of constitutional principles, appearing reenergized and much sharper than she had at the end of trial.

April argued that the 25-year sentence was "excessive" for what was clearly an "accident." She asked the judge to give Amber credit for her 15 months of time served and suspend the rest of her sentence. She cited the jury's shocking post-verdict question — "What does depraved mind mean?" — as undeniable proof the jury did not properly deliberate.

I then argued that Amber had never once changed her version of events, in response to the prosecutor having again asserted the contrary. I urged that Amber was "not a career criminal" but "a young, scared girl who has been through incomparable trauma."

Judge Glassco then imposed the sentence.

"Actions have consequences," he said. "I am not shocked by the verdict of the jury or of their sentence. I believe the Defendant has been treated fair, and like the jury I must follow my oath of office. The Defendant's request for modification of the jury's sentence is denied."

He concluded the hearing and adjourned the case. Amber was led away in handcuffs.

This time she walked head high, without tears. This time, she was ready.

Under current Oklahoma law, she will have to serve at least 85 percent of her sentence before being eligible for parole. She will be in an Oklahoma women's prison until they year 2033 at the earliest.

The day she walks out of prison, Levi will be at least 21 years old.

75

After the sentencing, I sent a handwritten card to Josh's father.

Mr. Hilberling,

Now that the criminal case is over, please accept my heartfelt sympathy for your loss of your beautiful boy. I have an 18 and a 16 year old, and I can't imagine the pain of losing a son.

I understand the resentment you must have of me and anybody else who assisted my client, which is a natural response to our obligation to be zealous advocates for our client. But please know that my heart always aches when I see the pain in the eyes of you and your family.

I hope the resolution of the criminal case has given you all a sense of justice and comfort.

I had felt the daggers Josh's family and friends had shot in our direction throughout the case, but I had more empathy for them than they could have known. Like Josh, my brother had been killed within days of his 23rd birthday, a bright future ripped away. I knew their pain and my heart had ached for them. While I had resented their pre-trial campaigning against my client, Amber herself had quickly forgiven them; who was I to not?

Patrick Hilberling responded to me soon after receiving the card, with an e-mail titled "Thank you."

"I received your card yesterday," he began. "I must say we are surprised. Yet, we are ready to forgive and move forward with life."

Out of respect for his privacy, I will not share the rest of the e-mail.

76

O ur final hopes rested on an appeal.

For that, we agreed Amber needed a new attorney. For one, an appeal of a criminal trial verdict should always include the standard claim that the defendant received "ineffective assistance at counsel" at trial. The trial attorney himself can't credibly make that argument.

One of the state's most respected criminal defense attorneys, Rob Nigh, would take the lead. Nigh was a partner at Brewster's firm, and well known for having represented Oklahoma City bomber Timothy McVeigh years earlier. I was honored to work for their excellent firm while in law school.

April and I soon met with Nigh and other attorneys at their firm to get them started. We shared our thoughts about opportunities for appeal, evidentiary rulings we believed were improper, and what we thought was the prosecutor's questionable behavior at trial.

We suggested numerous ways they could claim we made mistakes at trial, strategy decisions we ourselves had second guessed. If throwing ourselves under the bus would help Amber, neither April nor I were too proud to do it. Nigh made a point to tell us he respected our willingness to do so. Not every lawyer, he said, makes that offer.

Nigh filed his appellate brief on December 26, 2013, citing five grounds:

1) The evidence was insufficient to support the charge of second-degree murder;
2) The court erred in failing to give the jury the option of second-degree manslaughter;
3) Amber was denied a fair trial through the admission of gruesome photographs, improper character evidence, and prosecutorial misconduct;
4) The state offered improper opinion evidence that Amber was guilty;
5) Amber was denied effective assistance of counsel.

As to the first, Nigh argued that the state had failed to prove Amber's "conduct evidenced a depraved mind and extreme disregard for human life" as required of a second-degree murder conviction. "At most," Nigh wrote, "the state's theory proves a tragic accident." He cited numerous Oklahoma cases in support, arguing that there was "no evidence… that Ms. Hilberling acted in a way calculated to put life in jeopardy or perpetrated with full consciousness of the probable consequences."

As to the second ground, Nigh argued that the court should have given the jury an instruction that it could convict Amber of second-degree manslaughter, a death "caused by the culpable negligence of the defendant."

As to the third ground, the prosecutor's behavior, Nigh accurately captured what I felt were a few of the state's questionable tactics in the trial.

The state's repeated trumpeting of graphic, blown-up photographs of Josh's body on the parking garage concrete was improper, Nigh argued, because "cause of death was never an issue in the case, and there was no need to admit multiple photographs of his severely disfigured body." He alleged the prosecutor went to great lengths to remind the jury of the gruesome details of the photographs, creating "the inescapable conclusion," Nigh wrote, "that the photographs were simply offered to trigger an emotional response from the jury."

Nigh then argued that the state's repeated references to the temporary protective order, which had been dismissed in days, was unfairly prejudicial and improper character evidence.

Nigh singled out other instances of Keely's conduct, such as her seemingly inventing a new nickname for the white tank top Amber was wearing when Josh died, calling it a "spouse beater."

He argued that the court erred in allowing the state to play the partial video of the conversation between Amber and her grandmother because it showed Amber stating she wanted an attorney. Governing case law, Nigh argued, holds that the prosecution cannot use a defendant's exercise of the constitutional right to remain silent as an implication guilt.

The fourth ground was that Detective Felton should not have been allowed to offer his own personal opinion that Amber had not used self-defense.

Finally, Nigh asserted the standard claim for ineffective assistance of counsel. Nigh's own examination of the trial transcript, he wrote, found that April and I had been "skillful" in the trial, "and in many aspects of the case provided excellent representation." All he could manage to come up with was a claim that we had been ineffective in our objections to the video and protective order.

"Ms. Hilberling was denied a fair trial," Nigh wrote, "and her conviction should be reversed."

In its response, the state asserted that the eyewitness accounts of Antonio DePaz and Robert Baker — that they had seen Josh go through the window glass "face first" — corroborated the testimony Bonnie Lambdin had given about Amber catching Josh "off guard."

As to the protective order, the state began its argument with these words: "Curiously, the only item laying on the coffee table in the living room where the crime took place was a copy of a protective order the victim had filed and served against his wife, the defendant." The state argued that this "curious" presence of the document right there on the coffee table showed "it apparently was brought to the surface the day the fatal injury was inflicted."

This was yet another falsehood.

The only document on the coffee table was the search warrant the police had placed on it, as reflected in this photograph of the scene:

Another police photograph shows the real location of the dismissed protective order. It was folded up inside a bowl on a stand near the kitchen, next to Amber's purse, along with numerous other random papers, mailings, and assorted odds and ends:

The appeal process mirrored nearly everything else that had happened since June 7, 2011: truth was discarded where convenient, and no one seemed to care.

77

I asked God for help.

There were times I went to my knees on my bedroom floor and prayed the appeal would win. I envisioned the whole scenario often. The conviction would get reversed in time for Amber to be home with Levi for Christmas. I'd be there watching as she stepped out of prison, her family and friends waiting to embrace her. I'd stay in touch to try to help her restart her life on the straight and narrow. I'd always be there for her. She knew that.

If she won the appeal, I was sure the district attorney's office wouldn't want to go through another circus of a trial. They'd offer a deal. This time, I'd twist Amber's arm until she took it. Her time already served, I expected, would probably be sufficient.

But if the case did go to trial again, it'd be in the hands of a new attorney. I'd be sitting in the gallery watching.

There was no way I was getting pulled back into a long, hard case. Other than finishing up a few matters I had picked up for family and friends over the course of Amber's case, I was done with active practice. Just after the appeal was filed, I announced on my practice's website and Facebook page that my practice was now, finally, closed to new cases.

I was already burned out when Amber's case fell into my lap three years earlier. Back then, I had shut down my law office with a vague plan to finish up my remaining cases then get back to writing. I had also been considering a standing employment offer a client had been pushing me to accept for years: good money, and enough freedom to start writing again. Either path was more attractive than active litigation.

Before I closed my firm's doors, there were days I'd step into my office, merely look at my case files, and feel physically ill. Sometimes I couldn't even open them; I'd just stand in my doorway, frozen, and stare at them. Near the end I'd started to go days without listening to the voicemails or returning work calls.

I found myself fantasizing about just disappearing to the beach without telling anybody, start writing my novel, maybe tend bar in flip flops, live without a cell phone or computer, and give all my suits and ties to charity.

It was a scenario understood by the man who had most strongly supported my detour into law in the first place. My late stepfather, a non-practicing attorney who found success outside of law, had years ago encouraged both me and my cousin to go to law school. "A legal education will serve you for life," he often told us. But he hadn't expressed the same enthusiasm about the actual practice. He had quickly transitioned out of law and into ventures that brought him joy. My cousin then followed a similar path: law school, a few years of litigating, burnout, then the pursuit of work that made her smile.

They had both learned what I would later. While I had built a nice resumé of trial victories and settlements in my short time practicing, I found the work mostly miserable. Civil litigation is nothing more than suits bickering over how to divvy up some insurance company's money among unhappy people. That's it.

It wasn't just the nature of litigating itself that had disappointed me. It was often the hostility of the people involved. There were some attorneys who could be tough outs while still carrying themselves with dignity and grace, but they were hard to find. The vast majority of litigators struck me as guys who had been picked on in middle school, couldn't get the girl in high school, and were now spending their entire adult lives trying to get revenge. Alcohol and drug problems were prevalent in the practice, and it hadn't taken me long to understand why.

In civil litigation, most defense attorneys, getting paid by the hour, would drag cases on for years if they could. Along the way they'd do little more than call people names, harass, recycle old briefs originally written by somebody else, and run the meter on their insurance company clients for as long as possible. Usually it would be the eve of trial, after they had billed the file to the max, when they would finally agree to settle the case for terms predictable two or three years before.

Civil litigation was a tedious and ugly game, and I had grown tired of it.

Working Amber's grueling case had taught me something else: during the entire time I had been practicing law, the real litigators had actually been working on another courtroom floor. While I had been filing motions and taking depositions in long fights about money, underpaid prosecutors and hardened criminal defense lawyers had been spending their days fighting about justice and guilt and freedom. Their work changed lives. By comparison, their world made mine look silly.

I gained respect for their world, but wanted no part of it. I missed my original calling. I missed being creative rather than destructive. I missed smiling while I worked.

I had loved my days as a journalist in Nebraska and Wyoming, running a daily sports page then a small-town paper. In those days I felt I was touching lives and informing the public, making a difference, having fun and collecting a box full of journalism awards along the way. That was the life I had always planned, not dark suits and fights. Since I was 10 years old I had dreamt of someday writing for *Sports Illustrated* or the *New York Times*, writing the occasional novel or non-fiction on the side, maybe someday trying a screenplay. Journalists and authors had always been my heroes, not litigators.

But at 29, with three young mouths to feed, I chucked my dreams to go chase money.

If I had any lingering doubts about shutting down my law practice, my final trial confirmed it. I ended up with one more trial scheduled on my docket after Amber's, a nasty fight between neighboring landowners: all easements and property law and bitterness. As I finished up my closing argument, I was sure we had won on all counts yet I felt... indifferent. When the verdict came, the complete and total victory I knew was coming, my client was overjoyed. I felt like shrugging.

Having gone through Amber's case, litigating about money and property issues felt even more inconsequential than it had before. It had been just another stupid, unnecessary fight generating a ridiculous amount of legal fees. Like most lawsuits, I could have resolved it two years earlier with one good conversation over a few cold beers.

I was over it. I had a new plan.

It was all about to come together perfectly. I was sure of it.

Amber would win her appeal and go home to her son. Our trial loss would be reversed. I'd start sleeping at night again. I'd settle what was now my one last remaining case, federal court litigation over unpaid sales commissions, financial fraud, and bad blood, then go start writing my books on the beach.

But what happened next was something I never saw coming.

I remember looking up at the ceiling of the ambulance, unable to talk clearly, trying to understand what the paramedics were saying as we raced to the hospital, thinking about my kids, wondering if I was about to die.

78

On August 27, 2014, the Oklahoma Court of Criminal Appeals issued its ruling.

The court affirmed the conviction.

We had lost.

The appellate court rejected all five of Nigh's appeal arguments with little comment, holding that "any rational trier of fact" could have convicted Amber.

As to the judge's evidentiary rulings, the appellate court held that "even if we found the photograph and testimony concerning the protective order inadmissible," the verdict would have likely been the same. The appellate court never learned of the misrepresentation about the protective order being found on the living room coffee table, and its implication that the order was thus related to the couple's final conflict.

The court did agree with us that some of the prosecutor's behavior in trial had been "dubious," but excused it because it "did not deprive Hilberling of a fair trial."

The court rejected the claim of ineffective assistance of counsel, ruling that Amber had suffered "no prejudice" from the matters Nigh had raised on appeal.

It was over.

79

It was a Tuesday evening, soon after the appeal lost.

I had been having trouble sleeping again, the same problem I had the first few months after the trial. I'd toss and turn, reliving the case, picturing Amber in her cell, her son far away from his mommy. I felt partly responsible.

You got my daughter 25 years.

I had taken my four-year-old daughter to dinner at Chick-Fil-A, where her school was having a fundraiser. She ate, chatted with Daddy, then went into the play area with her friends.

I stayed at my seat and pulled out my iPhone, scrolling through my Twitter feed. I clicked on a college football article. It came up, but I couldn't read it. It was blurry, like the sensation after a camera flashes in your eyes. I tried to read it by looking at it sideways, out of the corner of my eyes.

But things felt... weird.

I looked around the restaurant. Everything else seemed blurry too. I couldn't focus. I tried to read a sign on the wall, but couldn't make it out.

I took some deep breaths and waited for my eyes to snap out of it. They didn't.

So I decided to do what men do: I'd just "walk it off." I stood up and tried to walk, but felt wobbly.

Something was going on. Definitely. But I didn't know what.

I walked to the counter to order the ice cream my daughter had wanted for dessert. I remember thinking that just doing that, ordering some ice cream, would snap me out of it. I opened my mouth and saw the words form – *kids' ice cream cone* – but I couldn't make anything come out.

I tried again. Nothing.

I felt uneasy and clutched the front edge of counter with both hands.

The teenager behind the counter looked scared.

"Are you OK?" he asked.

I realized I wasn't. I couldn't talk, so I shook my head. He yelled for his manager.

Two parents from my daughter's school saw the scene and rushed over. I wasn't sure what everyone was seeing, but it obviously wasn't good. The man grabbed hold of me and hustled me outside to his car, his wife telling me she would watch my daughter. I was unable to think or talk clearly. He sped me to the urgent care clinic directly across the street.

The doctor there rushed in our direction and started asking me questions. I could tell by her reaction I wasn't answering them well. She told me to lift my legs, then my arms. I looked down and watched myself try.

I couldn't lift my left leg. Or my left arm.

She looked up at me and said the word.

"Stroke."

Paramedics quickly arrived. They loaded me onto a stretcher and into their ambulance, then rushed me to a hospital emergency room.

"We're going hot," I remember one of them saying. The lights and sirens came on.

"We're hustling," he told me. "I don't have a good feeling about this one, buddy."

I looked up at the ambulance ceiling, confused. A stroke? At 42? *We're going hot?*

This all must be a mistake, I thought. I was in great health, ate well, and exercised regularly. Since the trial ended I'd been hitting the gym at least three times a week, had a personal trainer, had lost about 30 pounds and put on muscle, and finally looked how I wanted to without a shirt on. I was in the best shape of my life.

This can't be happening.

But it was.

From the ambulance to the emergency room to my own room, nurses and tests and bad food and more tests. I'd never been in the hospital before; I didn't even have a regular physician. Yet there I was, feeling like a caged zoo animal as friends and family shuffled in and out to stare at me uncomfortably over the next couple days.

I had a heart defect, a doctor finally told me, one that makes me more prone to strokes. A cardiologist then explained that I wasn't a typical candidate for a stroke, even with the defect. I had none of the usual risk factors. But there was, he said, likely one specific thing that would have triggered it.

"Have you been under an unusual amount of stress lately?" he asked.

I chuckled. I can't say for certain that any one case had contributed more than others. But no case had haunted me, staying with me on a personal level, more than Amber's. Losing her appeal had made the pain fresh.

The cardiologist's question was all I needed to hear.

As soon as I was out of the hospital, I called up another attorney and asked him to finish up my final case. I notified the court, deactivated my law license, and turned off my practice's e-mail addresses, phone lines, fax lines, and post office box. I did everything I could to eliminate the risk I'd be tempted to ever say yes again.

Finally. I was done.

Done fighting, done living for things that didn't really matter. I had a new mindset, a clear head, a sense of peace. If you had any drama for me, I wasn't even going to respond.

It was the strangest thing: I remember sitting in my backyard on a fall afternoon soon after, reading literature the cardiologist had sent home with me, getting strange prescriptions filled, scheduling an appointment with a heart surgeon... yet it was the lightest, happiest, most relaxed I had felt in years.

Then I did exactly what I always said I'd do. I sold my house and headed to the beach.

Instead of spending my days fighting about money with lawyers, I spent that winter on the Gulf of Mexico wearing shorts and flip-flops, following my cardiologist's orders and avoiding stress, savoring fresh seafood and the occasional mojito, and finally getting started on that first novel.

I was now a Florida resident, a recovering lawyer, and, best of all, when someone asked what I did, I could go back to the answer I had always loved giving more than a decade before: "I'm a writer."

It was the life I had dreamt of for years. So far, I haven't missed the lawyers once.

80

Rhonda called me out of the blue one night in 2015, well after dark, asking me if I would "fall on the sword" to get Amber out of prison.

"Please!" she said. "Just say it was all your fault! Fall on your sword!"

I had no idea what she meant. She was upset and difficult to understand. It sounded like she was asking me to file an "ineffective assistance of counsel" appeal. But we had already tried that, I told her. It hadn't worked.

She wasn't listening.

She said attorney Clark Brewster, whose law partner had filed the appeal, had told her Amber would get an "automatic retrial" if I would simply say everything was my fault.

It was ludicrous, of course. There were no magic words I could suddenly say to get Amber out of prison. If it was that easy, not only would I have already done it, but there'd be lawyers lining up to recite the lines after every lost trial. She insisted, and continued to say it was Brewster who had been telling her this. I called him the next morning. As expected, he assured me that not only had he never said anything of the sort, "I haven't talked to Rhonda Whitlock in over a year."

She called back days later, asking me again to "fall on your sword." Only this time, I heard a new explanation.

"Will you do it for Dr. Phil?" she asked. "Please? For Dr. Phil? Dr. Phil said he is going to help get her out! Will you fall on your sword? Please?"

"Whoa, Rhonda, wait," I said, trying to slow her down. "A TV show?"

"I'm going on his show!" she said excitedly. "He really cares about Amber, and he has done amazing things for so many people. He's going to get her out!"

"Rhonda, a talk-show host is not getting Amber out of prison. That's not how this works."

She didn't believe me. I remembered she had been trying to get on this same show since 2011. Now she was finally getting her wish. I wished her the best.

The show aired an episode about Amber's case in early 2016. I only learned about it when my cell phone started buzzing one afternoon with texts from friends, including lawyers, upset about, as one person put it: "Amber Hilberling's mom trashing you" during a segment of the show. Apparently Rhonda and Bryan had told the national television audience that after all this time, the one person they really blame for Amber being in prison was actually... me, her second-chair trial attorney.

It was this television show, not a new appeal, that Rhonda had in mind when she called me late that night, begging me to 'fall on my sword.'

For years I had heard them blame the media, the judge, the prosecutor, the jury, Josh, and even Josh's parents. But unlike their TV audience, I knew the real reason they had shifted their oft-moving vitriol in my direction. They had angrily turned on me the moment I blocked their attempt to take over the window lawsuit.

Some told me to fight back, to sue for defamation. There were false things said on the show, comments I won't dignify by repeating here. I chose to respond to them on my website rather than in court or this book.

But the people telling me to fight back didn't understand. Only family and a few close friends knew about my stroke and the heart diagnosis. I wasn't going to worry about gossip or lies or talk-show trash. It wasn't the first time false things had been said about me, and I was sure it wouldn't be the last. I didn't see the show and never will, and I know I didn't miss a damn thing that matters.

I knew the truths. About the case. About Amber and Josh. About the trial. About me. So did my co-counsel. So did the people who matter.

Most importantly, Amber herself.

She called me from prison and apologized. "I asked my parents not to do that," she said, making it clear she didn't share their opinions. Her trial verdict, she said, "didn't have anything to do with my counsel."

Her apology was unnecessary; she hadn't done or said a thing. But it gave me another reason to admire her.

Amber wasn't the only one to apologize for the debacle. I later received a call from an attorney who represented the Dr. Phil show. He called to apologize. He said the show had come to learn about the falsehoods aired about me in one particular segment of the broadcast, and wanted to make it right. He admitted the show's producers "hadn't done their homework" and had made the mistake of taking Bryan and Rhonda at their word.

I wasn't interested in either a fight or a settlement, I told him. Just an apology would do. He sent me a letter "writing you on behalf of the Dr. Phil Show to express our sincere apology" for the false statements broadcast. He also promised that "we will not rebroadcast the programs in question without removing references to you and have removed references to you from the DPS media site."

He was a gentleman, and handled the matter with class. There were a few good ones out there; he was one of them. I thanked him for the apology and wished him well.

About an hour after the show aired, Rhonda texted me: "Was so proud of Amber for defending you with her belief in you!"

"Didn't watch," I replied. "Hope it all helps."

"I thought it was positive for Amber and Levi," she texted back.

"I didn't watch. Anything I know is from friends who did and are pissed," I texted, letting my guard down a bit. I told her I "didn't see the correlation between" helping Amber and Levi and "defaming me with ugly lies."

She responded by denying that she said a single thing about me on the show.

"I didn't do shit," she texted. "Whatever!!! Amber believed in YOU and I'm to blame????? .... Show me one thing I said!!!!!!!!!!!!.... I never mentioned your name...I didn't say shit. But whatever!"

I rolled my eyes and chose to not engage her further.

Then, as if none of that had happened, as if she hadn't just betrayed and badmouthed me on national television, she finished her text messages with a friendly note that she would call me tomorrow.

81

I was sitting at a restaurant on the evening of July 11, 2016, when I received a surprise telephone call that could change everything.

In the course of working on this book, I had reached out to interview people involved with the case. One person I had wanted to talk to was Bonnie Lambdin, the inmate who had given the crucial testimony about Amber's alleged confession.

Her testimony at trial had never sat right with me. When I read the trial transcript three years later, it troubled me even more. Her words about Amber's alleged confession were just too perfectly matched, a verbatim replica of the "she caught him off guard" account the prosecutor had been struggling to make.

I wanted to know the truth. If Bonnie had lied. Or if the prosecutor had offered her something in exchange for her testimony, something they both had denied at trial. Or if Keely had flat out told her what to say on the stand. I hadn't forgotten Nicole Pasco's earlier revelation that the prosecutor had explicitly instructed her to withhold information favorable to Amber.

I tried to track her down through the Oklahoma Department of Corrections, eventually pinpointing her location to a halfway house. I left voicemails and hoped for a return call.

I was a few bites into my dinner when Bonnie called.

She first told me she didn't really want to talk about the case because she still felt "horrible" about what she had done.

"What do you feel horrible about, Bonnie?"

She talked about her time in custody with Amber, about being served a subpoena to testify at trial, and about meeting in person with the prosecutor before trial to discuss her testimony. She told me she regretted what she had done at trial, and had been upset for years about the way it "all got twisted around so bad."

Wait. Hold on, Bonnie.

What, exactly, got twisted around?

What Bonnie said next nearly floored me.

She said that before testifying at trial, she had told the prosecutor that she had been high on meth, out of her mind, when Amber had allegedly made the incriminating confession.

She said she told Keely that Amber had actually been joking the entire time, that nothing she said had been serious. They had been "playing round, being silly," Bonnie told me.

Then she said Amber herself had also been high when she made the joke. "I told Keely all this," Bonnie told me.

She said a group of inmates had been sitting around getting high together at the time. I remembered that time period, just after Amber's breakdown, her trying to escape from it all, barely sure she even wanted to live. Bonnie's memory made perfect sense.

The weight of Bonnie's revelation hit me.

This was the prosecution's key witness, the only person to testify that Amber had allegedly "confessed" to an act constituting murder.

And she had been high when she heard it? And Amber had actually been just kidding around? And Amber was high herself at the time?

And the prosecution knew all this?

And we didn't?

I realized, as Bonnie talked, that the prosecutor would have been required by law to have told us about all of this. But she hadn't told us any of it.

It got worse.

Not only had Keely not shared this information with us, Bonnie said the prosecutor expressly ordered her not to share it either. Bonnie said Keely "told me I wasn't allowed to say any of that at trial because of some ruling the judge had already made."

Any such instruction would have been false. There was no ruling preventing Bonnie from revealing these crucial facts, and certainly no ruling preventing the defense attorneys from knowing about them.

I stood up and walked out of the restaurant for air. I kept Bonnie talking as I paced back and forth on the sidewalk in front of the building, my mind racing at the implications.

Bonnie clearly had no idea about the legal significance of anything she had told me. She had simply been sharing her recollections of the entire matter, and had progressed to the part where she had met with the prosecutor. Her main purpose for the call was to ask me to reach out to Amber and apologize for her, which I later did.

I told her these details were important, and that I'd want to meet with her in person to get them on the record. She balked at that idea. She said she was afraid the state would retaliate against her for saying anything that could help Amber, so she wanted to wait until she completed her sentence in November. But once out of custody, she said, she'd go on the record.

She said had "more" to tell me but was too afraid to say it over the phone.

I don't know what she meant, but in my opinion she had already, unknowingly, said more than enough. By the time we finished our call, my adrenaline was rushing.

We had something.

It had been almost two years since I had retired from the active practice, and I hadn't handled many criminal cases in the first place. But I remembered the basics of this particular issue: the law requires the prosecution to turn over to the defense all exculpatory evidence — things that could help Amber — it obtains.

The reason is simple: the Constitution promises every defendant a fair trial. The state can't hide helpful evidence for the purpose of landing a conviction. It should only convict the guilty.

The evidence the prosecutor withheld from us was vital.

The fact that Bonnie had been high on meth at the time would have been a crucial part of our cross-examination of her. It went directly to her ability to perceive and remember Amber's alleged confession. Credibility of the witness is always a vital part of impeachment. We needed that evidence. The law guarantees our right to it. And there had been no pretrial ruling about evidence of drug use by testifying witnesses.

The same applies to Bonnie's statement that Amber had been joking when she made the alleged comment. Here was the state's lone evidence of a confession, and the witness had told the prosecutor it had actually been a joke. Of course we needed to know that.

The same even applies to the evidence that Amber herself had partaken in the group's drug usage. It offered an explanation as to why Amber had no memory of making the statement. It would have helped give context and clarity to any such exchange.

Though drug use in jail certainly wouldn't have reflected well on Amber's judgment at the time, its benefit may have outweighed the cost. And while the two sides had made a pretrial agreement about previous drug use by Josh or Amber, we certainly would have had the right to revisit that given Bonnie's surprise testimony.

We would have also needed this evidence in our cross-examination of the second jailhouse inmate who came in late to testify about Amber having made a window joke.

But most importantly, it would have torn apart Bonnie's testimony.

The prosecutor had built her entire trial around Bonnie's accusation. Bonnie was the one and only witness to testify that Amber had ever confessed to catching Josh "off guard" and shoving him through the window. The jury clearly believed Bonnie's version of what had happened.

The prosecutor repeated Bonnie's claim throughout both of her closing arguments, even expressly citing it as the reason the jury should give Amber a stiff sentence. Then at the formal sentencing, the prosecutor had once again relied heavily on Bonnie's testimony.

And it had all been a sham.

By the time I got off the phone with Bonnie, my dinner now cold, I was torn between anger and excitement for what this new evidence could mean for Amber.

I called Brewster, whose firm had handled the appeal, and told him what I had just learned, feeling out his thoughts on a new appeal. He called the revelation "explosive," the kind of bombshell, he said, that gets convictions overturned. I then called April, who agreed.

I left the restaurant and raced home to dig back into my case file and the governing law.

I found a Motion For Discovery I had filed on July 17, 2012, eight months before trial, in which I had demanded that the prosecution turn over "all evidence, information, statements, property, documents, witnesses, or other evidence of any sort in this case." I had identified 40 different categories of evidence, including all statements made by any person or witness, and "all evidence tending to impeach the credibility of each potential witness." Though the prosecution was obligated regardless, we had even demanded this very type of evidence in writing.

The state hadn't given it to us.

I pulled out the state's written summary of Bonnie's testimony, which we had received just before trial. It made no mention of the critical evidence Bonnie had just shared with me.

I researched the law, something I hadn't done in years. I had remembered the basics correctly. The "*Brady* Rule" requires prosecutors to disclose exculpatory evidence to the defense.

"*Brady* evidence" is anything that goes toward: (1) negating a defendant's guilt, (2) reducing the defendant's potential sentence, or (3) affecting the credibility of the witness. Withholding such evidence violates a defendant's right to due process.

The withheld evidence here met all three categories.

I kept researching. Oklahoma courts followed the *Brady* Rule. I read a United States Court of Appeals case, *Browning v. Trammel*, which governed in Oklahoma and was directly on point. In that case, the murder conviction of an Oklahoma man was overturned on appeal because the prosecution had withheld the fact that a crucial trial witness had a mental health issue the defense could have used to impeach her eyewitness testimony. That witness had suffered from "memory deficits" and a "blurring of reality and fantasy" which, the court of Appeals ruled, "is classic impeachment evidence" the defense needed.

"A witness's credibility may always be attacked by showing that his or her capacity to observe, remember, or narrate is impaired," the court held. "Consequently, the witness's capacity at the time of the event, as well as at the time of trial, is significant" and "relevant to impeachment." Because the prosecution had withheld evidence challenging the witness's capacity to recall the events she testified to, the conviction was thrown out.

The reasoning applied to our situation perfectly. We were entitled to this evidence.

I called Bonnie back the next morning and went through the crucial statements again, this time recording them. She agreed to meet in person after finishing her sentence and testify when asked. I shared her recording with an Oklahoma criminal appellate attorney whom April had strongly recommended.

As I finished this book in the fall of 2016, the attorney had started the work on a new appeal based on Bonnie's revelation.

I was hopeful.

82

Levi turned five years old on August 6, 2016. He has light brown hair, his mother's eyes, and his father's wide smile. He's happy, playful, healthy, tall, and strong. He carries his father's broad and athletic build. Just before his fifth birthday, he rode his first big-boy roller coaster at Six Flags Over Texas in Dallas.

He still lives with Rhonda and Bryan in Tulsa, his "Mi Mi" and "Da." The family's longtime nanny helps raise him.

Josh's mother, Rosa, asked to see her grandson while she was battling cancer. She met with him once and died soon after. As of Levi's fifth birthday, he had still never met Josh's father, step-mother, or brother.

In the years post-trial, Josh's sister Nikki was the exception. For a while she regularly spent time with Levi, with Amber's bless-ing. Amber told me that Levi "adores" his aunt. According to family friends, this relationship ended after Levi's aunt asked the Whitlocks for money.

Despite being incarcerated, Amber tries to be a regular part of Levi's life and stay involved in his parenting. It's her lifeblood, feeling like she's still his mom. She talks to him on the phone regu-larly, sees him at visitations, gets updates on his daily activities, and gives her input on his life. Though they don't see eye to eye on everything, Amber tells me how grateful she is for her mother's commitment to Levi.

The one topic she expresses the most concern about is Levi's exposure to ongoing volatility at home. Rhonda filed for divorce nine months after the trial, and she and Levi moved into the home of another man, a Tulsa attorney. That man then drove to meet Amber in prison, where he introduced himself as the "new father figure in Levi's life." He told Amber he intended to start spanking her two-year-old son as part of his discipline.

Amber was horrified but helpless. "I'm Levi's mom," she says. "I would never spank him."

Levi and Rhonda were then petitioners in a protective order Rhonda obtained against Bryan in 2014. The petition alleged "Bryan has been abusive for years," threatened to kill Rhonda, was suicidal and "drinking out of control." Rhonda alleged he had "repeatedly hit me, slapped me, and pushed me" and "put a loaded gun to my head when drunk." She also alleged Bryan had been drinking and driving with Levi in his car. On March 11, 2014, Bryan was arrested for violating the terms of the protective order.

They later reconciled. Rhonda and Levi moved out of the other man's house and back in with Bryan.

Amber says she's done a lot of thinking and reading inside, and has a better understanding of the cyclical nature of domestic violence than she did as a teenager. She talks about how she and Josh were products of their environments. From what I had seen and heard, she was right on both counts. If she ever gets out, she hopes to help educate others in similar situations. But more than anything, she says, she wants the cycle broken for her son.

Levi's exposure to domestic tumult isn't Amber's only concern. Having learned to distrust the media, Amber said, she'd prefer Levi grow up without television cameras. She doesn't want him in the spotlight or being recognizable in public.

But she may not be able to stop it. After finally landing her coveted Dr. Phil moment, Rhonda began working with a British television production company to film a reality-TV style "documentary" about her family and the case. At the time of this writing, she was planning to make an appearance on a talk show hosted by Piers Morgan, and publicly announcing plans to become a "podcast" talk-show host herself.

"I love my mom," Amber told me, "but she is who she is."

Rhonda put together a grand party for Levi's fifth birthday. He was surrounded by family, friends, gifts, cake, ice cream… and the British television crew filming it all.

83

Coiled rolls of razor wire guard both the bottom and top of the tall chain-link fence that surrounds Mabel Bassett Correctional Center, a women's prison just outside of McLoud, Oklahoma, some 90 miles west of Tulsa.

McLoud is a quiet, rural town of about 4,000, marked by double-wides, American flags, and "For Lease" signs on vacant Main Street windows. There aren't signs pointing visitors to the largest employer in the area, the women's prison. Just head west from the traffic light, turn right at the cemetery sign, then left onto Kickapoo Road.

There, at the top of a hill, sits the quiet fenced complex of concrete buildings. Outside the main entrance, visitors shuffle through two electronic sliding doors which are programmed to never be open at the same time. Once inside, armed guards run a scanner across each guest, pat down their bodies, and direct them through a metal detector.

Inside the gray walls, about 1,200 inmates are separated into minimum- and medium-security wings. They wear their assigned uniforms, loose-fitting pants and shirts. Their clothing, like the walls that surround them, are a drab, lifeless gray. Tattoos are prevalent, often illicitly obtained inside with ink and whatever sharp object will do the job.

On a visit one Sunday afternoon I watched as another visitor, some 20 feet from Amber and me, handed an inmate a small item from a clear bag. The inmate turned her back to guards, put her hand down the front of her pants, and appeared to insert the item into her body. I asked Amber about it. She told me it happens all the time. She said sometimes the guards look the other way, and other times they'll make deals themselves with the inmates, exchanging leniency and contraband for sexual favors. Shaking her head in disbelief, Amber told me about one girl who had recently had sex with a guard in exchange for a small make-up mirror.

Public records reflect such a history of sexual relations between guards and prisoners at the prison. At least three male Mabel Bassett officers had been criminally charged with sexually assaulting inmates since the beginning of Amber's case alone.

Every day, Amber is surrounded by convicted murderers, child abusers, drug dealers, violent criminals, and thieves. But there is one inmate everyone inside has heard of: Amber Hilberling. The notoriety hasn't made her life inside any easier.

She says she tried being more social for a while, making friends with other inmates. But the prison social scene inevitably involves drugs, fights, and drama. Amber senses the resentment others have of her high-profile stature; earlier in the year she was badly beaten up by another inmate. She says the constant flow of drugs throughout the prison offers a temptation, a brief escape from reality, that most inmates crave. She admits she's joined in herself a few times.

The best way to avoid the drugs and other troubles, she's learned, is to keep to herself and keep quiet.

Lately, Amber says, "I don't have very many friends. I'm a loner. I stay in my room and watch TV. I'm not really out on the scene."

On a typical day she wakes around 7 a.m., showers, and heads to class. She is a full-time college student, taking courses through two Oklahoma colleges. Some are taught in-person, others via video. She listens quietly, take notes, and studies later.

She'll go outside for sunlight when allowed.

She spends most of her time inside her two-bed cell on the second floor, where she lives alone. Her gray concrete walls are decorated with photographs of Levi, her reason to wake up each morning.

Three years removed from the public eye, most would probably not recognize her. She is significantly thinner than she was in the spotlight, having lost the weight that came from pregnancy and postpartum incarceration. Her hair is longer, her skin lighter, her cheekbones reemerged. She is pretty. She is still young; at the time of this writing, she is 24 years old.

She writes poetry. Some poems are to Levi, which she asked me to keep private.

Some are to Josh. She ends one of those, titled "Nightmares," with this line: "We are one… a vow not broken, a love never dead."

After losing her appeal, she penned one to God:

<u>Leftovers</u>
I trusted You to be my voice when all I felt was silence
I needed You to show me faith, join with me in alliance.
I wanted You to give my heart the safety that it sought;
I asked if You would grant my wish:
Restore the things for which I fought.

I dreamt that You would show Your might,
Your knowledge of my soul.
I thought that You could never die...
Your absence makes me cold.
I wished that You had counted
All the moments that I missed:
His crawl, his walk, his brand new teeth,
A first word and interests.

I begged for life at its fullest:
Levi and his Mommy.
I believed in You, God!
I believed that You could save me!

She reads. Books, schoolwork, the Bible, letters. She long ago lost count of the letters she'd receive from strangers. For the first couple years, she could expect at least one a day. She used to respond to each with a handwritten letter of her own.

Not anymore. The written exchanges led to more unwanted attention.

"Now," she says, "I've learned not to trust very many people."

There have been dark days. Days when she wasn't sure she wanted to keep going. She says praying helps. So does an anti-depressant.

But nothing helps more than the gift she receives twice a month.

Levi.

Her son visits the prison every other weekend during his mom's visitation hours. The visiting room has 32 tables, some round, some rectangular, and fills up quickly. There are eight vending machines, a table with books and games for younger visitors, and a small outdoor visiting area. During visiting hours, most inmates sit inside with their guests talking, hugging, eating, playing cards and board games, laughing, crying.

Not Levi. The patch of grass in the outdoor visiting area catches some sunlight between buildings. It's enough for him. Amber and Levi spend his visits out there, rolling around on the ground, sweating, running, piggybacking, playing, laughing.

"We play hardcore," Amber says. "He loves his mom."

If she sits on the grass with her back to the visiting area, her son in front of her, she can almost pretend they're at home in the backyard.

His visits, she says, are "the only thing that keeps me going, when it gets lonely and hard."

And it does get hard.

She misses her husband. She grieves for his family and always reminds me that she forgives them for their words. She aches constantly for what she has put her own family through.

She thinks back to the trial often. She has formed a strong opinion about why the jury was so eager to convict first and ask questions later.

The prosecutor's "whole case," Amber says, "was that one phrase taken out of part of the video ['he was messin' with the TV'] and the protective order."

Other than that, she believes, "the media did the rest of the job for her."

For 21 months she had waited for her day in court, confident she would have a fair trial. Reality was a shock.

She said she respects the work of the police officers and first responders who testified at trial, and knows they were just doing their job. She feels grateful to those who showed her care that June afternoon, particularly the paramedic who pulled her away from Josh and comforted her.

She even expresses compassion for the judge. "It was probably a hard case for him," she says. Some rulings still bother her, she admits, such as the jury only hearing about one of the couple's two protective orders against each other.

But she has a difficult time finding the same respect for the prosecutor's trial methods. "I couldn't believe the prosecutor was allowed to talk to me the way that she was," she says. "That's what I think about the most."

She is still particularly bothered by the memory of Keely ordering the lead detective to physically manhandle her on the courtroom floor. "The setting was so inappropriate," she says, "and nobody thought that this was wrong? She was just this mean girl from high school who was trying to pick at me while I was trying to save my life. The whole scene was disgusting."

She remembers the woman in the audience passing out during that dramatic scene, the atmosphere turning surreal.

"It was so inappropriate," she repeated.

Her one personal regret from trial, though, is how nervous she became when she took the stand to testify.

"Before and after the testimony," she remembers, "I felt this power. I was going to get up there and tell it like it is. I had nothing to hide, nothing to be nervous about. But getting up there, the whole scene, not only was I still in a state of mind of shock and grief over the whole situation, but Josh's family was sitting there staring at me and making faces. The pressure got to me."

She still resents the prosecutor for accusing her of lying when she couldn't recall the exact specifics of how Josh went up and out the window. "I couldn't piece it together," she says. "One minute we're standing there screaming at each other, and the next moment the glass is broken."

Looking back, she says now, it would have been easier to lie. Had she just come up with a story about how Josh went through the window, or not said a single thing, chances are she'd be home raising her child. There are times she wonders if telling the truth is what put her in prison. I told her I've wondered the same.

On August 9, 2016, I asked her a question she had heard many times before.

"Do you regret turning down the plea deal?"

Had she have taken it, she'd have already been home with Levi.

"I don't," she said. "It's crazy, but I don't. Every now and then someone will ask me that, and it takes me a minute to think about. But at the end of the day, I don't regret it. This is bigger than a lot of us understand. Bigger in a sense not only to change flaws in the legal system, but I've gotten letters from people all over saying that my story has inspired them to make a small decision in their life that has changed something for them."

Of every memory from trial, though, there is one in particular that haunts her the most: the shocking question the jury asked the judge – after already convicting her of the "depraved mind" murder and sentencing her to 25 years:

"So what does 'depraved mind' mean anyway?"

"You told me I'd think about that line every day for the rest of my life," she told me, more than three years after the verdict. "And I have."

84

At the trial, a police officer testifying about the details of the crime scene mentioned a handwritten note that had been folded up inside Josh's wallet.

Amber didn't know what it was.

During a trial break, I asked if I could see the note. I retrieved it and brought it to our table.

It was a note Amber had written to Josh just before she left Alaska for Tulsa, at the end of his Air Force tenure. He had kept it in his wallet.

Amber opened it up and quietly read it to herself.

Love,

I'm going to miss you so, so much, but we will get through it.

You don't have to worry about anything. I don't want you to. You're worth more to me than anything.

I'll always wait for you. Now and forever, I'll be here.

Love,
Amber
Xoxo

P.S. I love you so much.

She smiled to herself as she read it, then wiped her eyes.

Epilogue

It is nearly midnight on Monday, October 24, 2016.

Hours ago I was sitting in my living room performing a final review of the packaging of this book, which I had already finished writing. My MacBook was open on my lap, my daughter playing on the floor next to me, when I received a text message from Rhonda Whitlock.

I picked up my phone and opened the message. It contained exactly three words.

"Amber is dead."

I stared at the screen, frozen.

No.

I closed my eyes for a moment then looked at it again, hoping I had misread it. I hadn't.

No. No. No.

I stumbled to my feet and into my bedroom, closed the door, and called Rhonda. Though it was just a few hours ago, I don't remember anything either of us said. I just remember the sounds of her sobbing. I'm not sure either of us got a word out.

One of us finally hung up. I screamed out in anger, then sunk to my knees on my floor and wept.

———

Minutes after Rhonda texted me, Shawn Peters rushed to her house. When she arrived, Rhonda was on the floor wailing. Amber's sister Ariel was in the basement screaming and sobbing uncontrollably.

Levi was walking around the house blowing bubbles, smiling and unaware.

"Somebody died," Levi told Shawn. "Somebody died."

———

In the month before Amber's death, I had twice telephoned Debbie Aldridge, the Mabel Bassett Correctional Center warden, to warn her that I feared Amber was a suicide risk. I made the calls hoping the prison would initiate a suicide risk protocol.

Amber had just had her visitation rights suspended for 90 days as punishment for being in a particular prison building outside the allotted time. She had called me the evening she received the punishment, crying so hard I could barely make out her words. I tried to calm her down, to get her to breathe and talk more slowly. She begged me to help.

I had never heard her so upset.

The 90-day suspension would coincide with the holiday season, she was finally able to explain, which meant she wouldn't be able to see Levi over the holidays. She told me she didn't think she would be strong enough to survive the holidays without seeing him.

Her biggest fear was losing him, her son no longer looking at her as his mommy. She needed their relationship, their moments. They kept her going. Each Halloween, Levi would visit the prison in his costume and steal the show. Each December, they had their own little version of Christmas in the visitation area. She couldn't imagine not seeing him in his costume, not hugging him and telling him "Merry Christmas."

She was frantic. I tried to listen and comfort her. I told her the 90 days would go by before she knew it, and that she could do a Christmas visit with Levi right when it ends. I told her to be strong, and reminded her the new appeal had a good chance. It was the best I could come up with on the spot. But I knew it wasn't much.

She kept pressing me to help, to call someone up the chain of command, to try anything. I promised to try, but I was realistic with her. I told her I doubted anyone from the outside could make a difference in an internal discipline matter.

I called the warden's office the next morning. Her secretary asked what my call was about. I made my pitch, but it apparently wasn't compelling enough to be put through to the warden. I asked her to please have the warden return my call. She never did.

A few days later, I received some poetry in the mail from Amber. The final poem was, she had written me, "what I imagined of suicide."

I called the warden again, this time telling the secretary I wanted to talk to the warden about a book I was writing. That approach, though a half-truth at best, worked. The warden took my call. I offered some fake small talk about this book, then quickly told her about my real purpose: I was concerned Amber wouldn't make it through the holidays if she wasn't able to see her son.

"I'm not discussing this," she told me, quickly ending the call. She was not cordial.

Despite my warnings, the prison never initiated a suicide risk protocol. Had one been in place, the item Amber reportedly used to end her life – a curling iron with a long cord – would not have been in her cell.

———

Within a few hours of Amber's death, Zach Hilberling, Josh's brother, posted this on his Facebook page: "Muhahahahaha ding dong the witch is dead!! Muahaha."

Hours after that, Josh's stepmother made a point to insult both Amber and her family in the *Tulsa World* newspaper article first reporting Amber's death. Jeanne Hilberling suggested that Amber would have already been home – and thus alive – had she accepted the pre-trial plea offer, and said it was Amber's "greed or foolishness that caused her to not accept the deal." She inaccurately alleged that the plea "deal would've prevented her from personally suing the apartment building owners."

She's dead because she was greedy.

The *Tulsa World* printed this ugly lie without bothering to examine its accuracy. It was completely false, as had been most of the woman's other public statements about Amber. The referenced plea deal had actually offered a no-contest plea, rather than a guilty plea. Under the law, the no-contest plea would not have prevented Amber from continuing in the civil suit. But the more important truth was that Amber simply didn't care about the civil case, and it had not affected her decision at all. She had turned down the plea deal because she wanted to clear her name.

Jeanne then took a second shot, this one at Amber's family. "Amber loved her father, Mike Fields, and her Missouri family," she said, pointedly omitting Amber's mother, stepfather, siblings, and maternal grandparents from the observation. The *Tulsa World* printed this vicious statement despite its obvious intent to insult a grieving family.

Accompanying the same article, the *Tulsa World* also elected to prominently feature a graphic labeled: "Amber Hilberling's misconduct history in DOC custody." The graphic listed infractions Amber had allegedly committed in prison over the previous three and a half years, including charges of being in an "unauthorized area," "failure to obey verbal orders," "fighting with another inmate," and testing positive for drugs.

The newspaper rushed to publish this list, along with the above lies and insults, all before Amber's family had even begun to make arrangements for her funeral.

———

Amber seemed to be doing better the last time we spoke. It was just before her lunch on Friday, October 21. Three days before she died.

She told me she had met with one of the supervising officials in her unit and made an appeal of her loss of visitations. She was hopeful it would be reduced so she could at least have one Christmas visit with Levi. She expected a decision within the next few days. I now suspect she received her answer Monday, and that it wasn't good, and that she was gone soon after.

While we talked I could hear a growing commotion in the background. She told me it was "burger day" at the prison, and admitted she was excited. It was a rare treat – a cheeseburger with all the fixings. She was self-deprecating, laughing at herself for being so excited about a burger.

She told me how proud she was of a classroom speech she had just given that week. I knew she had been working on it for weeks and had been nervous; she had called me asking for advice on how

to handle nerves during public speaking. She said the classroom audience had loved it. She told me how people had even "clapped"
for her when she finished. In my mind I could see her beaming.

The topic of her speech: domestic violence.

She also said something that would impact me more later, after
I heard the news. She said Josh had appeared to her in a dream
the night before, and had asked her a question: "why aren't you
looking for me?" It was the first time she had dreamt about him
in a while, she said. She gave vivid descriptions of what he had
looked and sounded like in the dream. It was clear she found the
dream meaningful.

In the background, I could hear someone started to shout instructions. Amber told me her pod was being called to lunch, and
she had to go. She said she'd call again in a few days. I told her I
was looking forward to seeing her again soon.

It was the last time I spoke with her.

I look back now at the question she dreamt Josh asked her –
why aren't you looking for me? – and I believe I understand how
she interpreted it.

She was losing Levi. It was time to go find Josh.

———

Some time well before trial, I had started ending our conversations with the same two-word admonition: "be good." It had

become something of an inside joke between us, and it always made her smile. In early October, I received what would be my last letter from her. She signed off with the words: "<u>You</u> be good. ♡ Amber."

The letter was accompanied by some poems she had written. She asked me to "please keep them to yourself . . . at least for now." Her final poem was about her death:

<u>Auto-pilot</u>
So I finally jump into the abyss of the unknown,
silently as was my strength for so long.
Black pool at my feet quickly encasing me in its void.
Everything around me is the color of darkness!
I am still aware of my senses, though they
are hard to master in this place.
All I can see are distant pictures:
Pieces of my past lives that meant the
most; people I cannot bring with me.
What I can taste is the salt of my new tears;
hot and unrelenting...
as well as the bitter afterward of the tears
left behind from those who mourn.
Heard is only my screamed frustration
and (surprisingly) rushing water...
Maybe to take me under in the finality I've begged for,
Or maybe to cleanse me of what I feel:
Nothing but the sulfurous reek of death!
My decided destination?

Opposing Life's own selfish claim to me.
Now I embody the simple quiet that I need.
Waiting on God from here. . .
I am okay.

Amber was 25.

Author's Note

In March of 2013, just before she was hauled away to Mabel Bassett Correctional Center to serve her 25-year sentence, Amber asked me to write this book.

She knew the full story hadn't ever been told. She knew most of the things that had been said, and said often, weren't accurate. She gave me written consent to write the book, to disclose our confidential communications, and told me not to hold back.

I told her maybe.

I knew I was in a good position to report the full story, having both the first-hand knowledge of the case and experience as a journalist and attorney.

After she asked me in 2013, I tried. But I wasn't ready.

It was more than three full years before I could bring myself to reopen the case file and look at it all again. It had been that difficult for me.

Finally, in the summer of 2016, I went back in and re-examined everything. Thousands of pages of documents. Court transcripts. Police files. Handwritten notes. Photographs. Videos. Audio recordings. Pleadings. Text messages. Emails.

I was struck by how clearly one overarching theme presented itself: Amber Hilberling was treated unfairly. By a lot of people.

By her husband. Her parents. Josh's family. The media. The public. The prosecutor. The judge. The jury. The system.

There was no way to tell her story while avoiding this truth.

As I began to write, I worried that parts of the book would come off as an attorney trying to re-argue a lost case, which wasn't my intent. But facts are stubborn things. Any thorough report about this case is going to trouble rational readers and anyone interested in justice. There is no question that Amber did not receive a fair trial. The court transcripts, which provide the accounts of the courtroom proceedings throughout this book, speak for themselves.

I also realize certain revelations in this book will not reflect well on some, and I fully expect retaliation. You invite problems when you publicly criticize a district attorney, and I may come to regret opening that door. But I can't tell the entire story without going there.

This is not a happy story. It's real.

But I didn't finally agree to write this book to re-argue a case or point fingers. I wrote this book because Amber deserves to have the truth told. First and foremost, I wrote this book to inform. To correct the record.

I also hope it helps people, if even just a few, improve their own lives.

I hope it helps someone out there struggling with addiction realize how quickly drugs can change people, destroy relationships, and ruin lives. I hope some read this book and feel the push to get clean.

I hope it helps someone out there in a relationship with a drug addict finally realize how important it is to reverse course — either the addict's or their own — before it's too late.

I hope it helps someone in a physically abusive relationship better understand that it is not OK, is never OK, and cannot be minimized, rationalized, or tolerated. Ever.

I hope it helps some parents out there stop and think about what sort of home environment they are creating for their children. Abuse, whether it's physical abuse, drug or alcohol abuse, or emotional abuse, is a culture. It is a cycle. You can expect your kids to repeat your behavior.

I hope it helps remind police and prosecutors of the importance of pursuing justice while ensuring citizens receive due process and fair trials.

I hope it helps all readers understand the importance of knowing and exercising their constitutional rights, specifically their right to remain silent and speak to an attorney, and the risks of saying anything in or near the presence of law enforcement.

I hope it helps criminal defense attorneys glean some insight from what worked and what didn't in a high-profile murder case, a look inside that can help their own strategy decisions. From Mark Collier to April Seibert to myself, each of Amber's attorneys made decisions that can be second guessed. Such is the nature of the job. While Amber repeatedly said it wasn't our fault, you can be sure we have second-guessed our decisions plenty. We lost, so we deserve our share of the blame for the verdict. Learn from what we did and didn't do right.

I hope it helps attorneys, especially young ones who have dreamt of rushing into solo practice as I did, understand the risk of getting too close to your clients, of being too emotionally invested in their outcomes. Not keeping a distance creates all sorts of problems, a tough lesson I've learned the hard way. There is more to the practice than winning or losing cases.

I hope it helps some in the media appreciate the importance of doing their homework, of getting the details right, of demanding proof before they go public with damning allegations. I hope it helps them understand the massive impact they can have on lives, how they can dramatically threaten citizens' constitutional rights by influencing jury pools, and just how dangerous their day-to-day job decisions can be.

I hope it sparks people who spend time in high-rise buildings to ask about their window glass and demand not only strong safety glass but all reasonable safety precautions. Otherwise, death could be just a stumble away.

I hope it helps Amber's family. Her parents, her siblings, her grandparents, and mostly her beautiful son Levi. At least now there's one record out there that includes the other side of this tragedy, the one long ignored by the public, the media, and the legal system.

I hope it helps Levi understand, some day when he's older, that all those horrible things he can find on the Internet about his mom aren't the whole story. And in some cases, Levi, they're just outright lies. A portion of the profits from this book will go into a college fund for you.

Most of all, I had hoped this book would help Amber. She had wanted the full story finally told. Sadly, I had to come back in and amend this final part of my note.

Amber had read a draft of this book before it was published. She said it was hard, reading the details and reliving the pain. But she said she was finally ready for people to hear her voice, her side. I hope it gave her some comfort, knowing there would be at least one record out there of all the facts that had for so long been left out of the public narrative.

But it wasn't supposed to end this way.

When she read the draft, she praised the accuracy but told me I was too critical of a couple people in certain parts. I thought about her feedback for a while and concluded she was right. I made revisions. Notably, but not surprisingly, Amber never asked me to change a single word to make <u>her</u> look better. Just others. I had warned her from the start she wouldn't come across as an angel in these pages. She had made some bad decisions, and I told her I'd be telling the full story. To her credit, she told me not to keep any secrets. "Tell it all," she said, "maybe it will help somebody out there."

That's the Amber I knew for five years, four months, and 17 days. Honest, courageous, strong, funny, flawed, selfless, and fully aware that she was a sinner who had made mistakes. She wasn't perfect, but she wasn't the monster too many tried to make her out to be. I will never believe she was a murderer. She was an abused teenage girl who had the nerve to stand up for herself while being pushed and grabbed while pregnant.

All she did that day was push right back.

I hope that with this book, I've pushed back a little myself, pushed against the false narrative that was built around this young woman and her difficult case. I hope it's helped some form a more complete understanding of not just the case and the trial, but of Amber Michelle Hilberling.

She deserves it.

Her story is a tragedy. I am tormented by her fate and always will be.

But I feel blessed to have known her.

Author's Sources

The facts and details in this book came from official court transcripts, witness interviews, recorded witness statements, Tulsa Police records, Eielson Air Force Base Security Forces records, court filings and records, case exhibits, expert witness work product, photographs, video recordings, audio recordings, published news reports, and the author's first-hand observations. The author personally obtained, witnessed, or reviewed statements from dozens of people, including but not limited to the following:

Amber Hilberling	Joshua Hilberling
Mark Collier, Esq.	April Seibert, Esq.
Officer Don Holloway	Detective Jeff Felton
Gloria Bowers	Mike Fields
Rhonda Whitlock	Bryan Whitlock
Patrick Hilberling	Jeanne Hilberling
Judge Kurt Glassco	Ass't District Attorney Michelle Keeley
Bonnie Lambdin	Mark Meshulam
Armando Rosales	Antonio DePaz
Firefighter Dan Newbury	Paramedic Jason Whitlow
Paramedic Miriam Nichols	Officer Marcus Harper
Officer Joel Sense	Officer Diana Liedorff
Detective Vic Regalado	Detective Justin Ritter

Detective Christine Gardner
Joshua Lanter, M.D.
Bill Brown
Larry Rivers
Jolanda Cook
Nathan McGowan
Mary Chandler
Kenny Belford
Ashley Anacker
Anthony Mowry
Shannon Sherwin
Michael Lloyd
Sylvia Treat
Clark Brewster, Esq.
Brian Aspan, Esq.

Detective Darren Froemming
Carl Crager
William Lingnell
Michelle Hagerdorn
Brad Blake
Robert Baker
Ellen Henry
Nicole Pasco
Matthew Anacker
Roger Hansel
Joshua Starr
Brandon Morris
Courtney Dye
Rob Nigh, Esq.
Shawn Peters

About the Author

J.R. Elias, a native of Omaha, Nebraska, has journeyed through writing and law on his path from the Midwest to the white sands of the Gulf of Mexico.

Elias was an award-winning journalist in Nebraska, Wyoming, and Oklahoma, honored for excellence in investigative reporting, sports writing, opinion columns, news reporting, feature stories, and more.

He detoured into law in his 30s, opening a civil litigation practice before closing his office in 2010 to return to writing. He put his plans on hold to join Amber Hilberling's defense team, a venture that impacted him in more ways than he could have anticipated.

Elias is the proud father of Tanner, Dylan, Makenna, and Scarlett.

His debut novel, *The Bluejay Way*, is scheduled for release in late 2017.

You can read more about the author, contact him directly, read his blog, or purchase his books at his official website: www.jayelias.com.

Printed in Great Britain
by Amazon